THE MERIT MYTH

Also by Peter Schmidt

Color and Money

THE MERIT MYTH

HOW OUR COLLEGES FAVOR THE RICH
AND DIVIDE AMERICA

ANTHONY P. CARNEVALE
PETER SCHMIDT
JEFF STROHL

THE
NEW
PRESS

NEW YORK
LONDON

Requests for permission to reproduce selections from this book should be made through
our website: https://thenewpress.com/contact.

Published in the United States by The New Press, New York, 2020
Distributed by Two Rivers Distribution

ISBN 978-1-62097-486-5 (hc)
ISBN 978-1-62097-487-2 (ebook)

CIP data is available.

The New Press publishes books that promote and enrich public discussion and
understanding of the issues vital to our democracy and to a more equitable world. These
books are made possible by the enthusiasm of our readers; the support of a committed
group of donors, large and small; the collaboration of our many partners in the independent
media and the not-for-profit sector; booksellers, who often hand-sell New Press books;
librarians; and above all by our authors.

www.thenewpress.com

Book design and composition by Dix!
This book was set in Minion

Printed in the United States of America

10   9   8   7   6   5   4   3   2   1

To those for whom America's promise remains unfulfilled.

CONTENTS

THE MERIT MYTH

INTRODUCTION

JARRED AWAKE FROM THE AMERICAN DREAM

Thomas Jefferson would have been appalled by the chaos that erupted on the muggy night of August 11, 2017, at his beloved University of Virginia. For sure, many citizens of the nation he helped found viewed the events there with horror.

The fall semester had yet to begin, and the few students already on campus were either conducting or undergoing an orientation for the entering class. A University of Virginia orientation guide published for the occasion offered help to students who felt "a bit out of place in a sea of sundresses and ill-fitting khakis and pastel shorts." Few, if any, there actually had any sense of just how hostile the campus environment would soon be. The anti-fascist group It's Going Down had warned on social media of expected trouble, but the university's top administrators remained oblivious. The campus police had stayed in a business-as-usual mode that anticipated dealing with the usual: noise complaints or kids who'd downed too much alcohol.

Then, at about 9:30 p.m., the unthinkable happened: hundreds of white supremacists marched onto the normally idyllic campus. The tiki torches they carried framed their rage-contorted faces as they shouted racial slurs and chanted "Jews will not replace us!" They surrounded and menaced about twenty counter-protesting students at the base of a statue of Jefferson, the university's founder, before the police finally arrived to drive them off.[1]

The following day, the white supremacists skirmished on the nearby streets of Charlottesville with counter-protesters.[2] Tragedy ensued as a supporter of the racist group Vanguard America maniacally rammed his Dodge Challenger into a crowd, killing a thirty-two-year-old community activist, Heather D. Heyer, and injuring dozens of others.[3]

Photographs and videos from that weekend conveyed images that most Americans associate with the rise of the Nazis in 1930s Germany, the Ku Klux Klan's terrorization of the South, or coverage of foreign governments teetering on collapse. Not with the twenty-first-century United States, and definitely not with its universities, which typically espouse civility and seek to be models of inclusion for women and members of minority groups.

Yet there could be no denying reality: hundreds of well-organized, neo-fascist thugs had just mounted a disturbing show of force on the campus of a major public university and in the surrounding college town. The orchestrators of that weekend's events included Richard B. Spencer, a 2001 University of Virginia graduate who had gone on to lead the "alt-right" National Policy Institute, and Jason Kessler, a member of the university's class of 2009.

Expressing disbelief, many Americans asked: Can this actually be happening here? What is this country becoming? Is this really *us*? A socially aware University of Virginia professor could have seized a teachable moment and chided them for having failed to pay attention. Had they completely tuned out the 2016 presidential election, with its vitriol and racist rhetoric? Had they been oblivious to the headlines and newscasts about social unrest and disruption? Had they ignored the daily torrents of suspicion and hate on Twitter and Facebook?

A self-reflective and candid professor, with job protections afforded by tenure, might have dared to suggest the possibility of another teachable moment on how iconic elite colleges such as the University of Virginia had helped to create the conditions for what had just happened there.

Yes, despite lofty mission statements expressing their commitment to advancing the greater good, the University of Virginia and other colleges share some blame for the extremism and social unrest that had just been on display and remain likely to be features of American life for years to come. They are run by, serve, and perpetuate an elite whose members often have seen their self-interests advanced by excluding other segments of the population from political and economic power.

Using selective colleges as gatekeepers, that elite has shut large swaths of the American population out of having access to power, opportunity, and wealth. The effect has been to drive people of different ideologies and backgrounds apart rather than bring them together. Ideally, our colleges would encourage students to eschew prejudice not only as a matter of philosophy, but also in practice, by facilitating interaction among different students and different viewpoints. Higher education is hard-pressed to live up to that ideal, however: expressions of hate have risen on college campuses in recent years, leaving college and university leaders struggling to mount effective responses.[4]

Indeed, instead of being havens of diversity, where Americans of all walks of life can learn from one another, many of our colleges and universities have become isolated communities, where students and faculty largely interact with those who are like them. Many striving working-class and poor white, black, and Latino students find themselves stuck outside the gates—with the relatively few who get inside those gates feeling marginalized. It's understandable if these groups come to see colleges and universities as exclusive clubs focused on fast-tracking the elite to ever-higher status.

In a modern republic, colleges should do more than groom successive generations of governing elites. They should prepare student bodies that look like America for participation in a diverse civil society and equip them to reject authoritarian thinking that presumes one race, one faith, one leader, and one way of life. In a modern economy in which two-thirds of jobs require at least some postsecondary education, we rely on our colleges to help young adults achieve financial independence and move up the economic ladder.[5] We count on colleges to provide equal opportunity that fosters the social mobility that allows us the comforting presumption that differences in talent and effort alone are the underlying cause of America's disparities in income and power.

In the twenty-first century, a college education offers the best shot at the American Dream. That's what we tell our children, regardless of whether we immigrated ourselves, are descended from indigenous Native Americans or enslaved Africans, or have ancestors who came here to build railroads or to escape famine or persecution. We have entrusted our higher-education system with the primary responsibility of providing a path for upward mobility and see our colleges as indispensable in helping Americans find their way in our economy, culture, and political system.

We look to our colleges to validate our beliefs that we're responsible for our own destinies and that those who are broke or stuck in a lousy job have only themselves to blame. We support our colleges as legitimate social and economic sorting mechanisms because they validate our commitment to individual responsibility and merit. After all, we tend to believe, you have to do the homework and ace the tests to get into the best colleges and move on to the best jobs that confer wealth and power over others.

Fair enough? Not really. In a society where people start out unequal, educational attainment measured by test scores and grades can become a dodge—a way of laundering the found money that comes with being born into the right bank account or the dominant race. The college game is fixed long before the selective college admissions officers get involved, but college has become the capstone in an inequality machine that raises and perpetuates class and race hierarchies and sinks the lower classes.

In the long pathway from kindergarten to good jobs, the most talented disadvantaged youth doesn't end up doing nearly as well as the least talented advantaged youth. A child from a family in the top quartile of family income and parental education who has low test scores has a 71 percent chance of graduating from college and getting a good job by their mid-twenties. However, a child from a low-income family but with top test scores has only a 31 percent chance of graduating from college and getting a good job by then. And the numbers are even worse for talented low-income minorities.[6]

Even among students who make it to college, the reality is that colleges are failing to live up to our expectations that they will be equitable paths to the American Dream. Many college paths are, in fact, dead ends. Highly stratified in terms of selectivity and expenditures per student, our higher-education system reserves the best opportunities mainly for those already on top. The system then dishes out mediocrity and disappointment to the rest, who are tracked into non-selective two- and four-year institutions that are often underfunded dropout factories.

Top-tier colleges have admissions policies that are biased in favor of children of the affluent and powerful, often in ways that lack even the most tenuous educational justification. In an ascending spiral of wealth, they invest heavily in catering to families with the means to pay full tuition and donate healthy sums to finance institutional efforts to appeal to ever more such families down the road. The absurd degree to which they have exposed their admissions processes to corruption became the subject of public scandal in March 2019, when an extensive federal investigation dubbed "Operation Varsity Blues" resulted in criminal charges against fifty people accused of scheming to get students into prestigious universities, including Georgetown, Stanford, the University of Southern California, and Yale. Those charged included Hollywood celebrities and business leaders accused of bribing their children's way into colleges; SAT or ACT proctors who allegedly had been bribed to allow cheating on the tests; coaches at some of the colleges who had allegedly arranged to have unqualified recruits added to their teams; and an independent college-admissions counselor and nonprofit head who admitted to overseeing the nearly $6 million bribery scheme.[7]

The sensational revelations of "Operation Varsity Blues" distract, however, from broader problems more worthy of attention. The universities named weren't themselves accused of wrongdoing, and they characterized the current and former university employees who were charged as rogue actors engaged in unauthorized behaviors.

Admissions officers elsewhere argued that the scandal exposed vulnerabilities in colleges' admissions processes—including the undue deference often given coaches' assessments of applicants' athletic prowess—without implicating the admissions processes themselves.

But others in the field, including many champions of college access for low-income and minority students, said the problems brought to light are indicative of broader structural problems that produce unfair advantage. In interviews with the *Chronicle of Higher Education*, Marie Bigham, director of college counseling at the prestigious Isidore Newman School in New Orleans, said, "This fraud has just taken standard operating practice to a grotesque level." Nancy Leopold, executive director of CollegeTracks, a nonprofit organization that advises disadvantaged students, said the sensationalism stemming from the scandal's celebrity involvement and bribes as large as $500,000 makes it easier to miss a bigger truth: "The admissions system is rigged in favor of privileged students before any bribing or donating takes place to rig it more."[8]

The University of Virginia's 2017 orientation guide had been on the mark with its reference to ubiquitous preppy attire. About 7 percent of the university's students come from the richest 1 percent of America, and more than two-thirds of the students come from the most affluent fifth of the nation's families.[9] This university is not a place welcoming to the children of coal miners, store clerks, or laid-off autoworkers. Its black and Latino students often complain of having to endure the suspicion that they are imposters who gained admission solely through affirmative action.[10]

Despite all this, the University of Virginia's student body hardly ranks as the upper-crustiest out there. In fact, it does not even place in the top fifty among colleges with the greatest percentage of students from the nation's richest families. At Vanderbilt University, for example, nearly a quarter of all students are from the most affluent 1 percent of American families.[11] This exclusivity is common. Only 5 percent of the students at the nation's top five hundred colleges come from the bottom fourth of society as measured by family income.[12] Virtually all of the nation's selective colleges and universities disproportionately enroll young people who grew up advantaged, turning them into graduates who will have the means to have their own children follow their footsteps down the privileged path that winds through elite higher-education institutions. "If you walk around campus, you're most likely to get knocked down by a Range Rover or high-end Audi," quipped Ian Taplin, a sociology professor at Wake Forest University, one of the institutions caught up in the 2019 admissions scandal.[13]

On the whole, higher education serves to compound the advantages or disadvantages that people had as children. It is heavily segregated by race and class, plagued by inefficiencies tied to disparities in resources, and unable to prepare a sufficient share of the population for survival in the knowledge economy. It causes as much as it cures what ails this nation, including widening income gaps and social divisions. Recent economic research has linked 60 to 70 percent of the growth in earnings gaps since the 1980s to differences in access to and completion of college programs with real value in the labor market.[14]

Those differences in college access and completion serve to heighten the intergenerational reproduction of privilege tied to race and class. Children who live in households where the most educated parent has a master's degree have five times better odds of completing bachelor's degrees than children who live in households with parents who have a high school education.[15] Striving students who are from the bottom fourth of the nation in terms of family socioeconomic status but nonetheless end up with standardized test scores in the top half of their high school class have only a 30 percent chance of getting a bachelor's degree or higher.[16] By comparison, advantaged students from the most affluent fourth of families who end up with standardized test scores in the top half of their high school class have a 70 percent chance of getting such degrees.[17]

A higher-education system true to an overall mission of upward mobility would not allow such results. In such a system, students with equal abilities would succeed at equal rates, regardless of their families' wealth. Technically speaking, however, it's inaccurate to say that the United States has a higher-education system at all. Our colleges constitute a "system" only in the same sense that the term "ecosystem" covers a bunch of organisms in the same place. Colleges similarly feed off one another, compete with each other, or simply ignore each other, depending on their strengths or weaknesses and what they stand to lose or gain. They focus mostly on their own needs and survival, not the common good.

For decades, our society's divisions by class and race, between college-haves and college-have-nots, have been growing in tandem. The devastation of our high school–educated working class, the hollowing out of the blue-collar portion of our middle class, the rise of obstacles to social mobility, the malignancy and periodic metastasizing of America's congenital cancer of racism—all are hard to miss if one just turns on a television or drives more than a few miles. The ideal of upward mobility holds our society together, but as that mobility continues grinding to a halt, our nation will continue to come apart.

These trends stoked the populist uprising that upended the 2016 presidential race, lifting the strong insurgent candidacy of Vermont senator Bernie Sanders and handing real estate tycoon Donald Trump triumphs over his Republican challengers and former secretary of state Hillary Clinton. Our nation's colleges are viewed as part of the dysfunctional establishment that people are rebelling against. The disillusionment can be seen in the dwindling tax-dollar appropriations to public colleges, which send the message that higher education is best understood as a private commodity available only to those who can pay for it rather than a public good that should be offered to all. Federal and state lawmakers denigrate public colleges as fat and wasteful, faculty members end up stereotyped as lazy leftists who indoctrinate rather than teach, and students are dismissed as sensitive "snowflakes" who waste their time and tuition dollars taking worthless classes.

The 2016 presidential election cycle shed light on the widening of the divide between academe and America. People employed in higher education gave Donald Trump's campaign a tiny fraction of the support they showered upon Hillary Clinton and donated much less to him than they had to his GOP predecessors.[18] Clinton won the vote of the college-educated by a nine-point margin. Trump, who had declared his affection for "the poorly educated" in a victory speech after the Nevada caucuses, won more than 52 percent of all voters lacking a college degree and two-thirds of voters classified as non-college-educated whites, the highest share to go to a Republican candidate since Ronald Reagan's 1980 triumph.

In an interview with the *Chronicle of Higher Education*, Katherine J. Cramer, a political science professor at the University of Wisconsin at Madison, cautioned against talk of how Clinton would have fared better if only the electorate had been better educated. "That's the attitude that makes people who are not very warm toward higher education even less warm, because we are actually very elitist and not concerned about people from a different walk of life."[19]

In a 2013–14 national survey, just 14 percent of respondents reported having "a great deal" of confidence in the people running higher-education institutions, while 21 percent reported having hardly any at all. The responses reflected broader societal divisions, with political conservatives expressing much less confidence than political liberals, blacks much less than whites, Mormons and Evangelicals less than Catholics or atheists and agnostics.[20] This distrust in college leaders mirrors public distrust in other American institutions: only 18 percent of Americans trust the federal government to do the right thing "always" or "most of the time."[21]

On the whole, our nation's institutions, including our colleges and universities, need to change if they are to reestablish our trust in them. But how? Should we let the market sort them out? Should policymakers leave them intact and buttress them, or rebuild them from the bottom up? Either approach can bring unintended negative consequences. Thinkers across the ideological spectrum disagree on the answers, but many share the view that Americans' alienation from their institutions has become so deep and widespread that faith in them will be tough to restore. "The emotional disquiet plays in different registers on the right and left, but across the ideological divide you find a deep sense of alienation, anger, and betrayal directed at the elites who run the country," argues Christopher Hayes, a host on MSNBC and an editor-at-large of *The Nation*, a progressive magazine.[22] On the right,

National Review contributor J.D. Vance summarized the consensus in Trump-friendly Appalachia in his best-selling book *Hillbilly Elegy* as follows: "We can't trust the evening news. We can't trust our politicians. Our universities, the gateway to a better life, are rigged against us."[23] From the center, the prominent journalist Steven Brill contends that those who have come out on top have used their undue influence on the government to essentially build "moats that protected them from accountability and from the damage their triumphs caused in the larger community."[24]

With colleges under suspicion, their own scholars' calls for social and government reforms bump up against mistrust from the public and indifference from public officials. To hell with the Ivory Tower, the thinking goes. Who needs cloistered eggheads telling us what to do? When it comes to swaying voters, books and academic journals have ended up being no match for Twitter and Facebook.

It's too bad, because there are some trenchant analyses out there. Among the more widely read is *Our Kids*, in which Robert D. Putnam, a professor of public policy at Harvard, describes how unequal public schools have failed to stem rising income inequality and have helped cement the links between childhood privilege and economic destiny.[25] In *The Big Sort*, Bill Bishop, a journalist, teamed up with Robert G. Cushing, a sociologist and statistician, to show how Americans increasingly cluster together with people who share their education levels and values, concentrating wealthy degree-holders more heavily in big cities and leaving many voting districts redder or bluer.[26] In *Dream Hoarders*, Richard V. Reeves, a senior fellow at the Brookings Institution, cites upper-middle-class families' efforts to secure unfair advantages for their children as a chief reason why Americans are increasingly likely to end up in the same economic class as their parents. He describes as mechanisms for such "opportunity hoarding" both the "legacy" admissions preferences that colleges grant the children of their alumni and the hiring of interns based on personal connections, which plays a big role in determining who gets a running start into sought-after jobs.[27]

Most such authors share a common fear. It's that America has largely abandoned efforts to offer equal access to the American Dream—the attainment of success through hard work—and we'll end up living an American nightmare characterized by despair, social disorder, and unrest when people wake up to the reality of their relegation to the bottom of the heap from one generation to the next.

In hindsight, the events that transpired at the University of Virginia were less a challenge to Jefferson's views than an unintended consequence of them. The reasons extend well beyond Jefferson's personal ownership of slaves and his university's reliance on slaves to build its campus. As hypocritical as Jefferson's actions were, it's his influential ideas that helped get us where we are today.

Among our nation's founding fathers, Jefferson played a central role in establishing a constitutional democratic republic upon two distinct—and often conflicting—values: *democratic egalitarianism*, as expressed in the Declaration of Independence's assertion that "all men are created equal," and *liberal individualism*, promoted by the rights and freedoms enshrined in the Bill of Rights. Democratic egalitarianism represents our source of faith in our political system, offering the hope that our votes count and we all have the power to change the direction of government in a peaceful, civil manner. Liberal individualism holds that each of us has an unalienable right to "life, liberty, and the pursuit of happiness" and should be left free to pursue our ambitions. It's the value that protects a free market and unleashes the competitive and self-centered forces that drive our powerhouse capitalist economy, with a significant trade-off: the competitive capitalist economy that would loom as individualism's best-fed child produces and thrives on inequities in wealth and status.

Throughout America's history, tensions between egalitarianism and individualism—and swings in the balance between them—have repeatedly produced political instability and even, at times, threatened to tear our nation apart. The Civil War, the civil rights movement and the turbulence of the 1960s, various secessionist movements and outbreaks of radicalism—all these arose from conflicts over the definition of rights and the distribution of wealth and power.

For most of our founding fathers, there was one obvious answer to reconciling individualism and egalitarianism: equal opportunity. They believed its existence would enable us to attribute gaps in wealth and power to differences in individual talent and effort, rather than to any sort of unfairness or oppression.

If only it were that simple. Even as Jefferson espoused the importance of equal opportunity, he put forward a view of education that would undermine that ideal. He promoted assumptions about human intelligence that were deeply deterministic and elitist, steeped in the influence of the Calvinist ideas circulating widely at the time and in his slave-holder's blindness to his own bias.

In an 1813 letter to John Adams that would come to have a huge impact on the nation's higher-education system more than a century later, Jefferson posited that intellectual talent is innate, something we should be identifying in the lucky ones born with it rather than nurturing in everyone. He envisioned using America's education system as a sorting machine, a means of steering the best and brightest toward their proper station in society. He argued that there existed a "natural aristocracy" of the virtuous and talented, "the most precious gift of nature for the instruction, the trusts, and government of society." He believed its members might exist just about anywhere in this nation, and he wanted to see them elevated to positions of influence to replace the hereditary "artificial aristocracy" characteristic of the monarchies of Europe. He suggested that the best form of government is the one that best ensures such "natural aristocrats" are selected to hold its offices.[28]

Responding to the letter, Adams presciently argued that those who might qualify as natural aristocrats would bring into being exactly the sorts of governments our founding fathers were trying to prevent from arising here. He said "artificial aristocracy, and monarchy, and civil, military, political and hierarchical despotism, have all grown out of the natural aristocracy of 'virtues and talents.'" He acknowledged, "We, to be sure, are far remote from this. Many hundred years must roll away before we shall be corrupted." But, he said, "mankind have not yet discovered any remedy against irresistible corruption in elections to offices of great power and profit" other than "making them hereditary"—ironically, the very sort of system we had chosen to reject in rebelling against monarchy.[29]

More than two hundred years later, we're told that higher education produces a meritocracy. We're assured that colleges and universities elevate the brightest and hardest-working into a highly capable elite worthy of the power entrusted to it. We're taught as schoolchildren that everyone in the United States has an equal chance, independent of class background or demographic characteristics, of rising through the education system to become part of the upper classes.

Not true.

Even as higher education has become widely accessible, especially in recent decades, it also has become much more widely stratified by class and race. Our higher-education system has replicated the sort of academic tracking associated with elementary and secondary schools. Just as our K–12 system has long steered students onto separate tracks based on purported assessments of aptitude tainted by race or class bias, college students are now steered into institutions or programs in a manner that arguably gives consideration of potential less weight than assumptions based on family background. Affluent whites look to selective baccalaureate institutions as refuges to protect their offspring from the risk of downward social mobility. Indeed, at the top five hundred or so colleges that their children commonly attend, the graduation rate is 82 percent. Blacks, Latinos, and working-class whites are increasingly crammed into underfunded two-year colleges and four-year colleges with open admissions policies, where only about 49 percent of entering students go on to graduate.[30] Such low completion rates have been shown to stem from inadequate and declining resources at such institutions rather than, as is commonly asserted, worsening college preparation at many high schools.[31]

Driving selective colleges' exclusion of low-income and minority students are the SAT and ACT admissions tests, which such institutions rely on to give their favoritism toward the privileged the veneer of being based on science and quantitative metrics. We know from research that the socioeconomic characteristics of students predict the likelihood of students' admission to a selective college just as well as their scores on the SAT or the ACT.[32] These tests are also greatly overused as predictors of college grades, college completion, and success after college.[33] Marginal differences in students' test scores have negligible predictive value, despite sometimes meaning the difference between acceptance and rejection by a selective college. There are 1.5 million high school seniors with better than an 80 percent chance of graduating from one of the top 193 colleges, but those colleges annually admit only 250,000 freshmen.[34]

Selective colleges may seek to take into account the influence of advantage or disadvantage to more fairly weigh applicants, but those efforts have limited impact. Rather than seek to minimize the role that advantage plays in admission decisions, colleges usually magnify it by giving additional weight to attributes tied to privilege, such as the reputation of the applicants' high schools. In looking at applicants who fall short of being shoo-ins, they're more likely to lower the bar for a rich, connected kid whose borderline admissibility reflects a squandering of tremendous opportunity than for a kid from the wrong side of the tracks whose borderline status demonstrates impressive resilience and striving. They give preferential treatment to the children of alumni, administrators, and faculty members, and to applicants connected to deep-pocketed donors or to politicians they hope to flatter and influence.[35]

Even colleges' financial aid offices tend to favor the wealthy. They lavish money on students who don't need it—those from wealthy families shopping around for tuition discounts when deciding where to drop their kid off in the fall.[36] They often deny such aid to students whose families can't afford the place without it, and some go as far as deliberately trying to deter such students from enrolling by denying them the full amount of aid they'll need, a practice known as "gapping." There are still elite colleges that practice need-blind admissions, but their test-score requirements tend to ensure that most needy students will not qualify.

The eminent higher-education economist Caroline Hoxby describes the increasing concentration of elites at the top colleges as an intergenerational "dynasty." It is sustained by alumni contributions and other revenue sources that provide an institutional subsidy more than ten times the already high amounts students pay in tuition and fees, with the result being that just over a fifth of educational expenditures per student are covered by the students themselves.[37] Meanwhile, the less-advantaged students at open admissions institutions get only what they pay for, and oftentimes less.

Partly as a result of such practices within higher education, our society is becoming a meritocracy in name only, with that purported meritocracy's drawbacks outweighing its perceived benefits. In theory, every individual may have a chance to achieve greater status through educational attainment, but, in fact, one's chances depend more on where one starts in life than we'd like to admit. We're left with a detached leadership class propped up by privilege and overconfident in its own deservedness. Meanwhile, people on our society's lower rungs are concluding that their efforts won't get them anywhere, and they're either succumbing to apathy or lashing out.

Harvard law professor and civil rights theorist Lani Guinier says our society's new elite class passes on its privileges in much the same way as did the old white Anglo-Saxon Protestant (WASP) elite of the twentieth century, but with "an even more worrisome" twist. "The old elite recognized that it had been privileged by accident of birth, so that the message to those who were out of luck was that you were unfortunate but it was through no defect of your own." Its members, she says, "felt the need to give back through public service or financial commitment to the greater good" to defend the social oligarchy. "The new elite, on the other hand, feels that it has earned its privileges based on intrinsic, individual merit. The message, therefore, to those who are not part of this elite is 'You are stupid. You simply don't matter. I deserve all of the advantages I'm granted.'"[38]

The ideal of meritocracy assumes that the elite will be churned by social mobility, that people will rise into the elite through high performance or fall out of it from failure. In reality, our education system helps cement our elite into place, ensuring families' perpetuation of their favored status from one generation to the next. Cleverly summarizing what many educators and education researchers have long observed, Christopher Hayes posits in his book *Twilight of the Elites* the existence of an "Iron Law of Meritocracy." It holds that "eventually the inequality produced by a meritocratic system will grow large enough to subvert the mechanisms of mobility. Unequal outcomes will make equal opportunity impossible. . . . Those who are able to climb up the ladder will find ways to pull it up after them, or to selectively lower it to allow their friends, allies, and kin to scramble up."[39]

In the 2015 commencement address delivered to the graduates of Yale's law school, Daniel Markovits, one of Yale's star law school professors, offered this ironic encapsulation of how meritocracy had turned the individual virtues of hard work and talent into forces that undermine the common good: "American meritocracy has thus become precisely what it was invented to combat: a mechanism for the dynastic transmission of wealth and privilege across generations. Meritocracy now constitutes a modern-day aristocracy, one might even say, purpose-built for a world in which the greatest source of wealth is not land or factories but human capital, the free labor of skilled workers."[40]

It will not be easy to challenge the class- and race-based "meritocratic" juggernaut so as to revitalize and protect upward mobility. Judged individually according to the current rules of the college admissions game, most families of high socioeconomic status seem deserving. After all, their members consistently showed up at school, completed their homework, and scored high on tests on their way to attending the best colleges and obtaining the best jobs. All that seems fair. No wonder they feel entitled to defend their disproportionate claim to money and power and their right to pass those gains on to their children.

Elitism in higher education comes with convincing rationales and sophisticated apologists. As always, the best defenses are intuitively sound ideas that go largely unexamined. The post–World War II era has given rise to a widespread but largely unproven belief that we can somehow create ineffable synergies that serve the greater public interest by putting the young people with the highest test scores and the most published professors together on the most elite campuses with the highest per-student spending. There certainly are private benefits for the participants in elite education, but the public benefits are much smaller, and they're never measured against the public benefits of the economic and racial justice that elitism precludes.[41] Add to all that the general public's faith in the attainment of the American Dream through individual striving—a faith that treats individuals as abstractions, with no accounting for context—and you have top-to-bottom support for selective colleges' entrenched elitism, even as evidence mounts for public disillusionment with the higher-education system.

Educational privilege can even be portrayed as patriotic. Our nation's meritocratic higher-education system came into being largely to marshal the intellectual forces necessary to fight the Cold War and prevail in the race to explore space and other contests against communist nations. When James Bryant Conant, a Harvard president who had helped oversee the nation's World War II effort to develop the atomic bomb, heard qualms expressed about the elitist nature of the meritocratic admissions system he and others were creating in response to the Soviet threat, he said the nation had no time to waste fretting over such equity concerns, because "the fate of freedom hangs very much in the balance."[42]

Similarly, the Nation at Risk report of 1983 began the latest long wave of elementary and secondary education reform with a breathless call to arms to protect our national "preeminence in commerce, industry, science, and technological innovation."[43] The report—the product of a commission of business, government, and education leaders established by President Ronald Reagan—treated as an afterthought any concern about equality in the opportunity to learn. It instead fixated on improving education in a few fields that currently account for about 5 percent of the workforce but are seen as crucial for global economic domination: science, technology, engineering, and math.[44]

Policymakers and educational leaders at all levels are complicit. Separation by race and class begins in kindergarten, long before college admission officers get involved, and continues through twelfth grade. From there, the K–12 system's apportionment of educational opportunity based on race, ethnicity, and class becomes faithfully reproduced across the full range of American colleges and universities. The postsecondary system mimics and magnifies the inequalities of the K–12 system and then projects them into the labor market, ensuring that privilege linked to race and class gets reproduced from one generation to the next.

Can we look to America's higher-education leaders to restore the right balance between merit and opportunity? Clearly they have stepped up to help our nation deal with crises before. Led by Conant during the Cold War, they unseated East Coast WASP privilege by successfully advocating for the national administration of standardized college admissions tests so that top colleges could identify and enroll bright kids from the hinterlands. Conant wanted to use the test to scour America's highways and byways for academic talent and find the next Einstein behind a plow.[45] Selective colleges responded to the urban rebellions of the 1960s by adopting admissions policies that leveled the playing field for minority applicants, to send black Americans a message of hope for upward mobility and for a seat at the tables where decisions get made. Higher education has been a primary avenue for women's flight from patrimony. Women with bachelor's degrees now outnumber men with those credentials in the workforce.[46] At the time, these efforts opened the gates of higher education to a broader cross-section of qualified students. But, over time, they have lost their edge as court decisions have limited the use of affirmative action, federal policy has weakened enforcement of laws designed to promote equality on the basis of sex, and colleges have implemented policies that use standardized test scores to strengthen the gentry's hold on top colleges.

While the mechanisms for increasing diversity and equity on campus are changing, higher education's capacity to see the value of diversity and equity has not gone away. We've seen signs in recent years that at least some presidents of selective colleges are giving greater weight than in the recent past to considerations of opportunity. Among the institutions at the forefront, Franklin & Marshall College, under former president Daniel Porterfield, substantially increased its low-income enrollments with the help of a summer program that sought out talented students from relatively disadvantaged back-grounds and prepared them for college.[47] Amherst College, initially under the leadership of former president Anthony Marx, has brought about similar increases in enrollments of low-income students partly by aggressively soliciting the donations necessary to ensure they re-ceive sufficient financial aid.[48] At Vassar College, president emerita Catharine Bond Hill led the institution to significantly increase the shares of its students from low-income families and racial and eth-nic minority groups.[49] Even Ivy League member Princeton University, under President Christopher Eisgruber, has started to diversify its stu-dent body. It dramatically increased enrollments of both low-income and middle-class students by making socioeconomic diversity a much higher priority.[50]

For their part, some less-selective colleges have made big strides in ensuring such students graduate. Georgia State University, which serves a large number of low-income and minority students, raised its six-year graduation rate from 32 percent to more than 54 percent from 2003 to 2017.[51] Under President Mark P. Becker, it has become a pioneer at identifying risk factors that get in the way of students completing their degrees.

It seems unlikely, however, that most selective or somewhat selec-tive American colleges will reform themselves without being guided, coaxed, and prodded. The problem is that, by buying into a mad scramble for money and prestige, they have become obstacles to their own progress. They're too caught up in dealing with market forces, too focused on short-term competition, and too insulated from the strug-gles of average Americans to see the big picture and what's needed for the good of our nation and their own welfare in the long term. Even those with the best of intentions are trapped in the prestige game.

In their interests and our own, we will need to change that game's rules. Higher education has long equally valued the competing prom-ises of merit and opportunity at the heart of our educational system, but in the end, many students are shut out. Without the opportunity to attend a college from which they can graduate, higher education is just an empty promise.

In the chapters that follow, we examine the role that colleges and universities play as both some of the most aspirational places in our society and some of the institutions most accountable for persistent societal inequity. By going to college, a person can change his or her lot in life, but only if the system is based on opportunity, fairness, and merit. Instead of realizing that ideal, we as a country have built a system that is committed to sustaining a class- and race-based aristocracy through intense and imbalanced competition. Without serious reforms, the United States is in danger of becoming what Adams warned about more than two hundred years ago: a system more dedicated to maintaining a hereditary aristocracy than providing equal opportunity.

We begin in chapter 1, "What the Nation Needs," by describing the evolution of the distinctly American commitment to the balance between the competing ideals of individualism and equality. The pendulum swings between these ideals have been a driving force in our nation's history and profoundly influenced how our colleges respond to calls to reward test-based merit or provide equal opportunity. We look at competing beliefs that have shaped the relationship between education and American society, as well as the outsized roles that racism and classism have played. We trace how these ideas have played out throughout our nation's history, both shaping and being shaped by economic, social, and political trends. And we describe how rapid industrialization after the Civil War and more recent economic trends driven by international competition and the Information Age have reduced opportunity and social mobility and widened gaps between our nation's "have-nots" and "haves," most of whom have white skin. Often the "haves" assisted this process or, at least, deliberately refrained from taking steps to stop it.

We focus on the forces that have left us with today's stratified and unequal higher-education system in chapter 2, "The Rise of the Sorting Machine." A growing number of selective colleges compete fiercely for students from families with the financial means to fatten endowments and operating budgets. Colleges lower down the prestige ladder find themselves starved of resources, partly from paucities of students able and willing to pay much tuition, but also because they receive far too little support from neoliberal lawmakers, who have shown themselves perfectly willing to let an unfettered market cull the weakest, smallest, or least aggressive.

Chapter 3, "Understanding the Odds," takes an unflinching look at the inequalities that shape the applicants who knock on colleges' doors. It looks at deciding the proper role of higher education as a moral problem of balancing individual liberty with economic and racial justice. It maps out the huge obstacles that loom in the paths of those whose parents are not well educated and wealthy, and of those who find that no achievement can insulate them from discrimination based on their ethnicity or the color of their skin. It also makes clear that many more people surmount such obstacles—and end up fully qualified to enroll and succeed at even our best colleges—than ever actually pass through such institutions' doors.

The flaws built into the sorting machine's inner workings are laid bare in chapter 4, "Standardized Bias." In this chapter, we look under the machine's hood, showing just how miscalibrated and corrupted it has become in determining who is worthy of each level of education. We shed light on the tremendous harm done by our society's embrace of the view of intelligence as innate and by our excessive trust in standardized admissions tests as the measure of potential. We reveal how most tinkerers with the machine seek to perpetuate privilege rather than advance equity.

Chapter 5's title, "Separate and Unequal," sums up what kind of higher-education system we're left with as a result of market-driven institutional stratification, endemic socioeconomic inequality, pervasive admissions bias, and our nation's reluctance to recognize or try to remedy discrimination. That system has distinct tracks reminiscent of those once found in our nation's "comprehensive" high schools, which steered some students into college preparatory classes that groomed them for degrees and promising futures while consigning other students to training in how to fix cars, mop floors, or bake casseroles. Much as was the case in yesterday's comprehensive high schools, today's higher-education system has an upper track that is dominated by the wealthy and white, and a lower track that disproportionately serves those students who are members of racial and ethnic minority groups or from families of modest means.

The fights waged against inequity within our nation's education system are examined in chapter 6, "The Fight for Fairness." They include bitter legal and political struggles over the financing of education, the racial integration of public schools and colleges, and colleges' use of affirmative action to enroll lower-income and minority students. In each of these conflicts, the battle lines have ebbed and flowed, with all sides laying claim to righteousness steeped in our nation's core values. More importantly, each struggle has revolved around a distinct perceived injustice rather than considerations of the bigger picture. This antagonism has resulted in the expenditure of vast amounts of money and energy, and the stirring up of animosity and the loss of goodwill, without ever squarely confronting the establishment for allowing the injustices to occur. Each has hacked at an appendage of the dragon while failing to aim for the heart of the beast.

Chapter 7, "Built to Collapse," explains why our higher-education system is unsustainable in its current form. No public policy proposed so far seems capable of slowing its stratification and segregation as a result of unchecked market forces. It inefficiently spends vast sums subsidizing conspicuous consumption by the wealthy while it denies others the minimum postsecondary educations needed to fully participate in a postindustrial society and economy. It excludes and alienates enough people to undermine support for higher education as a public good, spurring public divestment that leaves colleges even more dependent on private revenue sources that incentivize further stratification. Its failures to provide equal educational opportunity or to foster social mobility strengthen the belief that individualism and equality of opportunity are irreconcilable. Our inability to find the sweet spot in balancing these equally valued but competing ideals will result in more political division and instability. The 2017 chaos in Charlottesville was only a harbinger of the trouble that is brewing, as evidenced by more recent outbreaks of violence inspired by radical ideology, such as the massacres at the Tree of Life synagogue in Pittsburgh, Pennsylvania, and a Walmart in El Paso, Texas.

In "College for All," this book's eighth and final chapter, we are realistic about likely opposition and barriers to needed reform in higher education, and yet we argue for the possibility of dramatic change. A first step is convincing the leaders of selective colleges that the rat race they're running threatens their institutions' long-term health and the viability of our democratic society. We suggest changes to selective colleges' admissions policies that will enable them to enroll students from a much broader cross-section of American society. We direct their attention to the large, untapped pool of academically talented students we call strivers—young people who have encountered hardship and deprivation and demonstrated determination and resilience that will enable them to do just fine at a tough, selective college.

Recognizing that we will only get so far by focusing on selective colleges, which educate just 18 percent of American students,[52] we call for changes in the entire postsecondary education system that will promote upward social mobility and ensure that colleges efficiently channel people from high schools into the workforce. Just as our nation flourished in its first one hundred years by offering access to free land, we urge providing at least some free postsecondary education as a way to renew the promise of opportunity for everyone.

We confront a fundamental question: how do we define educational adequacy in the twenty-first century? Many educators and policymakers in K–12 and higher education define adequacy as high school and college completion. But such completion goals raise a larger question: completion for what? We see the real measure of educational adequacy as the successful transition from youth dependency to independent adulthood and citizenship in a modern democracy and a capitalist economy.

But we recognize we will only get so far by appealing to the better angels of the higher-education leadership at the top of the selectivity pyramid. Elite colleges are key examples of the class- and race-based inequities permeating higher education, but they serve best not as mere targets of criticism but as points of leverage for the reform of postsecondary education. A little more affirmative action at the top has symbolic value and benefits those who get in, but really only makes a difference on the margins. Class and race inequity in higher education is a systemic problem requiring much bigger systemic solutions. With this in mind, we shift our attention away from the elite colleges to the entire postsecondary education and training system. And we argue further that effective solutions cannot be restricted to higher-education policy alone. If we are to maximize upward mobility, we will need our higher-education system to reach back into high schools and look ahead to labor markets to ensure students are getting the educations they need.

Completing the transition from education to the workforce—and flourishing in a system of democratic capitalism—requires an adequate general education and, at its conclusion, a good job. A general education spanning a range of broad subject areas, when combined with specific education in particular fields of study with labor-market value—ideally at the bachelor's degree level—is a crucial asset in an increasingly complex and diverse global society and economy. It is a means to economic independence as well as individual human flourishing, a necessity for informed democratic participation and a bulwark against authoritarianism.[53]

Many object to tying education to economic outcomes. But we believe that in the long term, the commodification at the core of the emerging mass system of higher education can be seen as the potential engine of its democratization, in that it creates financial incentives to provide at least some basic level of postsecondary education to everyone. It extends the reach of college education and the attendant increase in liberal learning to an increasing share of the population.

We are convinced that education reforms are not only the most effective, but also the politically preferred approach to finding a new balance between individualism and upward mobility. The American public regards the beneficence of education as gospel. We Americans welcome our increasing reliance on education as the arbiter of economic opportunity because, in theory, education allows us to expand merit-based opportunity without surrendering individual responsibility.

The cultural historian Richard Weiss teaches that in American history the belief that anyone can succeed "is a two-edged sword. Taken as a description of what is, it encourages complacency; taken as a description of what ought to be, it encourages the impulse to reform." [54] For the sake of needed reform, we call upon all sectors of education to take an "all-one-system" approach that connects the dots from high school through college to early careers. We urge the expenditure of more public resources on higher education's neglected tiers: the nonselective four-year colleges and community colleges that play an outsized role in training hundreds of thousands of Americans for success in a rapidly changing economy.

We seek to rebalance our education system's role as both a rewarder of merit *and* a provider of equal opportunity. We are hopeful that the growing gulf between individual merit and equal opportunity finally will get the attention it deserves.

1

WHAT THE NATION NEEDS

What do we want from our nation's colleges and universities? How should they balance the needs to provide preparation for a good life, for citizenship, and for economic independence? Should they focus on training people for specific careers, or should they seek to graduate lifelong learners? Should they foster social mobility, or simply accept that some families will never set foot on college campuses while others enroll generation upon generation at Harvard? Should they try to groom the best and brightest to make major contributions in their chosen fields, or cast a wide net and ensure that everyone can earn a living in our rapidly changing economy? Should they be allowed to continue offering separate and unequally funded college tracks, one for the racially and economically advantaged and another for the disadvantaged, even when such students are equally prepared?

It's worth asking these questions of ourselves if we are to subject our postsecondary institutions to scrutiny. After all, we'll find it hard to pass judgment on the colleges we have if we lack a clear vision of the colleges we want. And pursuing our vision of the colleges we want is a fool's errand if they won't be the colleges we need.

Ultimately, what we want out of our colleges boils down to a question rooted in the tension between individualism and democratic egalitarianism—a tension made inevitable by the contradictions that come with our historical efforts to balance the inequality produced by a

successful capitalist economy against the belief in equality underlying
a democratic society. Should our colleges be arenas for individualistic
competition that sort people into economic winners and losers, or
should they be promoters of social equality and the good of all?

To get a better sense of where we need to go, it helps to first focus
on how our nation's colleges, and our higher-education system as a
whole, were shaped by our nation's distinct culture and history and
by the persistent influence of race and class in America. It's safe to
say that both our colleges and our higher-education system would be
very different—maybe even unrecognizable—if not for the influences
of the Puritans, the American Revolution, westward conquest, slavery, immigration, the suffragettes, the civil rights movement, and our
long-standing devotion to the free market.

What our nation *didn't* experience also played a role in shaping our
higher-education system. In crossing the Atlantic, the early American
colonists left behind both feudal institutions and societies rigidly and
explicitly organized by hereditary class.[1] Our country was formed in
a revolution against an overseas monarchy, and the mythology that
arose around that originating event has encouraged us to believe that
we have a society in which opportunity is not dependent on heredity.
We have failed to develop the deep class consciousness that's a primary feature of politics in Europe and other places around the world.
Without the feudal past that provided a strong historical basis for
Europeans' demands that government engage in the redistribution of
wealth and power from the upper classes to the lower classes, we never
fully developed a comprehensive welfare state.[2]

Instead, our colleges were shaped by the philosophies that took root
in a land of new possibilities and competed for prominence: individualism and republicanism.

Our nation's colleges have also been buffeted by decisions and behavior arising from base impulses and prejudice. Racism, classism,
and sexism have been controlling and resilient forces throughout
the world's, and our nation's, history; like shape-shifting scavengers,
these intellectual pretenders have clung to whatever ideas seemed
to justify them at the time, and found new justifications to sustain

themselves when the old ones disappeared or got snatched away. Look no further than the fact that nearly all of our nation's colleges enrolled only white men in the period leading up to the Civil War, and many remained off-limits to African Americans and women well into the middle of the twentieth century. Our leaders, and the institutions they built, have been much more likely to espouse the value of equality and equal opportunity than they've been to seriously attempt to provide either.

Individualism: The Importance of Me

No belief has played a bigger role in our history and its education institutions than belief in the sanctity of the individual. Faith in individual striving is embedded in our education system's DNA. It was central to the faith-based worldview of the Puritans who founded the nation's first schools and played a central role in establishing the nation's first college, Harvard, in 1636.

Our nation's original Puritan settlers brought over with them a deep faith in individual striving as the means by which those predestined for salvation distinguish themselves. Their religious beliefs, arising from the sixteenth-century Protestant Reformation, saw individualism as having a moral basis, steeped in their belief that the source of moral authority was the individual conscience. Like the other Protestant sects that counted for most of the nation's early white settlers, they held that individuals should have their own private, direct relationship with God, unmediated by any church official or monarch. They regarded individual success as evidence that people had been born predestined for ascension into heaven. Their logic was tautological— being chosen by God meant success because those who succeeded must have been chosen. They preached values like industriousness, prudence, and sobriety as a means to stay on the right path, and in doing so imported the middle-class "Protestant work ethic" that became crucial to our economy.[3] To the extent they espoused equality, it was the equality to be found among the community of the virtuous in the service of the almighty.[4] They established schools to foster literacy and perpetuate the faith, seeing the ability to read the Bible as the best defense against false prophets, heresy, and church dogma.[5]

The individualism born out of the early settlers' religious beliefs would be honed for the self-reliance needed to carve out a life in the New World, and it would be ingrained enough to survive the secular shift in thinking that took place here as a result of the Enlightenment and the resulting American Revolution. Its faith-based underpinnings were replaced by an intellectual foundation derived from Enlightenment philosophy, the writings of Thomas Jefferson and other founding fathers, the teachings of the ancient Greek and Roman scholars who inspired those seeking to form a new republic, and the thinking of Adam Smith, whose writings on the free market helped create the intellectual framework for a thriving capitalist economy.

The emergence of individualism as a well-defined secular value came during the Enlightenment of the late 1600s, mainly through the writings of John Locke, the English philosopher who profoundly influenced our constitutional republic's founders.[6] Locke argued that all men have natural rights to life, liberty, and to any property derived through honest labor, and that governments rightfully exist mainly to secure such rights from encroachment by others. He wrote in his 1690 *Second Treatise of Civil Government* that all men are naturally in "a state of perfect freedom" to conduct themselves and handle their property as they see fit, "without asking leave, or depending upon the will of any other man."[7]

The liberalism of Locke blended two contradictory ideas—that we are all fundamentally equal before the law and that social inequalities stem from differences in our natural talents. In *Why Liberalism Failed*, the political scientist Patrick Deneen characterizes Locke's notion of individualism as amounting to what Plato defined as a "noble lie."[8] Plato argued in *The Republic* that societies subscribe to untruths about their creation because doing so leaves the populace more inclined to support the state and get along with each other. In proposing the creation of a republic made up of three distinct social classes, Plato recalled how Socrates told of a hypothetical society's embrace of an creation myth in which a god created an upper class of rulers made of gold, a second class of helpers made of silver, and a lower class of farmers and craftsmen made of iron and brass.[9] Liberal individualism created a similar social order based on its own version of the myth, which offers those on the bottom exaggerated hope of advancing and those on top false assurances that they legitimately occupy their high place, Deneen argues.[10] Such critics of Locke fault his individualism for having an inherent contradiction, in that it is based in a belief in equality even while being cited as a justification for social inequality. Noting how the laws governing liberal societies perpetuate imbalances of power, the French writer Anatole France wryly observed: "The law, in its majestic equality, forbids the rich as well as the poor to sleep under bridges, to beg in the streets, and to steal bread."[11]

Thomas Jefferson bought into Locke's belief that a mix of fundamental rights and equal opportunity would produce a society led by the worthiest. In writing in the Declaration of Independence that "all men are created equal," Jefferson meant that all men—or, at least, all white men—are born with an equal right to seek to make the most of themselves, not that they remain equal regardless of their subsequent successes or failures. He echoed Locke's thinking in envisioning a social order for our new republic. He called for a "natural aristocracy" of the virtuous and talented to replace the lineage-based "artificial aristocracy" characteristic of Europe.[12] In contrast to the Puritans who first landed on our shores, he trusted men, not God, to select the best among us. As the sociologist Daniel Bell observed in his influential 1972 essay "On Meritocracy and Equality," "Among the Founding Fathers the idea of virtue and of election by ability (if no longer by grace) predominated. . . . The central theme was independence, and the conditions whereby a man could be independent. But in the very use of Lockean language there was an implicit commitment to a hierarchy— the hierarchy of intellect."[13]

Jefferson and other founding fathers also embraced a more spiritual and deeply personal form of individualism, one that would shape the missions of our nation's education institutions in the centuries to come and serve as the foundation of college curriculums in the liberal arts. It likely stemmed from the ancient Greek Epicureans, whose philosophy argued that the greatest good is the pleasure each of us derives from pursuing knowledge in the course of a simple, modest life. Jefferson's assertion in the Declaration of Independence that the "pursuit of happiness" is "an unalienable right" stems from the Epicureans and, especially, the philosopher Lucretius.[14] Focused on individual flourishing, Lucretius and other Epicureans encouraged learning for its own sake, and saw immersion in the arts, the sciences, and the humanities as an antidote to ignorance and superstition.

Our history of deriving economic plenty from the conquest and exploitation of a new, resource-rich continent strengthened our individualist biases.[15] In 1776, the same year the Declaration of Independence was signed, the Scottish social philosopher and political economist Adam Smith published the seminal free-market text *An Inquiry into the Nature and Causes of the Wealth of Nations*, which argued that unfettered individual competition produces wealth and general human progress. It offered a strong case for seeing individual liberty as an economic imperative, and laid the intellectual foundation for our nation's reliance on the free market as the chief arena where individual striving plays out.[16] Our capitalist economy would emerge here as individualism's favored child.

The French diplomat and historian Alexis de Tocqueville saw the potential downside of our nation's individualist economic ethos when touring America in the early 1830s. In *Democracy in America*, published in 1835, he wrote:

> The first thing that strikes the observation is an innumerable multitude of men, all equal and alike, incessantly endeavoring to procure the petty and paltry pleasures with which they glut their lives. Each of them, living apart, is as a stranger to all the rest; his children and his private friends constitute to him the whole of mankind. As for the rest of his fellow citizens, he is close to them but does not see them; he touches them, but he does not feel them; he exists only in himself and for himself alone; and if his kindred still remain to him he may be said at any rate to have lost his country.[17]

Republicanism: The Importance of We

If there is a legitimate contender other than individualism for centrality in the history of education in America, it is republican virtue. From intense study of ancient Rome's poets and philosophers, a task common in their era, the founding fathers derived a deep faith in the venerable approach to governance known as republicanism.[18] Republicanism—the virtue, not the political party—starts from a different place than individualism. Republican virtue supersedes the sum of individual wants and needs. It is a governing creed that begins not with "me" but with "we," emphasizing our roles as citizens of a larger society.[19] It holds that our liberty depends on our involvement in self-government and our informed pursuit of the common good.[20] Ultimately, republics depend on public virtue, especially under stress.[21] Our founders tried to protect us from tyranny and mob rule by founding our republic on a constitution that enshrined individual rights and the separation of governing powers.

The inculcation of republican virtue has been a key mission of American education, helping to generate support for common elementary and secondary schools in the nineteenth century and the first half of the twentieth century, during the period before education became an economic necessity.[22] It led us to develop an education system that provides a general education covering a broad range of subjects to students from kindergarten through high school. That system culminates in the hybrid mix of specific majors and general education requirements that forms the signature curriculum in American two-year and four-year college degrees.

Since the 1980s, globalism and advances in technology have driven a surge in the complexity of our economy and the diversity of our culture, raising the bar in terms of the level of education needed for economic independence and to play a constructive role in the republic's life. No longer is a high school diploma sufficient. People generally need at least some form of postsecondary credential.[23] A growing share of us rely on the general education that comes with two-year and four-year college degrees to equip us to support ourselves and instill in us habits of mind such as critical thinking, the ability to consider multiple viewpoints, and competence in interacting with other cultures, all crucial if we are to advance and defend democracy.

There are many reasons why education—especially at the postsecondary level—stands as a friend to republics and a natural enemy of authoritarianism, especially in our current time. Some are purely financial. The greater income and financial security currently associated with educational attainment beyond high school generally leaves people feeling less threatened by the prospect of economic competition from immigrants and foreigners. People equipped by colleges to cope personally and economically with the various forces that buffet them through adulthood feel more control over their lives and value their personal autonomy as well as their economic security. The skeptical culture of higher education is itself anathema to authoritarianism, which looks with suspicion upon free societies, seeks to suppress dissident views, and often feeds off nativism, racism, xenophobia, ethnocentrism, religious tensions, and other sources of animosity. The available evidence tells us that higher education—and, especially, exposure to a humanistic curriculum focused on independent, critical, evidence-based thinking—mitigates authoritarian tendencies. There exists a strong correlation between a highly educated populace and democratic governance, both in the United States and across the world.[24]

While individualism and republicanism have always animated our society and education system, they have never competed on equal terms. As of the beginning of the industrial era in the late 1800s, the mutually reinforcing influence of individualism and our market economy have combined to make the individual the primary focus of our education system and our economy. This approach teaches us to view ourselves as responsible for our own destinies and to blame low social status on a lack of talent or effort rather than the forces of oppression. Americans tend to see K–12 education as a public good, but, despite evidence to the contrary, we also tend to see K–12 education more as the screener and revealer of talent than the creator of it.[25] In contrast, we treat higher education more as an individual responsibility, with students bearing responsibility for gaining admission and paying tuition.

The perception of higher education as an individual responsibility skews its social benefit. The best colleges—and the desired mix of specific and general education at the heart of liberal education, especially the bachelor's degree—are disproportionately the province of the most advantaged segments of our society.[26]

Selective higher education has always been reserved almost entirely for elites. To add insult to injury, elite higher education has always ruminated over the question of whether the benefits of liberal education are beyond the intellectual reach of the common folk, especially those who come from classes relegated to "menial work." It's hard to imagine having sat down for a beer with Washington, Jefferson, Hamilton, or any of the other founders if you didn't own a ruffled shirt and silk britches. The elites who govern modern higher education aren't quite as exclusive, but some still have their doubts about the worthiness of others.[27]

In summary, individualism—the "me" in the American psyche— exists in tension with republican civic values—the "we" needed to maintain support for a representative democracy. In a democratic and capitalist system such as ours, democracy assumes equality at the same time as capitalism relies on inequality to motivate workers and accumulate funds in the hands of investors. College could defuse such tension by being the great equalizer, the mechanism designed to ensure that anyone can pursue their dreams of upward social mobility. Yet colleges have generally shirked any responsibility for doing so, often because they themselves have been steered by market forces more than anything else.

From Free Land to Free College

The history of individual opportunity in America can be boiled down to a shift from access to free land to access to free education. Free land was made available to each white man in the colonies. Then, in the nineteenth-century republic, free education was offered first at the elementary level and then at public high schools, and now is increasingly discussed as necessary at the postsecondary level. Our republic began with a transactional relationship in which the government distributed land to help secure the support of the white male voting public. That relationship has evolved into one in which the government funds education as the preferred guarantee of equal opportunity, presumably preserving each individual's responsibility for his or her own upward mobility.

The new constitutional republic gave virtually all white men, regardless of their past circumstances, access to power, property, and the fruits of their own labor. It legally protected all white men but prison inmates from all forms of indentured servitude, including apprenticeship contracts.[28] It provided them access to free land to exploit, settle, and farm, and its rapid expansion perpetuated skill shortages that made work readily available.[29]

People here instinctively rejected credentialing, and states passed laws opening nearly every profession to anyone enterprising enough to seek to practice it.[30]

To participate in the economic expansion, "Americans made themselves literate," the prominent historian Robert H. Wiebe later noted. Even with little help from public schools, the literacy rate for white men soared between 1800 and 1840, from roughly 75 percent to 95 percent in the north and from roughly 50 percent to 80 percent in the south.[31]

White men used their newfound autonomy to tear down the elites. As white men became self-educated, self-governing, and eager to vote, populist sentiments arose among them. In the 1828 presidential race, populists lashed out at—and horrified—the nation's elites by handing a landslide victory to Andrew Jackson. A professed champion of the "common man," Jackson argued that the nation remained in the grip of a "corrupt aristocracy" and professed little patience for public officials who failed to yield to the popular will. His basic political approach— portraying himself as a Washington outsider determined to use the power of democracy to rein in a republic's entrenched elite—would be copied in the years to come by other presidential candidates, with varying degrees of sincerity and success.[32]

All white men were entitled to be their own bosses, cultivating the idea—still widely held today—that self-reliance is an essential element of individual worthiness, citizenship, and republican civic virtue. Thanks to the general availability of self-directed work, we entered an age of self-rule for white men.[33] It was an era that saw extraordinary levels of voter participation after even white males without property gained voting rights beginning in the late 1820s. Participation rates among eligible voters remained high, sometimes exceeding 80 percent, through most of the rest of the century, up until the beginning of the Industrial Era.[34]

The common school thrived in the nineteenth century, not so much because it was economically necessary but because it helped lay the groundwork for expansion. Fully armed frontiersmen scouted and conquered the land, farmers settled it, and school marms and preachers rendered it "civilized" in the view of the populations that came here from Europe. The precursors to today's public schools, common schools popped up in cities and towns everywhere, their construction financed heavily by revenue from land set aside for them through federal laws related to westward expansion. Every American town decided it needed a schoolmaster, every state a school system.[35]

Despite the rise of populist advocacy for the "common man," the nation continued to have a narrow view of who exactly deserved individual rights and access to education. Blacks were consigned to hundreds of years of slavery, followed by ninety years of Jim Crow and a failed commitment to forty acres and a mule after the Civil War.[36] Native Americans were subjected to genocidal conquest, and women were often relegated to the home and kept out of public life. As long as the institution of slavery persisted, teaching literacy to African Americans remained illegal in many states.

When the Union victory in the Civil War helped vanquish the belief that slavery could be reconciled with our morals and ideals, those certain of the inherent inferiority of others looked to new scientific developments to cobble together justifications for their prejudices. They found a scientific explanation for human inequality in the theory of natural selection posited by the evolutionary biologist Charles Darwin in his landmark 1859 book *On the Origin of Species*.[37] Although Darwin himself was an abolitionist, and his book deliberately omitted any application of his theory to mankind, his ideas nonetheless helped give rise to Social Darwinism, the controversial invocation of natural selection to explain human societies' disparate fortunes.[38]

It also inspired Darwin's cousin, Sir Francis Galton, to develop heredity-based explanations for variations in human intelligence and other traits and argue that some people are genetically superior to others, giving rise to a field Galton later dubbed "eugenics." Eugenics eventually would be researched and taught at many colleges and universities, and the popularization of eugenic beliefs in the early twentieth century would help inspire a preoccupation with marrying into the "right" families and an upsurge of marriages joining people within the same social class.[39] Practices aimed at "improving" the genetic quality of the human race live on today in a host of ways: dating services for elite colleges' graduates, the high premiums that fertility operations attach to the eggs and sperm of Ivy League graduates, and the role that racism and xenophobia continue to play in shaping everything from cultural attitudes and social interactions to political behavior and access to opportunity.

Raising Hierarchies and Sinking the Lower Classes

In his seminal 1893 essay, "The Significance of the Frontier in American History," the historian Frederick Jackson Turner expressed fears that the settlement of the American frontier's last vestiges would bring an end to our culture of striving, and that the industrialism on the rise here would crush individualism and foment class struggle as it had in nineteenth-century Europe.[40]

Together with the closing of the American frontier, which it helped bring about, the Second Industrial Revolution would trigger a wave of change in American society and in the role of the education system.

A period of profound technological, social, and economic transformation, the Second Industrial Revolution brought an end to the period of "self-made" white men who went through life on fairly equal footing, regardless of their education levels. In contrast to the First Industrial Revolution of the late 1700s and early 1800s—which mainly spawned inventions that simplified tasks and made few demands on education—the Second Industrial Revolution dramatically changed how Americans worked and lived and what they needed to be taught.

As American industry became national in scale, capital became concentrated in the hands of a few business leaders and robber barons, resulting in more-pronounced social stratification on the basis of wealth and skill.[41] Across the Atlantic, surging inequalities in wealth and social standing fostered sometimes violent movements espousing anti-capitalist ideologies. Communism, socialism, and syndicalism—in which workers' unions own the means of production—each found substantial support.[42] As a result, both in Europe and in America, democratic capitalism began to take hold, alongside regulation meant to mediate capitalism's harsh inequalities. In Europe, leaders began to create a comprehensive safety net, which become more complete following World War II, while the United States produced one that was more threadbare.[43]

Speaking at the Cambridge Reform Club in 1873, Alfred Marshall, a leading political economist of his time, argued that although capitalism and democracy were antagonists in theory, they could be made allies in practice by striking a balance between strong democratic governments and strong markets. Market economies, he reasoned, would generate the taxable wealth necessary to fund enough publicly provided education and social services, which in turn would guarantee citizens full membership in society and the ability to rise in the economy.[44] "The question," he said, "is not whether all men will ultimately be equal—that they certainly will not—but whether progress may not go on steadily, if slowly, till, by occupation at least, every man is a gentleman" who values education and leisure more than the "mere increase of wages and material comforts."[45] He assumed that a basic general education would be a universal common experience for the citizenry. He did not see education as a means of apportioning economic opportunity and power, because in his day the vast majority of people learned their occupations in the home or on the job.

Even as he spoke, the economy was changing in ways that would make capitalism and democracy harder to reconcile, and Marshall's views seem quaint. As the industrial era continued through the 1900s and gave way to the postindustrial knowledge economy of our current century, it became increasingly clear that the rising value of human capital had strengthened the link between education and capitalism. The two became mutually reinforcing mechanisms for fostering inequality based on race, class, and gender.

Four distinct classes can be seen as emerging during this period. On top stood wealthy industrialists and landowners; beneath them were managers and professionals, followed by a skilled working class and, finally, unskilled labor. White-collar workers on salaries became more distinct from blue-collar workers, who were largely paid by the hour. Industrialism not only created complex new hierarchies, it also sunk the lower classes as well as racial minorities to economic and political depths that ensured lives governed by constant economic necessity, with no payoff for political participation. Social status at birth became a much bigger determiner of personal, economic, and political power than it had been in the past. As those at the bottom of the pile became more alienated from the democratic elite,[46] participation in elections began to drop off.[47]

Voting regulations and Jim Crow discrimination amplified and calcified political and economic disenfranchisement. The suppression of voting is endemic in the United States, where the founders left it up to individual states to define voting eligibility. Black men did not acquire the right to vote until after the Civil War, and Jim Crow made casting their ballots rare and dangerous. Women were not guaranteed suffrage at the federal level until the passage of the Nineteenth Amendment in 1920. It took the Voting Rights Act of 1965 to fully guarantee all blacks access to the voting booth, and even now efforts to limit black political power through gerrymandering and voter suppression remain common.[48] The lowering of the minimum voting age from twenty-one to eighteen occurred only after the controversy over the Vietnam War highlighted the contradiction in deeming people both too young to vote and old enough to risk death in combat. Politicians have resisted the idea of making Election Day a holiday or otherwise ensuring people could leave work to vote.

This history of uneven voting rights and outright voter suppression has taken its toll. At the beginning of the 1900s, the United States led the democratic world in voter turnout. Now we rank twenty-sixth among advanced postindustrial nations.[49] The American University political scientist Allan Lichtman has observed: "A consequence of nonvoting, partisan gerrymandering, and public cynicism is an American government that is especially responsive to the wealthiest citizens, a throwback to the early republic when tax and property qualifications prevailed across the nation."[50]

As Turner predicted, the closing of the American frontier did, indeed, bring an end to visions of settling free land and living autonomously. Although some found success in the uneven fortunes of entrepreneurship, many resigned themselves to lifetimes of economic dependency on employers. Individualism took a turn inward, with people seeking personal fulfillment and retreating into their private and personal lives. They began compartmentalizing their lives in ways that divided the personal from the professional, the private from what was public, with personal fulfillment increasingly relegated to the vacations, weekends, and retirements that rose in importance in Americans' lives.[51] Especially among the affluent and highly educated, the standard of success broadened from economic self-sufficiency and control over one's own work to the achievement of a high level of personal self-fulfillment. To get on the path to such fulfillment, the privileged increasingly looked to colleges' liberal arts programs, especially their offerings in the humanities.

Although most Americans still learned their occupations on the farm or on the job in the early twentieth century, high school replaced grade school as the academic level a young person should reach to receive a general education that would both socialize them and teach them democratic citizenship.[52] Colleges, for their part, became finishing schools for ladies and gentlemen from well-off families. They also helped the emerging elite class of scientists and professionals keep pace with technological change and prepared a growing managerial class to handle rising organizational complexity. As the industrial era wore on, upward striving continued, but the actual journey from rags to riches became the exception that proved the rule. For most, it was the beginning of the end of America's free land and free labor, and the beginning of work as a lifelong dependency on others and a heightened fear of falling, either within or across generations.

In the industrial era, higher education's dual personality began to emerge. Universities grew as a safe haven for dissent and the intrinsic value of knowledge, even as the extrinsic economic value of knowledge blossomed. At the same time, however, they became more and more elitist in their selection of students, in their provision of access to the faculty guilds, and in their association with economic power.

Even in the early decades of the industrial economy, some higher-education leaders became apologists for the new industrial order. Among the earlier proponents of this view, Harvard University president A. Lawrence Lowell argued in 1913 that, although the public could have a say in setting the nation's general direction, specific decisions related to governing were too complicated for the masses and should be left to the nation's emerging population of university-trained experts.[53] The following decade, a graduate from Lowell's Harvard, Walter Lippmann, dismissed the idea of the rational citizen as a democratic myth in his enormously influential books *Public Opinion* and *The Phantom Public*.[54]

Since then, many university intellectuals have persisted in providing cover for democratic elitism. In the mid-1900s, the Columbia University historian Richard Hofstadter wrote several best-sellers that essentially marked the individual voter as paranoid and anti-intellectual.[55] The peak of the elite, university-based assault on the competence of the voting public probably came with intellectual critiques that argued that the public was prone to escape conflict in democracy by moving toward authoritarianism.[56] This judgment of the feckless citizenry only became harsher with the dawning of our current century.

Christopher H. Achen of Princeton University and Larry M. Bartels of Vanderbilt University updated the argument for the Trump era in their 2016 book, *Democracy for Realists*, which sought to expose the "folk theory" of the existence of rational voters.[57] In recent years, these arguments have reached their logical conclusion with academics' assertions that the golden age of democracy has ended because the citizenry stands innately incapable of rendering rational decisions on the issues of the day.[58]

Many academics came to agree that the individual voters didn't matter much, and that the increasingly vaunted stability of American democracy came not from widespread political participation but from competition among elite interest groups.[59] Such views have led our education system to be stratified in ways that have faithfully reinforced the class differences in our society.

The long American tradition of tracking students by race, class, and gender into either elite academic or lower-wage vocational pathways began early in the industrial era. By the end of World War I, the nation's emerging class stratification had seeped into thinking about how an adequate high school education should be defined. High schools developed separate academic tracks based on assumptions that some students needed to be prepared for college, others for skilled trades or left for menial work. Frequently, being assigned to a vocational track hinged less on ability than on students' race, family economic background, or sex. The Smith-Hughes National Vocational Education Act of 1917, which promoted vocational education in "agriculture, trades and industry, and homemaking," urged steering girls toward homemaking and a large share of boys toward non-supervisory working-class jobs.[60]

Despite growing class divisions and the proliferation of academic tracking, which helped cement those divisions into place, many Americans retained their faith in social mobility and the prospect of getting ahead, beliefs that deterred those on the bottom from rebelling against the educational trends of their day.

In the 1920s, Horatio Alger's widely read youth novels about boys who rose from rags to riches promoted the idea that anyone could succeed. Like our Puritan forebears who saw success as a measure of self-worth, we subscribed to a definition of success that is fundamentally moral, seeing it as a measure of our virtue and pluck. We became a nation—run on wage labor and by a wealthy elite—that perceived character flaws behind the struggles of the "undeserving poor" and the excesses of the "idle rich." The writer and historian James Truslow Adams popularized the term "American Dream" as shorthand for our aspirations. In his best-selling 1931 book, *The Epic of America*, he wrote:

> The American Dream is that dream of a land in which life should be better and richer and fuller for everyone, with opportunity for each according to ability or achievement. It is a difficult dream for the European upper classes to interpret adequately, and too many of us ourselves have grown weary and mistrustful of it. It is not a dream of motor cars and high wages merely, but a dream of social order in which each man and each woman shall be able to attain to the fullest stature of which they are innately capable, and be recognized by others for what they are, regardless of the fortuitous circumstances of birth or position.[61]

Seeking Salvation in the Best and Brightest

Even as *The Epic of America* hit bookstore shelves, the Great Depression was leaving a large share of the nation focused on mere survival, and giving rise to political forces opposed to capitalism and democracy. Some feared that our class disparities would generate class struggles and a socialist revolution on our soil. The sight of Nazis on the march raised the prospect of fascism arising here or invading our shores.

As the nation emerged from World War II, the education system was based on an expectation that most people would get through life with general or vocational educations from comprehensive high schools. It reserved colleges' rich mix of general and professional education for a select few.

Not everyone was convinced of the wisdom of this approach. The first president's commission on higher education, convened by President Harry S. Truman shortly after the war's conclusion, emphasized in its 1947 report the importance of higher education as a lever for equity in American democracy, and particularly its role in ensuring "equal liberty and equal opportunity to differing individuals and groups." Viewed from the present, the report seems prescient: it not only bemoaned elitism in higher education as well as unequal access by sex, race, class, and religion, but also called for tuition-free education through the fourteenth grade, a proposal that has significant political traction today. And it recognized the centrality of capitalist striving to American democracy, not only decrying the false binary between education for work and education for life, but also declaring that "to build a richly textured and gracious life is a desirable purpose, but few of us can make such a life without first making a living. Cultural values soon take wing when men cannot get and hold jobs." [62]

In contrast to the Truman Commission, Harvard president James Bryant Conant and other defenders of the new elitist system insisted that increased social stratification was a small price to pay to ensure that the best and brightest were in positions where they could steer our economy, advance science, and bolster our national defense.

The use of the SAT spread rapidly when massive new enrollments after World War II left colleges scrambling to find ways to assess students quickly.[63] The ACT test similarly caught on after being introduced in 1959.[64] Jefferson's "natural aristocracy" had posthumously given rise to an annual American tradition: the determination of individual college qualification based on which multiple-choice-test O's to darken with No. 2 pencils.

Of course, Americans were sorted by race, class, and gender long before the college admissions officers got involved. But the official great sorting of Americans by race, class, and gender gradually became attendant on the ritual admissions testing at the interface between high school and college. From the very beginning, the tests functioned as a political dodge, giving a false and superficial appearance of scientific validity to bias rooted in race, class, and gender.

Over the course of its history, the nation has gone from believing some were born chosen by God to succeed, to assuming that people gained status and wealth by dint of their own hard work, to believing that heredity played a big role in determining who made it, to deciding who could advance based on standardized test scores purporting to quantify academic potential. It has largely shrugged off any recognition of an overlap between the populations that fared well on standardized college admission tests—white men born into privilege—and the populations that Puritans or eugenicists would have identified as the worthiest.

The prominent British sociologist T.H. Marshall delivered a prophetic lecture in 1949, a commemoration of the lecture delivered by Alfred Marshall (no relation) in 1873. For the most part, he doubled down on Alfred's original argument. T.H. asserted that the equality implicit in democratic citizenship implied "a modicum of economic welfare and security" sufficient "to share to the full in the social heritage and to live the life of a civilized being according to the standards prevailing in the society." He said the institutions most closely connected with this notion of citizen equality in capitalist economies "are the educational system and the social services."[65] He expressed fear, however, that in the years since Alfred Marshall spoke, education had lost some of its power as a solution to the problem of inequality in market economies. Its role as a mediating force between citizenship and markets was increasingly compromised by the growing alignment between education and elite occupational preparation. Education made everyone equal as citizens, but those with the most education, especially at the college level and in lucrative fields, could accumulate more wealth and power at a faster rate than others.

T.H. Marshall expressed fear that industrial society already had "been accused of regarding elementary education solely as a means of providing capitalist employers with more valuable workers, and higher education merely as an instrument to increase the power of the nation to compete with its industrial rivals." He warned that education had evolved from an equalizer to "an instrument of social stratification."[66] His lecture became a widely recognized summary argument for the massive post–World War II expansion of public education to stave off Soviet and Chinese communism. Largely missed were his warnings about the growing inequality in public education.

Rather than have an expansive welfare state like those that emerged in Europe, the United States publicly finances education as a centrist strategy for providing opportunity and upward social mobility. Our social policy attests that we believe education allocates opportunity without surrendering individual responsibility, and that we can provide public support for education without running afoul of our commitments to an open economy and limited government.

We have become quite contented with our highly segmented society. We're comfortable with the knowledge that the poor and uneducated don't vote here at anywhere near the rate they do in European and other democracies, where the working class flocks to polls to try to preserve its hard-won gains from class struggle. Despite a professed belief in the importance of equal opportunity, Americans have always been reluctant to pay for the provision of education and other public benefits to people who don't look like them or who come from different backgrounds.[67] In America, educational success has become a marker of class.

In recent decades, the digital revolution and globalization have given rise to an entirely new educational and economic regime, changing the relationship between education and gainful employment. The result has been an increase of 35 million bachelor's degrees and 11 million associate's degrees attained by Americans since 1983.[68] The days when a high school education was enough to provide middle-class earnings are gone and not coming back.[69]

Economic and social disruption has created winners and losers. Postsecondary education has increasingly become a fountain of opportunity for economically advantaged whites, sometimes at the expense of blacks, Latinos, and whites who are working class. Whites' educational and economic momentum has grown enormously, suggesting the likelihood of a new surge in race and class inequality as we move further into the twenty-first century.[70]

Certainly, as the economic value of education continues to increase, we will need to remember that education and academic research are about more than dollars and cents. Public education should do more than provide new technology and foot soldiers for the American economy. Educators have a cultural and political mission to ensure an educated citizenry that can continue to defend and promote our democratic ideals.

The economic and democratic missions of higher education are intertwined. If secondary and postsecondary educators cannot fulfill their economic mission to help grow the economy and help youths and adults become successful workers, they also will fail in their cultural and political missions to create good neighbors, good citizens, and lifelong learners.

2

THE RISE OF THE
SORTING MACHINE

It was the sort of low-visibility conference where higher-education insiders share their secrets. Catherine E. Watt, who had been director of institutional research at Clemson University, was candid and matter-of-fact in detailing how Clemson had schemed to rise from number thirty-eight in the *U.S. News & World Report* rankings to almost the top twenty.[1]

Clemson, a well-regarded public university in South Carolina, had a multi-pronged strategy with the sole goal of influencing the metrics that *U.S. News* measures. Clemson reduced enrollment in as many classes as possible to fewer than twenty students, and strategically raised tuition so it could hire more professors to reduce its faculty-to-student ratio. Clemson leaders disparaged the reputations of other universities when asked to rate them. In short, the university followed a brazen strategy to game the system, even though that strategy was at odds with Clemson's mission. "We have favored merit over access in a poor state. We are more elite, more white, more privileged," Watt said unapologetically at the 2009 meeting of the Association of Institutional Research.[1]

Her comments at the conference, and the paper she presented giving more credence to her claims, provoked a public uproar. Aghast Clemson leaders threw her under the bus, calling her statements "outrageous" examples of "urban legends" that surrounded the university's quest to rise in the all-important university rankings.[2] Watt, unaware that reporters were in the room when she was speaking, admitted later, "I think I was just discussing publicly what we all say privately."[3] Her direction at the university, she said, came straight from the top: from then university president James F. Barker, who had come into office with the express goal of making Clemson a Top 20 university. "Every president's speech starts with the ranking; every policy starts there," said Watt. The university had a strategy to "affect every possible indicator (in the *U.S. News* rankings) to the greatest extent possible."[4]

What was Clemson after? Prestige, the all-encompassing goal of colleges at the top of the pecking order in American higher education, and also a chief concern of upper-middle-class or wealthy families in a mad scramble to get their children into the best colleges possible. The personal and institutional pursuit of prestige has given rise to an arms race in which students stress over small differences in their SAT scores and colleges warily guard their standings in the national rankings.

Students place their faith in the value of a college degree as the ticket to the life of their dreams. At their best, colleges are effective gateways to that better life, socially significant institutions that shore up students' prospects while enhancing the overall well-being of society.

But colleges are also businesses, and, as with all businesses, the interests of their stakeholders do not necessarily match those of the customers. If a college can become more prestigious, it can alter its course. Success attracts donors, alumni, and students. And as more students apply, more must be filtered out, resulting in higher rejection rates. The college's unavailability begets more yearning. And the yearning begets even more attention. The most prestigious colleges in America now reject ninety-five of every one hundred applicants.[5] In theory, the brightest take their rightful places at these elite colleges; but in practice, as at Clemson, these institutions' student bodies simply mirror the racial and class-based disparities in American society.

What happened at Clemson is emblematic of a larger shift in higher education's priorities. Among many elite institutions, and those on the threshold of the elite, rankings have gained outsized importance in the quest for ever-higher status. As a result, the rankings have created perverse incentives. Colleges looking to rise in prestige emphasize what is best for their ranking over almost any other considerations. And that has meant putting undue focus on the inputs that *U.S. News* uses to determine a college's "quality," including the average SAT score of accepted students, average class sizes, faculty salaries, financial resources, and the percentage of alumni who contribute to the institution.[6] The *U.S. News* ratings score college reputations by asking college presidents and other top college leaders to rate their institutions' peers. Throughout the history of the rankings, *U.S. News* had also counted among the criteria a college's applicant acceptance rate, which was blamed for incentivizing colleges to recruit students they had no intention of admitting. It finally stopped considering the acceptance rate starting with the 2019 rankings.[7]

For elite institutions and those lucky enough to be accepted by one, the rewards for skillfully playing the prestige game are huge. But for everyone else—even, arguably, for the nation itself, which depends on higher education to deliver on its promise of opportunity—the shortcomings of a system dedicated primarily to preserving America's hierarchy stifle education access and portend catastrophe.

Many families striving to get a child into an elite college fixate on the advantages that social status confers. While alumni magazines trumpet the educational and academic accomplishments of an institution's students and faculty, the real value of college in the minds of many aspirants is arguably in the college's reputation—its brand. The brand offers the promise of networks a student will plug into while enrolled and the doors the institution's name on a degree will open. Research shows that those effects dissipate over the course of a career, but colleges don't want you to know that.[8] They benefit from the idea that failure to be admitted is a life-changing setback.

Based on the attention that Ivy League institutions receive, one would think that they define American higher education. These colleges, however, collectively educate less than one percent of all college students.[9] Private selective colleges as a whole educate only slightly more of the college-going population—6 percent of all students.[10] The much larger share of students—especially those further down the economic ladder—attend public colleges or universities, which overall enroll three-quarters of America's college students.[11] Although some public colleges, especially state flagships, rank among the nation's most prestigious and well-financed higher-education institutions, many others are overcrowded, underfinanced, and, not surprisingly, ranked low—if they are ranked by *U.S. News* at all.

A modest ranking doesn't mean a college will provide a poor education. Excellent academic reputations have been earned by many regional public colleges, such as the University of Maryland–Baltimore County or the institutions in the California State University system.

Nevertheless, the fact is that students attending a selective college have a better chance of graduating, a higher likelihood of enrolling in and completing graduate programs, and, ultimately, more certain entry into the highest echelons of society. Meanwhile, their peers at less-selective institutions—even those no less qualified at the point of college entry—are less likely to ever earn the credentials they need to secure a place among the middle or upper classes.[12]

Students and families seeking the advantages conferred by elite colleges are sharply aware of the leaps and contortions necessary to gain acceptance to one. But the similar maneuvering for advantage that the top-ranked colleges themselves engage in takes place mainly out of the public view.

Pulling back the curtain reveals that our higher-education system has become a sorting machine that directs people along unequal pathways based as much on differences of birth as on so-called merit. Pressured by their business model's sensitivity to the rankings, colleges have adopted practices that, while intended to demonstrate their quality as institutions, instead divide students into haves and have-nots based on dubious metrics. The sorting machine takes in wave after wave of high school graduates and channels some toward prestigious doctorates and others toward community college certificates, some toward careers as highly paid professionals and others toward lives of low-wage menial work.

The sorting machine can be imprecise or inefficient, and its operation can be corrupted. Mediocre high school graduates get into top colleges with the help of behind-the-scenes tinkering with its gears. Large shares of students, including many who could do quite well at selective institutions, land at community colleges and open-access four-year colleges, where they may end up dropping out and thus wasting both their own tuition dollars and public or private money used to subsidize their education.

The sorting machine is heartless. It allows for the squandering of opportunity more readily than it affords second chances, at least for those without access to its inner workings.

But breaking free of the sorting machine takes extraordinary effort, and those who succeed in doing so are rare exceptions. Being steered toward colleges at the bottom of the pile consigns one to a track defined by limited resources, where the ladder to upward mobility has only a few flimsy rungs.

The machine's gravest consequence may be its intergenerational perpetuation of advantage or disadvantage. The machine works in favor of those with money and status, who sometimes even get to manipulate its gears, transferring their social and economic capital to the next generation. Meanwhile, those without the social and financial capital to avoid running afoul of the sorting machine usually find themselves tossed into reject bins.

In short, it's a system with the veneer of meritocracy that in fact ensures that members of the modern aristocracy will pass along their advantages to their children.

But it hasn't always been this way.

The Machine's Construction

The emergence of the sorting machine reflects a shift in the relative weights assigned to the fundamental yet conflicting American values of individualism and equality. As a nation, we've generally decided that higher education is a private good rather than a public one, a privilege rather than a right, despite protestations to the contrary by many college leaders. Decades of declining tax-dollar support have left many colleges under pressure to recruit students from families wealthy enough to pay full tuition and donate. Many colleges court families with deep pockets by jacking up tuition and admission standards to convey exclusivity, essentially selling membership to an elite club. Those colleges that can't compete on the basis of exclusivity and prestige often struggle just to get by, lacking the resources necessary to provide enough support services to students to ensure they have a good chance of graduating and earning a decent living.

Both federal and state governments have had a hand in this shift. The basic choice our higher-education system now offers—between elitist prestige and everyone else—is not just a historic artifact of market forces, but the product of deliberate policymaking and planning. State leaders consciously chose to structure public-college systems into tiered hierarchies, with flagship universities on top and community or technical colleges on the bottom. Lawmakers closed gaps in state budgets by hacking away at appropriations for higher education, based on the assumption that public colleges could offset lost support from tax dollars by raising tuition or soliciting donated funds.[13] Federal officials have pumped tax revenues into scientific research at big-name universities while appropriating too little money to the ordinary public colleges and financial aid programs that make college widely accessible.

As a result of public disinvestment, colleges need to build a corps of families and future alumni willing and eager to pay high tuition and invest in the alma mater. At the same time, to attract the wealthy candidates likely to yield those donations, colleges need to stay at the top of the rankings—meaning that they give undue weight to SAT scores and other metrics favored by the ranking apparatus.

The quest for academic prestige has merged with the quest for economic survival—for colleges, and for students and their families as well.

The emphasis on prestige in higher education is actually a rather recent phenomenon. As of 1900, few colleges had more applicants who met their minimum requirements than seats available to fill. Admissions decisions hinged mainly on whether the applicant had showed too high a risk of failure. The decisions erred on the side of giving a chance to those who might make it through. Dropout rates were high at the public colleges and universities that cropped up after the Morrill Act of 1862, which adopted forerunners of today's "open admissions" policies, taking in any graduates of state-approved high schools with the requisite number and distribution of courses on their transcripts.

Higher-education leaders soon recognized the need to adapt. Ivy League colleges resolved to admit more-qualified students and to draw them from a larger swath of society than the private boarding schools in the Northeast that most of them depended on. They raised their overall standards while no longer requiring applicants to have taken Latin and other subjects taught almost exclusively at elite college preparatory schools.[14] In December 1899, twelve colleges—including Columbia, Rutgers, Princeton, and Vassar—joined three college preparatory high schools in an effort to mesh the curricular offerings of high schools with the entrance requirements of colleges. They established the College Entrance Examination Board—a predecessor of the College Board, overseer of the SAT—and forged an agreement to use common entrance examinations to broaden the pool of qualified applicants.[15]

A new potential means of identifying bright students emerged with the 1905 invention of the "intelligence quotient" (IQ) test by the French psychologist Alfred Binet. The U.S. Army used the IQ test to select officers during World War I, and a Princeton University psychology professor, Carl Campbell Brigham, subsequently adapted the instrument into the Scholastic Aptitude Test, or SAT, to screen college students. In 1926, the College Entrance Examination Board administered the SAT to about eight thousand high school students on an experimental basis.[16] But the SAT would not be used widely until World War II. Its rise came almost entirely through the efforts of James Bryant Conant, who served as Harvard's president from 1933 to 1953 and loomed as a leading public intellectual of his day. Conant promoted the SAT to its current role as the chief sifting mechanism (alongside the ACT) within the sorting machine.

Conant was a fascinating and conflicted figure. Although a

Protestant New Englander, he did not come from one of that region's wealthy families, having been raised in Dorchester, a working-class Boston neighborhood.[17] He had managed to gain admission to Harvard by graduating at the top of his class at one of the nation's most prestigious boys' schools, Roxbury Latin School, which he had gotten into by besting others at its highly competitive entrance exam. He had gone on to have a distinguished career as a chemist before taking Harvard's top job.

As someone who had risen above his circumstances, Conant firmly believed talent ought to trump social standing as a determinant of how far people advance in life. He thought America needed an education system that fairly and efficiently lifted up its best and brightest, rather than letting its leaders emerge from the white, Anglo-Saxon, Protestant old-boy networks that had held sway for two centuries. As Harvard's president, he was determined to help the nation create a leadership class consisting of the most academically gifted, wherever they might have been raised.[18]

The financial miscalculations and policymaking follies that triggered and fueled the Great Depression had exposed the ineptitude of many graduates of prestigious higher-education institutions. In Europe, the economic crisis had triggered rebellions against the old order and given rise to communism and fascism. Conant, seeing such ideologies as a profound threat, hoped that the promotion of social mobility would enable the United States to stave off extremism and remain true to its fundamental values.

America had already made substantial progress in expanding access to higher education. From 1870 to 1940, the number of higher-education institutions had more than tripled, from just over 560 to more than 1,700. Over this same period, as the population more than doubled, total enrollment in higher-education institutions rose nearly thirty-fold, from 52,000 to nearly 1.5 million, thanks in large part to the construction of large land-grant public universities financed by the Morrill Act.[19] Elite colleges, however, remained dominated by old, wealthy families. As of 1940, the children of the richest 2.7 percent of the population accounted for 60 percent of the freshmen who entered

Harvard, which accepted virtually any applicant from the elite boarding schools with which it had long-standing ties.[20]

Determined to transform the nation's education system into an engine of meritocracy, Conant persuaded the leaders of other Ivy League
colleges to join him in establishing a new scholarship program to take
in bright students from all over the country. They chose the SAT as
their instrument for identifying high schoolers with academic talent
who would receive the scholarship. Later, as the national emergency
created by World War II made it impractical for colleges to continue to
put applicants through days-long batteries of admissions tests, the College Board turned to the SAT as a means to assess students quickly.[21]
Demand for the SAT grew so rapidly that the College Board felt compelled in 1947 to work with other higher-education groups to set up
the nonprofit Educational Testing Service to separately administer the
assessment. It took less than a year for ETS to be administering the
LSAT for law-school applicants and the MCAT for medical-school applicants, expanding the reach of standardized testing into judgments
of who was qualified to train for professions.[22]

College enrollments surged as a result of the Servicemen's Readjustment Act of 1944, also known as the G.I. Bill. It subsidized college
tuition for returning veterans, established a federal role in ensuring
college access, and helped bring a cultural change by convincing
Americans that higher education should be widely available. The Cold
War had a huge impact on colleges as well. To stay ahead in the arms
and space races against the Soviet Union, the federal government
poured money into university research and pushed colleges to enroll
students who showed talent in science, mathematics, and engineering,
even if it meant giving seats previously reserved for "well-rounded
kids" to those whose only talent was solving equations.[23]

Conant, who had chaired a federal committee overseeing World
War II defense research, assumed a Cold War role marshalling American education against the threat of communism. Over the next two
decades, he wrote several best-selling books on education that profoundly influenced the operation of colleges and high schools.[24]

Conant argued that a meritocratic education system would serve as an "engine of democracy" by nurturing an upwardly mobile, well-informed, economically powerful society that would best communism in the Cold War's contest of cultures. Instead of choosing the membership of our elite based on parentage, he proposed completely reinventing the education pipeline to use tests, grades, and other education metrics as the basis for an open competition, one that essentially begins at birth. By relying on our education system to be our arbiter of individual opportunity, he argued, the country could avoid having either the economic plutocracy of the right or a leftist welfare state that preemptively equalized outcomes.[25]

But for all his talk, Conant was not a champion of equity. Conant believed that only about a fifth of the population was college material. Convinced that human intelligence was largely innate, fixed at birth, and one-dimensional, he dismissed as "too small to bother with" the share of the population that undergoes an intellectual awakening later in life. He called for comprehensive high schools to identify the 15 to 20 percent of students who were college material and groom them for liberal arts colleges and graduate or professional education.[26]

As for the 80 to 85 percent of students at a comprehensive high school whom he regarded as unsuited for college, they should be provided vocational training to ensure their economic independence and personal stake in capitalism, Conant argued. On top of that, they also should take courses like history, English, and civics to familiarize themselves with their heritage.[27] He proposed that comprehensive high schools maintain a separate academic track for young people with IQs over 115, above the normal range of intelligence, to prepare them for entry into selective colleges and, subsequently, our meritocracy's leadership positions.[28]

America Goes to College

Conant's belief that only about one in five people were college material did not deter a much larger share from knocking on the college door. By 1960, the share of American children whose educations extended into high school had risen to about nine in ten, largely because a diploma increasingly became seen as a prerequisite for getting any decent job.[29] Applications to colleges continued to increase, with growing shares of women and members of minority groups seeking postsecondary education. The number of community colleges grew briskly to meet the needs of an expanding population of college-going students.[30] We were shifting from an elite higher-education system to a mass one, and states struggled to figure out how to accommodate demand. California led the way, enshrining a meritocratic sorting mechanism into law with the *California Master Plan for Higher Education* that it adopted in 1960.[31]

The California plan established a hierarchal system of public higher education. Its top tier consisted of research institutions, the various campuses of the University of California. Beneath them was a system of comprehensive state colleges (now known as the California State University system), and beneath them, a separate system of community colleges. The highest tier that applicants could enter depended on their academic qualifications.

The California plan sought to promote social mobility by making research universities accessible and affordable, by providing access to at least some form of postsecondary education to every high school graduate, and by assigning two-year colleges a primary function of preparing students to transfer to four-year institutions. It sought to maximize return on public investment by allocating resources according to students' perceived ability to benefit, as measured by college applicants' test scores and grades. It assumed that the most money per student should flow toward the highest-quality institutions with the greatest concentration of students with top test scores.[32]

State governments throughout the nation implemented plans with similar characteristics. Today, most states have at least one public, research-focused, "flagship" university, accompanied by geographically scattered regional public universities and colleges, and a network of local two-year community or technical colleges.

The population of private colleges mushroomed primarily during the second half of the nineteenth century. Even though they educate only a quarter of college students, we have more private colleges in the

United States than public ones.[33] Many private colleges were founded
by religions to educate the children of those in the faith, while others grew out of bequests from wealthy industrialists. They have taken
off in many directions since. Some of these colleges would grow into
large national research universities—think Emory, Duke, Stanford,
and Notre Dame—and others have been content to remain small. The
average private college has 1,920 students.[34] Think Colby, Occidental,
Lubbock Christian, and St. Bonaventure.

Colleges' competition for students and resources has helped turn
American higher education into a more complex and powerful sorting machine than anything Conant envisioned. Colleges seem to have
arrived at two strategies for survival: either marketing conspicuous
consumption and exclusivity, or constantly expanding enrollment
while finding ways to educate students at a lower cost. They have continued on this path even as their approaches to doing business have
been rendered obsolete by broader economic trends transforming the
world around them.

To understand the reactions of colleges to market pressures, it's
helpful to keep in mind their distinct nature in business terms. Technically speaking, any college that is not a for-profit proprietary school
is a "donative-commercial nonprofit." The "donative" part of that label
means that the funds for its operations come partly from outside financial support in the form of donations, earnings on investments of
past donations, and government funds. The "commercial" part means
that a college also derives funds for its operations from the sale of
goods and services, its chief product being the education it offers in
exchange for tuition. Classification as a nonprofit does not preclude
an organization from making a profit, but requires that such money
be plowed back into the organization's budget.

Often, nonprofit organizations provide goods or services for which
there is little consensus on market value. We assume such organizations' good will—that being precluded from personally profiting
leaves those who lead or staff them with little incentive to take advantage of donors or customers. In many cases, outside subsidization

enables nonprofits to offer goods or services for a fraction of what a for-profit would need to charge just to recover its costs.

So it is with public or nonprofit private colleges that offer education—a good whose worth is difficult to evaluate—at a price substantially less than what it actually costs to produce. Because the subsidization of public-college students' education generally comes largely from state appropriations tied to enrollment counts, such colleges have financial incentives to enroll as many students as possible. Because private colleges rely mainly on tuition, private donations, and endowment investments to subsidize their educational services, they have a financial incentive to enroll students from families wealthy enough to make big contributions.[35]

There's another wrinkle in the operation of colleges that, in some ways, makes them a little like country clubs. Their customers actually are a feature of the product they sell. Just as people join a country club partly to hobnob with its members, a college points to the students it enrolls as a key part of its offerings. It's a shrewd move. Savvy students and their families often shop for a college where the student will be surrounded by bright, driven young people and will end up plugged into social networks offering lifetime benefits. The best way for colleges to enroll students whose presence draws others is to generate excess demand and then cherry-pick from an oversized applicant pool. As a sales ploy, colleges offer deep tuition discounts to highly desired students who actually have no need for financial aid.[36]

The dynamics of the higher-education market send colleges into either upward or downward spirals. Colleges that are well-subsidized by donors or the government can offer high-value educations for much less than what they cost. This makes it easier for them to draw students from wealthy backgrounds, who, in turn, will attract more students from wealthy backgrounds. The end result is expansion of their pool of potential donors and growth in their subsidies—and a campus and culture dominated by young people from wealthy, privileged backgrounds. Colleges with relatively little support from donors or the government have less money to spend on faculty or amenities.

They come under financial pressure to admit any student who can or *may* be able to pay tuition—whether through personal means or loans. They fail to build substantial bases of philanthropic support and end up having to cuts costs in ways that devalue their product.[37]

No matter how lofty their stated missions, colleges' desire to climb and their fear of going into a tailspin keep them focused on doing whatever is necessary to take in more money. In a seminal paper on the industry, the late Gordon Winston, a Williams College economist, described higher education as a place "in which very different educational quality is produced in very different schools at very different cost and sold at very different prices—gross and net—to students with very different input characteristics who get very different subsidies and are often selected from very long queues of applicants, leaving a lot of unsatisfied demand." Decrying what he saw as "massive ignorance about what is being bought and sold," he declared that colleges are "part church and part car dealer—devoted partly to charity and partly to commerce, to 'ideology' and 'rationality.'" He said, "The result is a tension between doing good and doing well. It plagues administrators trying to decide which behaviors—those of the charity or those of the firm—are appropriate to a college or university. It also creates real if often unrecognized ambiguities for society's evaluation of such an industry."[38]

The College-Ranking Juggernaut

The volatility and competitiveness of the higher-education market intensified with the emergence of the *U.S. News* rankings. Before the *U.S. News* rankings debuted in 1983, college-goers based their judgments of which colleges were best mainly on impressions rather than on numerical data like SAT scores. *U.S. News* changed the game by purporting to rank America's top colleges objectively, immediately spurring demand for seats at those institutions among students seeking to get into the best college possible.

The popularity of the *U.S. News* rankings exploded, and colleges that had already been difficult to get into soon became almost impenetrable for anyone but legacy applicants, athletes, and wealthy students who attended top college prep schools. To wit, before the rankings, Stanford, Princeton, and Harvard accepted about 20 percent of applicants in 1980, and Yale accepted about 26 percent. Now all those universities accept about 5 percent of applicants. Just a bit further down the exclusivity chain, many colleges—both public and private—have continued to strive for greater prestige, sometimes increasing their selectivity dramatically in very short periods of time. Boston University, for example, accepted more than 70 percent of applicants in 2002; in 2017, it accepted just 25 percent.[39] The tendency of students to apply to many more colleges than they did before has contributed to the surge in applications and helped lower acceptance rates.

The leaders of colleges criticized the magazine's methodology, but there was no denying the rankings' appeal to students, parents, and employers. Their popularity soon led U.S. News to begin ranking various types of professional schools and inspired other publications to develop their own college rankings and ratings.[40] Most profoundly, the U.S. News rankings helped give rise to the now common belief that colleges can be judged based on inputs—the students they admit, the faculty members they hire, the financial support they receive—rather than on the output that is their raison d'être, the learning and growth they produce in their students.[41]

The power that U.S. News asserted over colleges was immense. Those that dropped in the rankings could experience steep declines in applications, find it harder to recruit faculty or solicit donations, and even suffer a downgrading of their bond rating that forced them to pay higher interest rates in borrowing. To pressure colleges into providing it with information, U.S. News assigned lower rankings to those that refused to cooperate, for reasons that college leaders denounced as arbitrary.[42] Most colleges decided that they were better off trying to improve their rankings than fighting the magazine's efforts.[43]

Not all colleges have competed in the rankings honestly. Clemson is hardly an exception. Many colleges have been found over the years to have submitted false data to the magazine. Others have sought to skew their numbers upward by withholding data on certain segments of the student population, such as legacies, recruited athletes, or those who arrived on campus early via summer remediation programs or through mid-year admissions in January.[44]

Many colleges have embraced strategies intended to game the metrics. For example, to improve yield rates, colleges adopted "early action" or "early decision" admissions policies that encouraged students to apply and commit early.[45] To appear more selective, they brought about a reduction in the share of students admitted through marketing efforts that enticed many more students to apply, even if it meant dangling false hope before high schoolers who stood no chance of acceptance.[46]

To raise the average SAT scores of entering classes, many colleges gave applicants' SAT scores much more weight in admissions decisions, in some cases establishing rigid and statistically meaningless cutoff scores against the advice of ETS experts and others in the field.[47] Although dozens of selective liberal arts colleges have bucked this trend by making the submission of SAT or ACT scores optional, these test-optional policies have been shown mainly to serve the selfish interests of the institutions by helping them climb in the rankings. They entice larger numbers of students to apply, thus lowering acceptance rates. Because applicants with lower SAT or ACT scores typically withhold such information, the policies skew upward the average test scores of entering classes.[48]

Richard Freeland, a former president of Northeastern University, told *Boston Magazine* he and his team had successfully engineered a huge leap in his institution's *U.S. News* rankings partly by schmoozing administrators at peer universities so they'd comment more favorably on Northeastern in rating peer institutions for the magazine.[49] The practices and strategies Northeastern used for its ascent often served little or no educational purpose.

Broader political and economic trends have put added pressure on colleges to rise in the rankings and on families to secure their children's admission to highly ranked colleges.[50] The globalization of markets, the evaporation of manufacturing as a supplier of decent blue-collar jobs, and rising technological demands all have placed a higher premium on degrees. The sorting machine has caused our society to conflate class and merit. As of the 1980s, it became more and more difficult for anyone who had not gone to college to go anywhere in the job market and have a real shot at a middle-class existence.

Incomes of the wealthiest, most educated segments of society have surged, while others' annual earnings have remained flat or declined. Employers have increasingly considered not only how much post-secondary education applicants have attained, but also the selectivity of the institutions or programs that awarded credentials to them. Multi-billion-dollar industries have arisen around devising college rankings, administering standardized admissions tests, and preparing students to have an edge in taking such assessments. All serve to "reinforce a delusion that equates personal success with admission to one particular institution—and that causes a student to interpret a rejection from that pinnacle of all hopes as a catastrophic life failure," concluded one 2011 report by college admissions experts.[51]

Other outside factors were ushering in a new age of austerity in higher education. The 1980 election of Ronald Reagan signaled a rise in public support for fiscal conservatism and a backlash against the use of progressive taxation to finance ambitious social programs. Even the Democratic Party, under President Bill Clinton, came to demand more accountability for public expenditures and to espouse a neoliberal faith in free-market forces as the most efficient means of meeting society's needs. Public colleges came under pressure to show they were stretching dollars and teaching practical skills, which generally meant operating more like commercial businesses and less like charities.

In the 2016 book *Austerity Blues: Fighting for the Soul of Public Higher Education*, Michael Fabricant and Stephen Brier said austerity policies "created a need for universities and other public agencies to develop 'efficient practices' that do more with less because of drastically reduced state funding." Corporate and for-profit business practices were "imported wholesale into public university management, no matter their fit or misfit with higher education's core mission or larger contributions to the public good."[52]

In many ways, the 1980s ushered in a period of Dickensian contrast between wealthy colleges and others. While ordinary public colleges fell on lean times, elite public and private colleges "entered into a period of unprecedented prosperity," observes Charles T. Clotfelter, a professor of public policy, economics, and law at Duke University who has extensively studied higher-education financing trends. The gap in donations received between the top quartile and bottom quartile of universities more than doubled from 1970 to 2010. Average faculty salaries at the most competitive colleges rose, while those at the least competitive fell.[53] Clotfelter writes:

> Over the last 40 years, no one has proposed that the guiding purpose of higher education should be to aggravate inequality. Indeed, policy makers and college leaders have declared the opposite aspiration. They have spoken of colleges as meritocratic engines of opportunity. Yet the historical record tells a contrary story, one of widening disparities in the college market. The richest colleges have become richer, gathering an increasing share of the most in-demand students and exposing them to the most sought-after faculty and the highest-quality facilities and campus resources. In short, the leaders of rich colleges have presided over a remarkable increase in inequality.[54]

College leaders concluded that their institutions' fates hinged on catering to students from the upper-middle class, and, accordingly, they pumped money into amenities and tuition discounts to appeal to that population. Lawmakers in several states established lotteries, disproportionately played by the poor and poorly educated, to finance merit-based scholarship programs to keep in the state bright young people who disproportionately came from wealthy families.[55] A 2006 report by the Education Trust documented how flagship universities were awarding much more financial aid to students from high-income families than to students whose families were poor. It concluded that flagships were relentlessly pursuing selectivity, rather than opportunity, and were becoming "disproportionately whiter and richer" as a result of being "rated less for what they accomplish with the students they let in than by how many students they keep out."[56]

The number of four-year colleges in the top three tiers of Barron's guide to colleges—"most competitive," "highly competitive," and "very competitive"—has surged in recent decades.[57] Selective four-year colleges have opted to compete principally on the basis of their place in selectivity tiers and the prestige of their institutional brand, not on the basis of having specialized programs or distinctive teaching methods or missions. In doing so, they've undermined one of the distinct advantages our market-based education system had over those of nations where the governance of higher education is centralized: the diversity of our colleges in terms of size, approach, emphasis, and the composition of their student body.

Today, a growing number of selective colleges' presidents are raising alarms about the sorting machine and its overall impact on American higher education. They recognize that it perpetuates class-based inequity and does not, in fact, efficiently identify those who are most capable of succeeding in college. For the most part, however, they've been reluctant to have their colleges buck prevailing practices, out of fear that doing so will hurt their competitive standing.[58] As Richard Reeves of the Brookings Institution observed in his 2017 book *Dream Hoarders*, "The trouble is that the market is locked into an equilibrium that militates against serious reform efforts. It is simply not in the interest of the most powerful institutions to change things very much, at least not at the individual college level. Asking a single college operating in a competitive market to do a better job of attracting and retaining students from poorer backgrounds is to ask them to act against their own interests."[59]

Syracuse University, for example, under then chancellor Nancy Cantor, openly defied the metrics that the rankings value, admitting more low-income students and members of minority groups who often had lower SAT scores than other applicants. As a result, it slid in the *U.S. News* rankings from fifty-second to sixty-second. A new chancellor, Kent Syverud, took over in 2014, pledging to pay more attention to the rankings amid a clamor from alumni and faculty concerned over the direction of the university.[60]

The sorting machine has taken on a life of its own. It has shrewdly incorporated those with the power to alter or resist its operations and offered them incentives to ensure it keeps humming. The segments of the population with the most incentive to change it are those it has cast off and denied power in a political system where clout is derived from wealth and expertise.

The simple truth is that the rankings are what stand out in people's minds, not the ways in which such rankings are manipulated. Watt, the truth-teller behind Clemson's rise, has said that all things being equal, the university's efforts to game the rankings were worth it. "We have been criticized for not fulfilling the mission of a public land-grant institution," she said. "On the other hand, we have gotten really good press. We have walked the fine line between illegal, unethical, and really interesting."[61]

3

UNDERSTANDING THE ODDS

Picture a playground in New York's Central Park on an idyllic Sunday afternoon.

Given the city's diversity and appeal to tourists, you'd almost certainly find families from all walks of life gathered there. You might see the children of investment bankers romping near the children of cab drivers, factory workers, university professors, and janitors. Swings and slides accept all.

Now, picture those children as adults. What sorts of lives do you see them living?

Belief in the American Dream leads many of us to think that the possibilities are endless, that each child will find opportunity every bit as accessible as that public playground. We like to imagine that the struggling cab driver's daughter can become a highly paid investment banker, or that the janitor's son can earn distinction as a professor, even if we're inclined to be surprised when we actually meet people from humble backgrounds in such positions. We assume that the children of wealthy families can end up in low-paying jobs as a result of personal failure or choice. Someone needs to mop floors when the janitor quits or retires, and it won't be the janitor's son if the lad grows up to teach at a college. As much as people fear and regret downward social mobility, it fits into the great scheme of things in a capitalist economy. At least theoretically it keeps people on top under pressure to perform and creates vacancies for others when they don't.

The message that we live in a meritocracy gets constantly reiterated by our nation's employers and education institutions. Elite colleges boast of admitting the best applicants while neglecting to mention the academically subpar students they've accepted based on factors like their relationship to big donors.

American society embraces meritocracy because we see it as a mechanism for promoting both social mobility and efficiency. We want the best and brightest holding government posts, conducting medical research, or running big corporations, and we like the idea that anyone with the necessary talent and drive can rise to such a position. Among parents, the belief that their children will be rewarded for hard work and intelligence strengthens meritocracy's appeal.

The truth, however, is that our faith in meritocracy is out of touch with reality. People don't start out with the same odds of making it. Fates are shaped by a host of factors over which individuals have little or no control, including race, ethnicity, gender, class, family background, and geographic location.

Our support for meritocracy rests on a belief in individual talent and striving. The Protestant work ethic underlying our nation's founding compels us to attribute success or failure to personal strengths or weaknesses, while overlooking the roles that favoritism, discrimination, and social and economic inequality play in determining how much opportunity we'll have. Although Thomas Jefferson spoke of the need for our nation to be led by a "natural aristocracy," there is little that's natural about the competition that decides who gets how far in life.

The Interlocking Mechanisms That Limit Mobility

To understand inequality and its impact, we need first to account for the different forms it can take. The Harvard public-policy scholar Robert Putnam argues that we create confusion by conflating two types of equality: equality of income and wealth, and equality of opportunity and social mobility. "The two types of equality are obviously related, because the distribution of income in one generation may affect the distribution of opportunity in the next generation—but they are not the same thing," Putnam notes in *Our Kids: The American Dream in Crisis.*[1]

Surveys over the past half century have consistently found that more than nine out of ten respondents favor the proposition that every American should have an equal opportunity to get ahead. The same proportion similarly expressed support for spending more on public education if necessary to ensure everyone gets a fair start.[2]

Understanding how inequality of opportunity affects our prospects in life requires understanding the various forms of social mobility: absolute or relative, *intra*generational or *inter*generational.

Absolute social mobility refers to what happens when overall economic change leaves just about everyone either better off, as during economic booms, or worse off, as when we have a recession. *Relative social mobility* refers to changes in relative position on the economic ladder, as when a person gets a big pay raise or receives an inheritance. *Intragenerational mobility* happens in the course of one's lifetime, when one's own status changes for better or worse. *Intergenerational mobility* happens from one generation to the next, giving one's children a status different from one's own.[3] All four forms of mobility can be upward or downward, and multiple forms can occur at the same time.

If on the Monday after our visit to Central Park a stock market crash triggered a severe recession, just about every family there would be financially worse off within a few months. They would experience downward mobility in both absolute and intragenerational terms. If we look at economic change over a timeframe covering the past four hundred years, we see that over the long term Americans, as a whole, have experienced upward mobility in absolute and intergenerational terms. Pockets of extreme poverty remain, but, as a general rule, life is much more comfortable.[4] Less than one percent of U.S. homes lack indoor plumbing or electricity. A century ago, more than half of homes had neither.[5]

The story that America typically tells about itself is a tale of absolute

and intergenerational upward mobility, where each generation is at
least a little better off than the one before it. This story has made belief
in inevitable, if slow, progress an article of faith in American culture,
leaving us more accepting of inequality than we otherwise might be.
We look at disparities in college access less with outrage than with
hope that black, Latino, and low-income white students eventually
will have as much access to higher education as economically privileged white students have now.[6]

In contrast with absolute mobility, which lifts or drops everyone,
relative mobility is a zero-sum game. For someone to rise into the
top 10 percent, someone else needs to fall out of it.[7] Richard Reeves,
a Brookings Institution scholar who sees himself as solidly upper-
middle-class, jokes in his book *Dream Hoarders* that he has "ruined
a few dinner parties" by arguing that "we need more downward mobility from the top." He suggests, "We would likely be more relaxed if
society were more equal, since the fall would not be so great."[8]

Indeed, the prospect of downward relative mobility can be terrifying, and it incentivizes those with relatively high status to do what
they can to retain their place of privilege. But the fact is that inequality of opportunity is more than the creation of a self-protective upper
class; it's the product of interlocking social mechanisms that work
in tandem to sustain it. Such mechanisms ensure that indifferent
forces—social change, economic trends, even natural forces such as
hurricanes—have very different impacts on the privileged than on the
disadvantaged.

The social forces at work can be broken down into six types of
mechanisms:

- **Cognitive mechanisms**, which cause us to inaccurately judge
  and categorize each other
- **Spatial mechanisms**, which segregate us into very different
  living conditions
- **Market mechanisms**, which generally leave the disadvantaged disproportionately likely to suffer—and unlikely to
  benefit—from economic change

- **Policy mechanisms,** which arise from decisions by government agencies or private institutions that can have the effect of either reducing or increasing inequality
- **Cultural mechanisms,** reflected in the views and behaviors that we take on in adapting to our distinct circumstances
- **Educational mechanisms,** through which our education system puts us on separate tracks and replicates advantage or disadvantage from one generation to the next.

Together, these six interlocking mechanisms ensure that equal opportunity exists in name only. The chances are extremely slim that a person born into circumstances of mutually reinforcing disadvantages will be able to overcome the odds stacked against him and gain upward mobility relative to others of the same generation. And the chances are good that a person born into privilege will be able to maintain her advantages, avoiding any downward movement in relative social status or material advantage.

The **cognitive mechanisms** at work stem from the mental process through which we gather, organize, and make sense of information. As social beings, we rely on *social cognition* as a means of survival. It's hard-wired into us, the basic process through which we decide which groups to join and which people to trust or avoid.[9] It can be instantaneous and involuntary, as when we step away from a wild-eyed and ranting stranger, or it can take the form of a conscious and deliberate decision, as when we ignore emails from foreigners offering us a cut of stolen fortunes. We organize people into mental categories based on the availability and salience of information, and our ability to easily see defining traits has led us to create socially constructed categories like race, ethnicity, class, and gender. The result can be prejudice and discrimination as we divide people into in-groups or out-groups. Stereotyping biases not only how we see others, but also how we see ourselves, and can prompt us to behave in ways that confirm our self-image.[10] Research has shown that children develop awareness of gender and ethnic differences before the age of five and by first grade begin to form beliefs based on traditional cultural stereotypes.[11] Tell a young boy often enough that boys are loud, and he's likely to earn the label.

Because stereotypes are socially constructed, they can change over time. Few in this country still cling to negative stereotypes about white ethnic groups, such as the Polish or the Irish, that were prevalent a century ago. Stereotypes also can remain fairly stable. Prejudice and discrimination against African Americans have remained especially persistent over generations, lingering in the form of unconscious and implicit bias even as conscious and explicit bias has faded. These biases have real effects on opportunity: research has shown, for example, that African Americans are less likely than whites or Latinos to receive a callback for a job interview, and that discrimination against African American job applicants remains unchanged since 1989.[12]

Other research has found that teachers attend to cues that identify the social status of students in making decisions about them. For example, they are more likely to place a student in a program for the gifted and talented purely because the student's name is more common among families with money.[13] Unconscious biases are especially difficult to overcome because we have to be aware of them, motivated to correct them, and able to gauge their strength accurately enough to avoid overcorrecting by patronizing people or giving them special treatment.[14] Perceptions that past victims of bias are receiving excessively favorable treatment can and often do trigger a backlash and inflame racial tensions, as has occurred in the debate over affirmative action.

The prejudice and discrimination that result from social cognition are among the forces that drive the **spatial mechanisms** that separate people into specific geographic locations or social groups. Housing markets are a classic example. People—especially those with children—tend to move toward the best neighborhood they can afford, and demand for housing in highly desired neighborhoods drives up homes' prices and perceived exclusivity, rendering them even more desirable. Redlining—practices such as steering homebuyers toward certain neighborhoods based on their race or denying investments and services including federal mortgage insurance to buyers in primarily black neighborhoods—was officially banned in 1968, but discriminatory practices with very similar effects remain widespread in the housing market.[15]

Self-segregation also plays a role, with one 1990s study finding clear differences between whites, Asians, blacks, and Latinos in terms of what racial or ethnic groups they wanted to live alongside. Asked to react to cards abstractly depicting neighborhoods with varying racial and ethnic compositions, whites desired less integrated neighborhoods than did members of other groups and were especially averse to neighborhoods with relatively large numbers of black residents. Asians most desired integration if their neighbors would be white, and blacks desired integration most with whites and least with Asians.[16] Race trumps class as a determinant of where Americans live. A 2000 study found that, among people who earned $60,000 annually, the average white lived in a neighborhood where the median income was $60,363, the average Asian where the median income was $64,129, and average blacks and Latinos lived in neighborhoods where the median income was well less than $50,000.[17]

On a large scale, such patterns sort in-groups and out-groups into distinct geographic areas based on the locations' desirability.[18] Politics also plays a large role. Local decision makers have a long history in this country of wiping out low-income neighborhoods to build sports stadiums, factories, and other infrastructure, and of using highways to separate races from one another.[19] The residents of low-income and minority neighborhoods generally lack the clout to stop such actions, though they are left perfectly free to repopulate areas once they are made undesirable to others. That's why low-income people often can be found living near railroad tracks or factories, and why poor black residents of New Orleans were disproportionately concentrated in the low-lying quarters devastated by Hurricane Katrina.

The decisions made by people with wealth and power leave low-income and minority families concentrated in neighborhoods and tax jurisdictions with the least ability to generate the various forms of capital that provide opportunity. To an even greater extent, they leave white and wealthier families concentrated in neighborhoods and tax jurisdictions with the most resources. The constant shift of employers away from jurisdictions with high taxes and high levels of public need and toward jurisdictions with low taxes and high levels of consumption creates spatial mismatches that leave jobs and consumer goods inaccessible to minority and low-income residents.

Since 1970, the share of Americans living in neighborhoods that are middle income or mixed has shrunk from about two-in-three to two-in-five, with the shares living in uniformly poor or uniformly affluent communities growing.[20] In his book *The Big Sort*, Bill Bishop notes that, with the exception of Las Vegas, the cities that grew the fastest and richest in recent decades were those where people with college degrees had been congregating. Per-capita incomes in the ten metropolitan areas with the most-educated residents rose during the 1990s at about twice the annual rate as in the least-educated cities.[21]

The advantages and disadvantages caused by other mechanisms tend to be exacerbated by the **market mechanisms** that circulate wealth in our economy. Left to themselves, markets distribute wealth and power unequally as a means of their own self-perpetuation, because the unequal accumulation of income and capital is what provides people resources to invest. In growing the economy, the market tends to reward and expand the advantages of those who already have the most financial, human, social, and cultural capital, helping them increase their relative share of the pie. Stock dividends are only paid to those who had the money to buy dividend-paying stocks. Mortgage companies offer much more favorable terms to the financially well-off, allowing them to make stronger bids for houses in neighborhoods served by good public schools.

Expansion increases markets' complexity, creating new job titles associated with varying degrees of status. The U.S. Department of Labor now tracks well over 840 distinct occupations, up from 270 in 1950.[22] Our education and training systems have become significantly more complex to meet the needs associated with the widening array of positions in the modern economy. The knowledge economy has been especially aggressive in its demands for new abilities, and the government's failure to sufficiently fund training for emerging fields leaves people dependent mainly on private sources—their employers or their own bank accounts—to finance the acquisition of new skills. Relative wealth is a key determinant of whether someone gains access to the education they need to cope with such change. The knowledge economy not only requires more formal education, but also emphasizes skills, such as the ability to interact easily with coworkers and customers, most associated with the cultural capital possessed by people who are middle class or above. The unskilled labor pool—which predominately consists of people who are racial and ethnic minorities or from low-income backgrounds—has been increasingly left behind.

Government and private institutions can either mitigate or exacerbate inequality through **policy mechanisms**, which include tax policies, workforce and training programs, and direct investments. Some policies have negative consequences. For example, the U.S. Department of Housing and Urban Development promoted spatial deconcentration—the practice of relocating poor and minority populations away from urban centers—in response to rioting in the 1960s. This practice ended up hollowing out several of the specific urban communities that had been targeted and actually left more poverty concentrated in them than had been there before, until it was struck down by a U.S. district court for undermining the 1974 Housing and Community Development Act.[23] Inequality has also been promoted through zoning laws that have the effect of concentrating low-income or high-income housing, and through states' reliance on local property taxes to finance public schools.

More-positive examples can be seen in programs that provide free children's books to low-income parents or financial aid to economically disadvantaged college students. Enterprise Zones make use of tax policy to encourage local development and employment in economically depressed areas.[24] Youth Opportunity Grants, which aim to strengthen low-income communities through widespread federal investments in the development of community social and human capital, have produced some gains but show mixed effects overall.[25]

Cultural mechanisms come into play as we consciously and unconsciously adjust our expectations, social perspectives, and behaviors in response to our position in society's racial and economic hierarchy. People play the hands they are dealt. The various mechanisms being discussed here can fragment us into populations that take on distinct mixes of adaptive behavior in response to our daily experiences. Family, friends, and the media also influence how we think and act.[26] For example, segments of society that are downtrodden or marginalized sometimes rebel against the dominant cultural paradigm in America by stigmatizing academic achievement.[27]

A community's relationship to education or other formal institutions can be greatly hampered when the exposure to those institutions has been negative or inadequate, as is often the case in underresourced areas. Such mistrust of educational institutions may have little to do with whether a community values education: many minority communities have fought for equal education because of how deeply they valued it. Slaves risked life and limb to become literate, and many educators fought steady—and largely unrewarded—behind-the-scenes battles to equalize school funding in the South.[28]

Parents who are middle class or wealthier typically have the resources to ensure that their children have the best experience possible with the educational system. They have adapted to their environment by developing a distinct childrearing style that gives their offspring an educational advantage, according to the findings of the sociologist Annette Lareau. In the 1990s, Lareau and a team of research assistants extensively interviewed and visited white or black families from different economic backgrounds to study how they handled parenting. The researchers found that parents who were working class or poor still reared their children as pretty much everyone did fifty years ago, leaving them plenty of unstructured leisure time. Such parents sternly punished misbehavior and deferred to perceived authority in communicating with teachers and school administrators. The wealthier parents, by contrast, filled their children's days with structured activities intended to develop talents, responded to their children's misbehavior by trying to reason with them, and viewed educators as equals or subordinates who could be circumvented or challenged. Their children walked into school with "a robust sense of entitlement" and were far more comfortable in hallways and classrooms than the less advantaged.[29]

As Reeves of the Brookings Institution writes, "In the modern economy, human capital has become vital for success. The most educated and affluent parents got the memo. Upper-middle-class families have become greenhouses for the cultivation of human capital. Children raised in them are on a different track than ordinary Americans, right from the very beginning."[30]

American culture, with its emphasis on freedom, competition, and personal responsibility, fosters *cultural individualism*, an adaptive bias that leads us to blame racial and economic inequalities on differences in motivation rather than on structural problems. We see it in both sides of the affirmative action debate, with the right often blaming low black representation at selective colleges on insufficient effort by students, and the left often blaming low black enrollments on conscious racial discrimination.

Part of this disconnect may stem from differences between the individualistic values prioritized by mainstream American educational institutions and the communal priorities that are predominant in some cultures. Or it may relate to the fact that racial and ethnic minority students are less likely to see themselves and their cultures reflected in educational content.[31] A culturally centered curriculum and pedagogy has been shown to improve outcomes for students from specific racial and ethnic minority groups. A teacher who sees resourcefulness and emotional intelligence in a student who helps raise younger siblings, rather than registering the situation only as a deficit tied to a culture of poverty, can make a big difference in building up that student's intelligence and self-esteem.[32]

Educational mechanisms serve to legitimize inequality among the races and classes by linking it to unequal academic credentials from unequal institutions. As Douglas Massey has written, education is "the ultimate scarce resource in a knowledge-based economy."[33] The advantages and disadvantages that people have as children play a central role in determining their access to educational opportunities, which then shape their careers and their ability to pass advantages on to their own children. Race-, ethnicity-, and class-based gaps in the educational resources devoted to young people exist throughout the educational pipeline.[34]

In general, white children from high-income families go to better-equipped schools with better teachers, smaller student–teacher ratios, more adequate student-support programs, and enrollments consisting mainly of other privileged kids.[35] Academic tracking is growing stronger among and within K–12 schools, despite the muting of the past division of high school students into distinct college preparatory, vocational education, and general education programs.[36] Ostensibly linked to ability, but often biased by considerations of advantage, such placements restrict mobility within the educational system, limiting how far students rise or fall as a result of effort and achievement.

Low-income and racial-minority children have the odds stacked against them even before they enter kindergarten, and the odds against them remain high as they travel through the K–12 system.[37] The transition from high school to college, however, stands as the juncture in life when the tracking of Americans into a hierarchy becomes most apparent. Guidance counselors who can advise students on applying to the right college are much more prevalent at high schools where the enrollments are predominantly white and college-bound.[38] Nearly half of young adults who don't go on to college end up not working full-time, year-round jobs, and those who do work full-time have little chance of achieving middle-class earnings.[39]

One way to understand how educational sorting mechanisms work is to measure how different observed advantages and disadvantages help explain differences in SAT scores. This can be done through regression analysis, crunching statistical data using formulas intended to quantify the relationship between specific variables. In 2010, the Georgetown University Center on Education and the Workforce conducted an analysis that attempted to quantify the relationship between certain traits or experiences and SAT scores.[40] The findings of its analysis suggested that

- being black meant 56 fewer points on the SAT compared to being white;

- being in a household led by a high school dropout reduced SAT scores by 43 points compared to being in a household led by a college degree holder;
- attending a public school reduced SAT scores by 28 points compared to attending a private school;
- having friends who planned to attend a four-year college lifted SAT scores by 39 points; and
- taking an Advanced Placement course was associated with an 81-point score increase on the SAT.

In total, the study identified twenty-four significant factors that helped explain how intertwined disadvantages reduced some students' overall performance while similarly connected advantages helped propel others.* Overall, those who had every factor going for them could be expected to score 784 points higher on the SAT than those who had every factor going against them. Whereas the average student scored a 1054, those disadvantaged in every respect scored a 544, or 510 points fewer. Those advantaged in every respect scored a 1328, or 274 points above average.[41]

The Realities of Zero-Sum Competition

Movement through the education pipeline is determined partly by socially constructed differences in the opportunity to learn, with young people constantly directed toward either success or failure based on their class and various forms of discrimination or favoritism. The great

---

* These factors include racial and ethnic factors (black; Hispanic; Hispanic, interacted with percent of enrolled students who are Hispanic); family socioeconomic factors (low-income, parent's highest education is high school dropout, parent's highest education is a high school diploma, sibling dropped out of high school, wealth, occupational prestige); neighborhood factors (percentage of households headed by a high school dropout; percentage of households headed by a high school graduate; living in the South, living in rural area); school factors (percentage of students in the school eligible for free and reduced-price lunch, whether the school is Catholic, whether the school is public); peer factors (percentage of enrolled students who are Asian, having friends attending a four-year school); and non-environmental factors (having children, taking an Advanced Placement course, taking an Advanced Placement test, taking honors courses, not being arrested, worked during school).

sorting begins at birth, when people come into the world as members of racial, ethnic, and socioeconomic groups already ensnared in—and advantaged or disadvantaged by—the mechanisms outlined in this chapter. These same mechanisms then go to work on the next generation, helping to lift them up or keep them down.[42] While the mechanisms are heavily buttressed by individual behaviors, behavior is never divorced from context. These mechanisms are shaping the context in which individuals work, eat, travel, commune, shop, and make choices about everything in their lives—including education.

Although we often speak of the "ceilings" imposed on people by discrimination, it is crucial also to consider the impact of "floors," the barriers to downward mobility created when the mechanisms just described combine with the lengths to which advantaged families will go to prop up and protect their children. The construction of such floors stems from natural and socially accepted protective instincts, rather than discrimination. Nevertheless, floors can have the same impact as ceilings in any zero-sum competition for a limited educational resource. When disadvantaged but deserving students are denied admission to a selective college, it's partly because some seats in the entering class were taken by less-qualified students whose parents used their cash or connections to unduly influence the admissions process. Parental wealth also fosters the upward social mobility of young people by enabling them to take unpaid internships or extend searches for the perfect job rather than leaping at the first offer that will pay the bills.[43]

The competition for relative status can get especially ugly when waged in the educational arena, where social capital and money can convey strong advantages, especially when combined with dubious conduct. The outright bribery and fraud alleged in 2019 as a result of the "Operation Varsity Blues" investigation represents only the obvious tip of a very large iceberg, its criminality established mainly through admissions of deliberate misconduct by people entering plea deals. Much else that transpires never triggers prosecution, because the conduct at issue falls into a gray area where it is difficult to establish criminality or criminal intent. Arguably, students and their parents in well-heeled areas simply have become adept at working the system.

In the aftermath of the Varsity Blues scandal, the *Wall Street Journal* used data from nine thousand public school districts to analyze the rates of students who have so-called 504 plans, established under a federal law requiring that students with learning disabilities receive educational accommodations, including additional time to take standardized tests like the SAT. It found that in wealthy residential school districts an average of 4.2 percent of students had 504 plans. In wealthy suburbs in New York, Connecticut, and Massachusetts, the *Journal* identified at least three high schools where more than 20 percent of students had the accommodations, which often result after a child gets diagnosed with anxiety or attention deficit hyperactivity disorder (ADHD). Meanwhile, in low-income districts, only 1.6 percent of students had such plans.[44]

The *Journal* findings largely mirrored a similar investigation by the *Los Angeles Times* from 2000, which found that a tenth of the students at twenty prominent private schools in the Northeast received accommodations even as no students received them at many inner-city public schools. There is no reason to believe that anxiety and ADHD are more prevalent among wealthy students than poor ones—in fact, research generally shows the opposite to be true. Some disability-rights advocates argued that wealthy parents simply have more resources to get their kids diagnosed. But high school officials told the *Los Angeles Times* of parents who shopped around for a psychologist who would declare their child to have a learning disability. And tutors who specialized in SAT test preparation recalled watching parents circulate the names of those predisposed to give such a diagnosis.[45]

More commonly, parents try to secure their children an edge in applying to college by paying for SAT preparation services, hiring companies that edit or even write college application essays, paying consultants to secure their children's admission into the elite private schools that function as pipelines to top colleges, or even sending their teenagers off to summer camps devoted solely to grooming them for the college admission process.[46]

Espousing lofty, egalitarian ideals does not seem to immunize parents from descending into cutthroat behavior to secure their kids an edge. Ellen Brantlinger, a professor of curriculum and instruction at Indiana University, spent weeks extensively interviewing mothers in a Midwestern university town.* Nearly all worked as public school teachers, as college professors, or as administrators at social service agencies, and thus were "esteemed as the most intelligent, liberal, well-meaning people in society," she wrote in summarizing her study. Their ideals went out the window, however, when sticking to them meant sacrificing their own children's relative advantages. They engaged in all-out efforts to ensure their children attended the public schools with the smallest enrollments of economically disadvantaged students, even if it meant fighting or manipulating the school-assignment process. They held negative views of the poor and blamed poor children's problems on bad home environments rather than on the educational inequalities that they themselves helped foster.[47]

The mismatch between our ideals and our reality has become a hallmark of the American experience. The Swedish economist Gunnar Myrdal titled his landmark 1944 study of race relations in the United States *An American Dilemma* specifically because he saw our nation as torn between its high-minded ideals and the lesser motives of individuals and groups focused on their selfish interests.[48]

Looking back at our imagined Central Park playground, it's quite possible to imagine the consequences of these systemic pressures and hypocrisies. Many of the low-income and minority children on that playground will eventually perceive that they're subject to low expectations, which renders them more susceptible to internalizing those expectations in the form of low self-esteem. The wealthy white children on the playground are likely to receive the message from parents, teachers, and other adults in their lives that they can live their dreams and are entitled to education at prestigious schools and colleges, even if their parents have to intervene for them to gain admission.

---

* Brantlinger withheld the identity of the location where her research took place. Such an omission is standard procedure among social scientists seeking to protect the anonymity of research subjects and ensure their cooperation and candor.

The effects of the odds aren't lost either on those who play them to their benefit or on those who overcome them. In giving the 2015 commencement address for Yale's law school, Daniel Markovits, one of the school's professors, distilled how much most of the graduates on hand had been groomed for that day. "For your entire lives," he said, "you have studied, worked, practiced, trained, and drilled: and then you've been inspected, and finally—you made it here after all—selected." He observed: "A pervasive, effortful, and studied competition . . . dominates and even overwhelms virtually every year of the first three decades of an elite professional's life. The competition has become so ingrained that it is hard for you to imagine life without it." [49]

A far more stunning commentary on advantage came during a 2010 commencement speech by a student at Hunter College High School, not far from New York's Central Park. The school for the intellectually gifted takes in only the top scorers on a notoriously competitive and difficult admissions test. A similarly competitive process, using an IQ test, determines who enters as a kindergartener into Hunter College Elementary School, which feeds the high school. About a fourth of the high school's graduates go on to the Ivy League. It has an overwhelmingly white and Asian enrollment in a city that is mostly black and Latino.

Being both black and Latino, Justin Hudson, the student giving the speech, stood as an example of someone who had overcome the odds. He wasn't sounding celebratory, though.[50] He told his 183 fellow graduates: "I feel guilty because I don't deserve any of this. And neither do any of you. We received an outstanding education at no charge based solely on our performance on a test we took when we were eleven-year-olds, or four-year-olds. We received superior teachers and additional resources based on our status as 'gifted,' while kids who naturally needed those resources much more than us wallowed in the mire of a broken system. And now, we stand on the precipice of our lives, in control of our lives, based purely and simply on luck and circumstance."

He argued, "If you truly believe that the demographics of Hunter represent the distribution of intelligence in this city, then you must

believe that the Upper West Side, Bayside and Flushing are intrinsi-
cally more intelligent than the South Bronx, Bedford-Stuyvesant and
Washington Heights, and I refuse to accept that. It is certainly not
Hunter's fault that socioeconomic factors inhibit the educational opportunities of some children from birth, and in some ways I forgive
colleges and universities that are forced to review eighteen-year-olds,
the end results of a broken system. But we are talking about eleven-
year-olds. Four-year-olds. We are deciding children's fates before they
even had a chance."

"We are playing God, and we are losing," he said. "Kids are losing
the opportunity to go to college or obtain a career, because no one
taught them long division or colors. Hunter is perpetuating a system
in which children, who contain unbridled and untapped intellect and
creativity, are discarded like refuse. And we have the audacity to say
they deserved it, because we're smarter than them."[51]

4

STANDARDIZED BIAS

Selective colleges wouldn't dare send out completely honest rejection letters. If they did, those letters might go something like this:

Dear Tom,
Thank you for your interest, and congratulations for having a 4.0 grade point average and being at the top of your class. Unfortunately, we don't think much of your Midwestern small-town high school, so your achievements there mean little to us. The reality is that you never stood a chance of getting accepted here. We knew that from the start and recruited you specifically to set you up for the rejection that you're experiencing now. You see, the more applicants we reject, the more selective we look, which bolsters our reputation. And seriously, an 1100 SAT score? Do you have any idea what admitting students like you would do to our class average?

Or:

Dear Sarah:
For a moment there, it looked like we might accept you. Then, however, our director of development told us to make space for the grandchild of a donor who has pumped more money into our

endowment fund than you're ever going to earn. Someone had to be bumped off the list, and that someone was you.

No college would ever send out such letters, because, of course, they'd have hell to pay. Knowing exactly what drove a selective college to admit or reject each applicant would leave applicants and their families outraged. These colleges would be bombarded with angry letters, emails, and phone calls; they might face lawsuits, pressure from lawmakers to reform, and even threats to their tax-exempt status.

The truth is that selective colleges have some idea of the makeup of their incoming class before the applications arrive. These colleges will set aside places for a certain number of athletes, a share of "legacies" (the children or other relatives of alumni), the children of staff members and faculty, the children of large donors, and so on. Applicants with no such connections cast their lot thinking that their obvious attributes and carefully choreographed essays will win over the admissions staff. These unconnected applicants expect selective colleges to admit students with the greatest demonstrated promise—those who merit admission on the basis of their accomplishments, not their social status. Some will win a spot solely on the basis of their merits, but the odds are undoubtedly weighted in favor of the wealthy and well-connected. In fact, 60 percent of all seats in the most selective colleges go to students from the most affluent families. Of these students, 46 percent would not have been admitted if required to meet a minimum test score of 1250 on the SAT.[1]

Selecting a college class involves a set of interconnected decisions. Colleges say they consider a host of qualifications, including high school GPA and class rank, SAT or ACT scores, application essays, letters of recommendation, and records of involvement in athletics or extracurricular activities. They also consider how each applicant's presence on campus would contribute to the goal of having the right mix of students, with racial and geographic diversity, sufficient numbers of budding scientists and aspiring artists, and young people who can play trumpet in the marching band or sink three-pointers for the basketball team.

Scores on the SAT or ACT have outsized importance in the process, as colleges use test scores to maintain an air of exclusivity. In a recent confessional blog post, Sara Harberson, a former associate dean of admissions at the University of Pennsylvania, wrote:

> I used to give the same canned speech that my boss gave to prospective families and college counselors. Test scores are just one piece of the puzzle, I would say.
>
> What I didn't say was that the first thing I saw when I opened up an application to read or make an admissions decision on, was the student's test scores. It dictated how much time we would spend on that application and the likelihood of admission.
>
> No matter how good the student's grades were, how much of a trailblazer I thought they could be, how moving their essays were, nothing could "make up" for low test scores unless they were lucky enough to fall into a rare category of students that the institution wanted for political reasons.[2]

But colleges also ignore SAT and ACT scores when convenient. Admissions offices often find themselves under pressure to make decisions that will help their institutions take in money and build prestige, with considerations of applicants' merit and the greater good of society relegated to afterthoughts. Selective colleges are so focused on enrolling students from well-off families that they maintain admissions criteria that systematically reward advantage and punish disadvantage, compounding the effects of social and economic inequality.

While insisting that they only admit qualified students, selective colleges structure their admissions processes to be most easily navigated by applicants from families with money and insider knowledge, and they show outright favoritism toward applicants with cash and connections. Unsurprisingly, the applicants these selective colleges favor are disproportionately white.

The colleges mask this behavior by blending data from two very different admissions tracks: a highly competitive and demanding track for regular applicants, and a separate, less-demanding one for those who have what admissions officers call a "hook." The first is for outsiders they're looking for excuses to keep out, the second for insiders—children of alumni or employees—as well as athletes, people tied to powerful politicians or generous donors, and other recruited applicants. So many students gain admission through some sort of "hook" status that "among very, very good schools, a huge percentage of the class is not in play on academic grounds," William M. Shain, an educational consultant and former admissions dean at three private colleges, told the *Chronicle of Higher Education.*[3]

Selective colleges follow what sociologist Jerome Karabel describes as an "iron law of admissions." It holds that "a university will retain a particular admissions policy only so long as it produces outcomes that correspond to perceived institutional interests," Karabel writes in his book *The Chosen,* an extensively researched history of admissions at Harvard, Yale, and Princeton. Elite colleges built their admissions systems with two cornerstones: "discretion so that gatekeepers would be free to do what they wished and opacity so that how they used their discretion would not be subject to public scrutiny."[4] That combination of discretion and opacity masks the standardized bias that governs selective admissions and enables upper-tier colleges to make admissions decisions driven less by considerations of merit than by calculations of how they can enrich themselves and improve their institutional status.

The Use and Misuse of Enrollment Management

Understanding how the admissions process really works requires us to scrutinize the practice of enrollment management, a data-driven approach to admissions that has revolutionized the field since the 1980s. Enrollment management involves using strategic planning, insights from social science research, and computer simulations to tweak standards and practices to get the right mix of students. Rather than passively admitting the most qualified applicants, colleges seek to systematically shape the student body's composition to meet certain goals, such as increases in net tuition revenue, improvements in academic reputation, or larger enrollments of minority students. They meticulously monitor market position and how they're perceived by prospective students.[5]

Enrollment management treats various policies and practices as knobs that can be adjusted to get desired results. If previous decisions seem to be yielding an undesired student mix, it allows for recalibrations in the midst of the current admissions cycle or at the beginning of the new one. Colleges can tweak marketing and recruitment practices to target some population segments while skirting others. They might alter their mix of need- versus merit-based aid to become more accessible or, conversely, to drive up enrollments of valedictorians.[6]

The relationship between institutional priorities and enrollment management is one in which influence flows both ways. Just as institutional priorities determine enrollment managers' calibrations, the data gathered by enrollment managers can inspire shifts in institutional priorities, affecting almost any aspect of college operations. If an enrollment manager calculates that a university can attract larger numbers of desired students by offering more courses in business, there's a good chance that the institution will end up hiring more business instructors and advertising their course offerings. Back in 2005, writer Matthew Quirk observed in *The Atlantic*:

> Over the past twenty years, often under cover of the euphemisms with which the industry abounds, enrollment management has transformed admissions and financial aid, and in some cases the entire mission of a college or a university. At its most advanced it has a hand in every interaction between a student and a school, from the crafting of a school's image all the way through to the student's successful graduation. Any aspect of university life that bears on a school's place in the collegiate pecking order is fair game: academic advising, student services, even the curriculum itself. Borrowing the most sophisticated techniques of business strategy, enrollment managers have installed market-driven competition at the heart of the university.[7]

While the weight that admissions officers give to various applicant characteristics is open to adjustment, the set of factors that American colleges consider in filling seats in freshman classes have remained fairly consistent over the past twenty years, according to the National Association for College Admission Counseling. Generally deemed most important are standardized test scores, overall grade point average, grades in college preparatory courses, and the strength of the applicants' high school curriculum. Further down the list, but still likely to carry significant weight, are students' application essays, demonstrated interest in the college, counselor and teacher recommendations, and extracurricular activities and class rank in high school. Private colleges in general give more weight than public ones to high school attended, first-generation status, alumni relations, ability to pay, and race, ethnicity, or gender. Smaller colleges give more weight than larger ones to ability to pay, a likely reflection of the financial pressure that many are under.[8]

Decisions about the "right mix" of students—and thus the right factors to emphasize—are particular to each college. They are rooted in value judgments that put self-interest before the common good, prestige before fairness. And when selfish gain and prestige drive admissions decisions, colleges end up shutting out many low-income students.

That result isn't inherent to enrollment management; rather, enrollment management allows colleges to mask a deliberate choice made in pursuing their institutional interests. College officials who would never admit outright to wanting to reduce numbers of low-income students can use enrollment management to twist the knobs to produce such a result.[9] Enrollment management can cause suspicion because it's carried out through complex mathematical analyses and often produces results best explained in cynical terms, yet the mischief stems not from the tools used, but from the ends pursued.

At the end of the day, it's people who are driving the admissions process, and they come to it with different agendas, constraints, and relative levels of power. Many in the admissions offices sincerely care about students from less-advantaged backgrounds. But they're stuck working within a system that's defined by its own biases; that applies admissions criteria to meet shifting institutional priorities rather than to enforce rigid standards of merit; that has few, if any, firewalls to maintain its integrity and prevent inappropriate interference; and that allows market pressures and bottom-line concerns to overrule good deeds.

To understand how well-meaning people can end up greasing the gears of the sorting machine, it's helpful to look at how admissions offices are structured. The titles of their employees vary, but these offices are typically led by officers who oversee student recruitment and selection, with staff who recruit applicants and guide them and their parents through the application process. Increasingly, they fall under the command of some high-level administrator who also oversees at least one related administrative function, such as the financial aid office.[10] And their leadership most typically represents white and male privilege: women are overrepresented at the entry-level and mid-level positions and underrepresented at the senior ones, while blacks and Latinos are underrepresented at all levels, especially at the top.[11]

On the whole, these employees didn't get into the admissions game to rig the deck against marginalized students. There's no well-defined career path for admissions professionals, and many say they simply fell into the job. The main skills that colleges rank as important for chief enrollment officers are statistics and data analysis, marketing and public relations, higher education administration, writing, and business management.[12] About half of colleges rate having an advanced degree as "very important" for an admissions professional, but experience on a faculty is nowhere on the list, prompting concern that too many admissions officers think in business-focused rather than educational terms.[13]

In recent years, the profession "has changed dramatically in scope, responsibility and complexity and become more important to the university's bottom line," according to a 2014 National Association for College Admission Counseling report based on a survey of people in the field. The survey found that traditional recruitment responsibilities "have not gone away" but rather "have been made more complicated" by new technologies and other developments.[14]

"Conversations pertaining to admission and enrollment targets, retention, financial aid, tuition setting and annual budgets take place in the same room," noted Greg W. Roberts, dean of admissions for the University of Virginia.[15] Pressure to improve rankings and add to bottom lines is intense enough to have produced an upsurge in the turnover rate among top admissions and enrollment officers in recent years.[16]

That pressure is having an impact, and it often places enrollment managers and other admissions employees in impossible positions. According to Michael Bastedo, who extensively studied enrollment management at two flagship public universities as director of the University of Michigan Center for the Study of Higher and Postsecondary Education:

> Enrollment managers are often blamed on campus for pursuing goals that were set by presidents and boards. College presidents can publicly claim that they want more racially and economically diverse incoming classes, while privately demanding that their chief enrollment officer increase revenues and prestige. Enrollment managers become the faceless, pragmatic technocrats of the institution, while everyone else gets to pretend that all enrollment goals can be pursued simultaneously.[17]

College leaders are well aware that college rankings are based heavily on criteria linked to students' socioeconomic status, such as average SAT or ACT scores, alumni giving rates, and university financial resources.[18] The admissions staff acting under these leaders' direction use enrollment management to adjust admissions criteria. These adjustments can set the stage for a rise in the rankings or at least avoid downward spirals in which declines in a college's ranking, enrollment, and financial health feed off each other.

Enrollment management can be used to provide greater access to disadvantaged students, but market pressures and bottom-line concerns generally discourage colleges' pursuit of any goal that does not produce immediate, tangible benefits. As enrollment management was becoming ubiquitous in higher education a decade ago, Donald R. Hossler, a senior scholar at the University of Southern California's Center for Enrollment Research, Policy, and Practice, called its emergence "one small indicator of the ascendancy of capitalism and the extent to which the market metaphor has taken hold throughout the United States and the rest of the world."[19]

The Undue Influence of Political Pressure

Enrollment management hardly represents the only means by which admissions offices do the bidding of other administrative divisions. In some ways, the most shocking thing about the "Operation Varsity Blues" scandal of 2019 was that the parents involved resorted to blatant bribery and fraud when the system already strongly favored people with their level of wealth and connections.[20] On an informal basis, admissions offices' judgments of individual applicants often reflect meddling by trustees, presidents, athletics departments, and members of the administration who solicit gifts, handle alumni relations, oversee faculty, or handle government relations.[21]

When levels of such interference at a public college seem to violate the public trust, the backlash can be intense. Such was the case when a 1996 *Los Angeles Times* investigation found that the University of California at Los Angeles had for years maintained a backdoor admissions system for applicants connected to university regents and other public officials. Over a period of fifteen years, more than eighty public officials had pulled strings, seeking the admission of their own children or the children of friends, business associates, and political allies. As a result, UCLA admitted applicants who were poorly qualified or, in some cases, had already been rejected.[22] In 2009, members of the University of Illinois Board of Trustees faced calls to resign after the *Chicago Tribune* exposed how the flagship campus at Urbana-Champaign had bowed to political pressure in admitting several applicants who were well-connected and had questionable qualifications.[23] In 2015, an independent investigation commissioned by the University of Texas system found that William C. Powers, the

president of the University of Texas at Austin, had intervened in—
and even overruled—admissions decisions at the behest of lawmakers, donors, and board members. The investigative commission
accused staff members of destroying evidence of secret deliberations
on behalf of applicants.[24]

A study based on interviews with fifty-nine public university presidents found they commonly fielded requests from trustees to admit
politically connected applicants. Presidents often feel pressure when
they get requests from those who have the power to vote to fire them
at will.[25] Separately, the *Chronicle of Higher Education* reported that
trustees and some presidents "inquire routinely about the fates of individual applicants," a finding based on its review of nearly two thousand
pages of emails obtained from public universities under open-records
laws. At one institution, Florida State University, the president and
trustees had asked the admissions director to give special attention to
nearly forty individual applicants during a ten-month span.[26]

At a separate public institution, the New College of Florida, William R. Johnston, a trustee and former president of the New York
Stock Exchange, acknowledged that he comes out "with all guns fir-
ing" when someone brings a promising applicant to his attention.
The newspaper said, "At many institutions few if any rules govern
how much college leaders can influence admissions decisions, and
some admissions officials must deal with a deluge of such correspondence." Its investigation could not ascertain just how often or
far the universities had lowered the bar for favored applicants, because the documents it obtained had been heavily redacted and its
records request could not take phone calls into account.[27] Most college officials learned long ago to avoid written discussions of controversial decisions that could become part of the public record. "I am
rarely on a conference call with other public university presidents
that doesn't include someone reminding the group: 'No emails!'"
Mitch Daniels, the president of Purdue University, said in a 2018
Washington Post op-ed.[28]

Another study, this one based on the investigation of the University of Illinois admissions scandal, concluded that the potential for

such misconduct "pervades colleges and universities more than we assume—and even more than we feel comfortable acknowledging." It stems from a confluence of common psychological tendencies, such as self-deception; environmental pressures, such as financial concerns; and organizational structures, such as enrollment-management systems. The study used the term "ethical fading" to describe how the culture or structure of an organization causes those within it to lose sight of ethical considerations.

At Illinois, tough economic times had produced both increased demand for admission and budget cuts that threatened the bottom line. The administration avoided open conflict between its ethical purists and those who wanted to do favors for politicians and donors by creating a separate "shadow" admissions system. University leaders reassured themselves that their behavior was common at competing institutions. Each step away from their ethical moorings made the next one easier. Those involved made peace with themselves by using euphemistic language and focusing their attention on any good consequences of their behavior, such as the enrollments of connected applicants who were black, Latino, or from underserved geographic regions. Trustees adopted a "hear no evil, see no evil" attitude to avoid confronting the misconduct taking place under their noses and, in some cases, at their behest.[29]

More broadly, and less controversially, some colleges—especially public ones—alter admissions criteria and practices at the behest of various constituencies for political reasons. A group of forty-nine different higher-education associations suggested as much in a 2013 brief submitted to the U.S. Supreme Court in opposition to Michigan's ban on public colleges' use of race-conscious admissions. Echoing a central argument made by lawyers for the minority students who were challenging the ban, the associations said the ban violated the minority students' constitutional right to equal protection by precluding them alone from lobbying public colleges for the same preferential admissions treatment sought by alumni, wealthy donors, powerful politicians, and residents of various regions of the state. (The Supreme Court overwhelmingly upheld the ban.)[30]

Bias and Discrimination

Personal biases also factor heavily into admissions decisions, both in colleges' choices and calibration of admissions policies and in their evaluations of individual applicants.[31]

Many such biases are rooted in unconscious cognitive processes. People tend to attribute positive traits to themselves and their own group, even at times when that group is arbitrarily and artificially defined, as in the context of a psychological experiment. When told that there is a link between eye color and character, many will start thinking up virtues that those with their eye color possess.[32] People will project their own characteristics, or their group's, onto a prototype that connotes merit and predicts success. They'll credit the successes of members of their own group to permanent, personal, and pervasive strengths while discounting the successes of members of other groups as atypical and due to temporary, impersonal, and non-pervasive causes. Their own kids' success in business will be cheered as the result of brains and hard work, the Smiths' kids' to being in the right place at the right time. The reverse holds true for failure. They'll say their son is unemployed because there are no jobs, while the Smiths' son is simply lazy.[33] College admissions officers will almost naturally blur judgments of applicants' qualifications with judgments of applicants' ability to "fit in," favoring traits common among those already on campus.[34] Asian American students who accused Harvard of discriminating against them in a lawsuit filed in 2014 have uncovered documents showing that many were dinged for lacking personality traits associated with extroverts—such as likability or the ability to command respect—despite a lack of any evidence that extroverts are more intelligent or successful. People from cultures that stressed humility were getting docked for not being cocky glad-handers.[35]

In his fieldwork at flagship universities, Bastedo observed admissions officers exhibiting two distinct cognitive biases: *anchoring bias* and *correspondence bias*. Anchoring bias occurs when previously heard information skews our estimations, as when the second person guessing how many pennies are in a piggy bank will guess higher if the first person said one hundred than if the first said five. Bastedo concluded that this kind of bias "potentially plays a role in the disproportionate influence of standardized test scores on admissions decisions." Correspondence bias describes the tendency to attribute people's decisions to their dispositions rather than to broader context; this kind of bias potentially explains admissions officers' failure to account for how home or school environments have shaped applicants.[36]

How admissions officers' personal backgrounds skew their judgments was explored in a 2014 experiment involving admissions officers at 174 institutions that *Barron's Profiles of American Colleges* lists among those in its top three selectivity tiers. When presented with fictitious engineering school applications from three white men who varied in terms of their academic credentials and economic backgrounds, admissions officers who were female or members of minority groups tended more than others to look favorably upon applications depicted as coming from those with low-income backgrounds, suggesting greater concern for equity. Nearly half of admissions officers who worked at their alma mater showed a greater predisposition toward favoring applicants depicted as high-achieving and wealthy, although it was unclear from the data whether this tendency stemmed from a lack of concern over equity or a desire to increase their alma mater's prestige.[37]

Of course, the discrimination practiced by America's colleges has not always been subtle. Historically black colleges exist because many other colleges remained off-limits to blacks until the 1950s. Women's colleges came into being mainly because many colleges excluded women until the 1960s or even later.[38] These institutions were founded and attended by people who determinedly created their own opportunities to pursue higher learning, even in the face of widespread exclusion.

A shocking number of the admissions criteria widely used by colleges today have origins in another form of discrimination: anti-Semitism. They include considerations of legacy status or geographic diversity, requirements for letters of recommendation, and personal interviews, all of which elite colleges widely adopted in the first

decades of the twentieth century as means of keeping out Jewish applicants, who were presumed to be lacking in character and concentrated in major East Coast cities.[39] Colleges had previously primarily
accepted students from widely known feeder schools, but turned to
screening applicants using admissions tests. In doing so, the colleges
inadvertently leveled the playing field in ways that gave a fair chance
to talented Jewish applicants, many of whom came from families that
deeply valued education. Those who had attended competitive public schools in Boston, Philadelphia, and New York had little trouble
posting high admissions-test scores, but their growing presence on
campus rattled the wealthy Congregationalists, Episcopalians, and
Presbyterians who long had regarded the institutions as their own.[40]
The colleges' administrators faced backlash for spurning the children
of alumni—whose donations accounted for an increasing share of
their revenues—while admitting Jews, Catholics, and other recent
immigrants.[41]

John Albert Cousens, then the president of Tufts University, argued
that its academic reputation hinged on enrolling students from the
"best families" and not being "a poor man's college and an asylum for
the children of the foreign-born."[42] Princeton was hailed by Robert
Corwin, the chairman of its Board of Admissions, as having solved
its "Jewish problem" through its 1922 adoption of a comprehensive
admissions system that used personal interviews to judge "character."
Harvard and Yale considered capping Jewish enrollment before turning to legacy preferences and subjective admissions criteria to keep
numbers down.[43] Harvard jacked up its tuition to try to reserve access
for the wealthy graduates of private preparatory schools.[44] Some selective colleges went so far as to ask applicants for photographs or their
mother's maiden name. Liberal arts colleges that were beginning to
recruit nationally avoided reaching out to areas with populations they
viewed as undesirable.[45]

A 1945 survey of the nation's colleges documented the widespread
use of preferences for legacies and for applicants recommended by
alumni and other insiders. "Home influence" was cited as highly important by 4 percent of those surveyed, "character" as an essential

quality by 45 percent.[46] Our confrontation with the horrors of the Holocaust, however, would trigger a backlash against anti-Semitism that led to the abandonment of admissions policies that blatantly discriminated against Jewish applicants. Jewish enrollment at leading colleges has since soared. As of 2006, Jewish students accounted for more than 20 percent of the enrollment at most Ivy League institutions and at least 10 percent of the enrollment at about half the colleges that *Barron's* ranks as "highly competitive" or "most competitive," with their numbers lower mainly at Christian colleges, military service academies, and small liberal arts colleges in the hinterlands.[47] Nevertheless, admissions practices that once enabled anti-Semitic discrimination— by either favoring entrenched constituencies or enabling bias masked as legitimate subjectivity—remain in widespread use. If they disproportionately help or hurt certain segments of the population, it should be kept in mind that such was their original intended purpose.

Standardized Test Scores: Shortcuts to Nowhere

The number of students applying to selective colleges has surged in recent years as a result of the Common Application, which lets students apply to several colleges at once, and other online apps that can make applying as easy as visiting a Facebook page. Well over a third of the college freshmen of fall 2016 had applied to at least seven colleges.[48] Selective colleges certainly benefit from rising application rates, which drive down their acceptance rates and make them seem more exclusive, but a deluge of applications also puts tremendous pressure on college bureaucracies, especially at the top. Colleges that accept fewer than half of applicants enroll just over two-tenths of the nation's undergraduates but end up receiving nearly 40 percent of all college applications.[49] Donald Hossler said first-tier colleges generally have more resources, which enable them to give applicants individual consideration, while second- and third-tier colleges feel pressure to enroll applicants with objectively strong profiles in hopes of rising in the rankings.[50] In 2016, the mean number of applications handled annually by admissions officers at top-tier colleges (those that accept fewer than 50 percent of applicants) stood at just over 2,000. Colleges that accepted 50 to 70 percent of applicants handled an average of 800 applications annually, and colleges that accepted 71 to 85 percent handled an average of 460 applications.[51]

To cope with this surging volume, most selective colleges have had to tweak their admissions practices, devising fairly rough and mechanistic processes to winnow applicant files. A large share of the colleges initially assign applicants scores based on grades, standardized test results, or the academic rigor of their high school courses, and then use those scores as cutoffs to pull sure admits or sure rejects out of the pile. A 2014 survey of admissions officers in *Barron's* top three tiers found that 5 percent in the first tier, 28 percent in the second, and 37 percent in the third had set upper-range cutoffs above which applicants were virtually guaranteed admission. Lower-range cutoffs to weed out applicants who stood no chance were significantly more common, being used by 35 percent of admissions officers in the top tier, 52 percent in the second tier, and 47 percent in the third.[52]

This isn't to say that standardized tests like the SAT and the ACT can't be useful measures for admissions officers seeking to compare very different applicants. At the same time, however, these tests are entirely overused. Neither test was created to do much more than predict freshman GPA, but they are too often assumed to predict college and even career success. And while they do predict freshman GPA, they don't do a very good job. According to a large study of freshmen at the University of California, the SAT, by itself, predicts about 16 percent of first-year GPA; in combination with high school GPA, it explains about 23 percent of first-year outcomes.[53] The idea that we might use the tests to predict performance beyond the first year is a fallacy, one that requires us to ignore the multiple events that occur in a student's life between taking the test and college graduation, and between college graduation and entry into a career.

More important, although the SAT and ACT sometimes indeed identify highly capable young people from disadvantaged settings, they mainly serve the opposite function: legitimizing as differences in measured ability the effects of illegitimate differences in children's opportunities to learn before reaching college age.[54] They're a way for colleges to dodge accounting for racial and socioeconomic inequality. They're mechanisms for laundering race and class behind a scientific façade of quantitative metrics.

Consider the first test on the college admissions scene, the SAT. Its developer and early advocates of its use knew from the start that performance on it varies by race and class. The IQ test, from which it was adapted, had produced results that mirrored the stratification of American society when first widely administered during World War I as an officer-screening device. The sons of well-established families with roots in northern Europe outscored the sons of recent eastern or southern European immigrants, who, in turn, outscored the descendants of African slaves. Given the wide acceptance of eugenics at that time—when it was commonly believed that the human race could be perfected through selective reproduction, sometimes enacted through forced sterilization—the test's scoring gaps linked to race and ethnicity were seen as a feature rather than a bug.

Carl Campbell Brigham, the Princeton University psychology professor who adapted the IQ test into the SAT, was himself an outspoken eugenicist. His influential 1923 book, A Study of American Intelligence, classified white Americans into three distinct groups. He argued that northern European "Nordics" were intellectually superior to eastern European "Alpines," whom he regarded as superior to the southern European "Mediterraneans," whose high rates of immigration and reproduction alarmed him. In later promoting the SAT, he disavowed his eugenicist writings and his previous assertions that the test's results measured innate "native intelligence." Instead, he argued that its value stemmed from its ability to measure the effects of schooling, family background, and other environmental factors. His reversal did not deter those who remained eugenicists from championing the test as an innate-ability measure.[55]

Although the SAT has evolved over time, it has continued to come under fire for outright racial bias, primarily in respect to questions on the verbal portion that disproportionately trip up black students who match their white peers' performance elsewhere.[56] The Educational

Testing Service, which has administered the SAT since the late 1940s, has disputed some criticisms of the test being biased while responding to others by tweaking the instrument. It has never, however, completely solved the problem.[57] "The rhetoric that accompanied the birth of ETS was one of mass opportunity and classlessness, yet the main purpose of the organization was to select the few and not to improve the lives of the many," Nicholas Lemann concluded in his landmark history of the SAT, *The Big Test*.[58] In *None of the Above*, another acclaimed examination of the SAT, David Owen and Marilyn Doerr went so far as to allege, "The meritocracy, as interpreted by ETS, is eugenics by other means."[59]

Separate from the question of whether racial bias taints some SAT questions is the problem of broader performance gaps associated with race, ethnicity, and class. Such factors are strongly linked to educational advantage, and educational advantage, in turn, is strongly linked to SAT performance. As a result, whites and Asians end up heavily clustered at the top of the score distribution, blacks and Latinos at the bottom.

The ACT, introduced in 1959, billed itself as an alternative that measured academic achievement rather than innate ability.[60] Based on the Iowa Tests of Educational Development and developed from curriculum surveys, it initially included four sections tied to the high school curriculum: English, mathematics, social sciences reading, and natural sciences reading.[61] Before launching it, its developer, E.F. Lindquist, told participants at an ETS conference:

> If the examination is to have the maximum motivating value for the high school student, it must impress upon him the fact that his chances of being admitted to college . . . depend not only on his "brightness" or "intelligence" or other innate qualities or factors for which he is not personally responsible, but even more upon how hard he has worked at the task of getting ready for college. . . . The examination must make him feel that he has *earned* the right to go to college by his own efforts, not that he

is entitled to college because of his innate abilities or aptitudes, regardless of what he has done in high school.[62]

In reality, the ACT has failed to live up to such rhetoric. Among the researchers reaching such a conclusion, Richard C. Atkinson, president emeritus of the University of California, and Saul Geiser, former director of admissions research for the University of California system, concluded that the ACT "falls short of a true achievement test in several ways." Like the SAT, it is norm-referenced and used primarily to compare students against one another rather than to assess curriculum mastery. Some sections require little content knowledge of the disciplines covered and, like the SAT, mainly reward mental agility and test-taking skill. The ACT increasingly emphasizes time-management skills and, over time, has converged so much with the SAT that almost all U.S. colleges accept both and treat their scores as interchangeable.[63]

What do the SAT and ACT actually measure? The answer to that question lies down a rabbit hole. The ACT only somewhat measures achievement. Neither instrument precisely measures aptitude—a point the College Board conceded in 1990 by changing the SAT's formal name from Scholastic Aptitude Test to Scholastic Assessment Test (later trimmed down to the abbreviation SAT and nothing more). Official descriptions of what the SAT measures have changed from "aptitude" to "generalized reasoning ability" to "critical thinking."[64]

Press the organizations on what the tests do in fact measure, and you may get the response "G." Ask what "G" means, and you might hear something like "G is G." Down the rabbit hole you've gone. "G" is self-referential. It stands for itself and nothing else. When really pushed to demonstrate validity, the organizations behind the tests turn to the ability of the tests to predict freshman performance. For example, the College Board has said that the SAT's validity should be understood in the context of its primary use in admissions and placement: that is, with a focus on "the relationship between scores . . . and first-year grade point average."[65] So much for the claims that the tests measure intelligence.

While the tests do have some predictive value, that value is often overstated: by itself, the SAT has little ability to explain differences in freshman grades.[66] And it is an even weaker determinant of students' likelihood of college graduation. In fact, after controlling for institutional selectivity (since more-selective institutions tend to have higher graduation rates), we find that the likelihood of college graduation increases only modestly with increases in SAT and ACT scores.[67]

It is not a student's scores, but the selectivity of the college where the student ends up that matters more: people with the exact same standardized test scores and grades in high school graduate from colleges at remarkably different rates based on the selectivity of the colleges they attend.[68] A student who scores between 1100 and 1200 on the SAT and attends a third-tier school has a 68 percent chance of graduating; at a top-tier school, that student's chance of graduating rises nearly 20 percentage points, to 85 percent.[69]

While the tests have only weak predictive power, they do correlate with socioeconomic status, to the point that *Wall Street Journal* reporter Josh Zumburn labeled the SAT the "Student Affluence Test."[70] Knowing someone's SAT or ACT scores, it's possible to tell with remarkable accuracy how much their parents earn. In fact, admissions systems that consider grades and family incomes would be nearly as effective at predicting first-year college performance as are current systems that consider high school grades and standardized test scores.[71]

The biological determinists have it exactly backward in this case. Social inequality is a cause, rather than the result, of gaps in how members of different races, classes, and sexes perform on standardized admissions tests. The measured ability of children explains about 70 percent of the developed ability of adolescents from affluent families but only about 10 percent of the developed ability of adolescents from low-income families.[72] A seminal long-term study by University of Virginia researchers found that environmental factors help produce major gaps between the innate abilities measured in low-income children and their aptitudes at college age, but did almost nothing to hinder young people from middle- and upper-income families, whose aptitudes later in life reflected innate abilities displayed in childhood.

The bottom line: privileged kids get a chance to develop their talents, while most kids from poor or working-class families don't.[73]

Holistically Privileged

Other admissions criteria used by selective colleges in holistic evaluations have some educational basis, but also are inextricably tied to advantage or disadvantage.

High school reputation falls into that category. Public schools in wealthy communities and expensive private schools are much likelier to possess all the elements of a strong academic reputation: well-paid and experienced teachers, new facilities, small class sizes, few disciplinary problems, challenging and advanced instruction, high expectations of students, and active and involved parents.[74]

Along related lines, colleges give substantial weight to the strength of the high school curriculum and the number of Advanced Placement courses on applicants' transcripts. Students from affluent families are likelier to attend high schools where advanced courses are offered and to take any such courses offered by their schools.[75] Students at small, rural high schools often have no access to such courses.[76] Schools that serve low-income students have been expanding their AP offerings, but schools that serve the affluent have expanded their offerings at an equal or greater pace, maintaining or widening their students' advantage.[77] Colleges don't need to put such a premium on curriculum strength—high school GPA in all academic courses has been shown to be a decent overall predictor of performance in college, better even than standardized admissions test scores. Yet colleges continue to shy away from this relatively egalitarian measure because they assume grading standards differ and reliance on GPA fails to account for the grade inflation that occurs at more prestigious high schools when affluent parents pressure teachers.[78]

Colleges' consideration of students' involvement in extracurricular activities also gives an edge to the advantaged. Taking part in such activities often requires parents who can cover the costs of equipment and fees and can provide a car or shuttle the student around. Above all, it requires that students not be spending their after-school hours working to earn money for college.[79] The size of a high school and the wealth of its student body are strong predictors of whether it will offer a wide range of well-supported extracurricular activities. Students at small high schools in low-income communities tend to be out of luck.[80] Moreover, "it is not uncommon for the low-income families of high-achieving students to be unaware of the importance of extracurricular activities, or even to discourage them as a distraction from academic endeavors," Michael Bastedo from the University of Michigan notes.[81]

Affluent applicants also tend to get an edge through selective colleges' systematic consideration of recommendations from high school counselors. Private and public schools in affluent communities tend to have much better-staffed counseling offices with more time to advise students through the college application process and write glowing letters about them.[82] The most extreme advantages from counseling are enjoyed by students at the East Coast's most elite private schools, whose counselors have historically enjoyed cozy relationships with admissions officers at top colleges interested in maintaining good relations with their feeders. As part of relationships nurtured through reciprocal campus visits and, often, wining and dining, the college admissions officers tip the college counselors off to the types of students being sought that year, and the counselors often hand over thick dossiers on applicants, with selling points flagged.[83]

Selective colleges pay a lot of attention to the interest that applicants showed in a college before applying, because they're highly invested in maintaining a high "yield rate"—the term applied to the share of admitted students who actually matriculate as freshmen in the fall. Mainly because their institutional budgets can suffer if too few admitted applicants actually show up, many colleges try to gauge students' demonstrated interest. About a fifth of selective colleges describe it as a considerably important factor.[84] They look favorably upon applicants who have visited campus with their parents, which gives an edge to those who can easily afford travel. (More than a third of upper-income students visit more than six colleges, but just over 4 percent of low-income students do the same.[85])

Children of privilege are also advantaged by "early action" and "early decision" programs that have been adopted by a plethora of selective colleges. "Early action" admissions policies let students apply early and receive early word on the college's decision without being bound to enroll if accepted; "early decision" applicants must meet an earlier deadline and agree to enroll if they are accepted. One analysis of data from fourteen selective colleges found that applicants with SAT scores ranging from 1300 to 1390 on a 1600-point scale increased their chances of admission by 50 percent when they applied under early action and by 70 percent when they applied under early decision.[86] As of 2016, 49 percent of colleges that accepted fewer than half of applicants gave students the option of applying "early decision," which would preclude needy students from considering other colleges' financial aid offers before they commit.[87]

Both "early action" and "early decision" policies give an edge to applicants from families with the savvy to know about them—generally people with access to good counselors or inside knowledge of the institution.[88] And those applicants aren't always the most deserving of the pool. Jason England, a former assistant dean of admissions at Wesleyan University in Connecticut, wrote a confessional essay in which he described early decision as "a way to admit wealthy, undistinguished white students with often not much more in their favor than high SAT scores." He elaborated:

> That's *not* to say they are weak candidates; they just wouldn't stand out in the general pool. These students tend to have savvy private-high-school counselors who understand that the early-decision applicant pool is weaker and the acceptance rate higher. These students also tend to be from wealthier families who got a head start on the college search: They could afford campus visits the previous summer; financial aid isn't an issue, so they don't have to wait for and weigh packages; their scores are high enough

they don't have to wait to take a test again. Disproportionately, they come from elite feeder schools that have slickly tailored their students to suit the admissions standards at top colleges.

The Power of Money

If the long list of admissions policies biased in their favor isn't enough to ensure that students from wealthy families get into their desired college, their families always have several ways to use their cash and connections as leverage.

The political interference in public-college admissions that gave rise to scandals in California, Illinois, and Texas may only represent the tip of that iceberg. Public-college lobbyists in state capitals and Washington, DC, acknowledge spending substantial amounts of their time lobbying their own institutions' admissions offices on behalf of elected officials.[89]

Donors hold sway as well. A 2003 *Wall Street Journal* investigation concluded, based on interviews with education consultants, that applicants could get into a small liberal arts college through a donation of as little as $20,000 and into one of the nation's top ten universities with a gift of at least $250,000.[90] It's bribery that can be written off come tax time. Middlebury College's dean of enrollment separately told the *New York Times* that "every admissions office in the country is paying attention to families' ability to make a major donation."[91] Duke University acknowledged annually accepting 100 to 125 students based on family wealth and connections.[92] A former Duke admissions officer has described getting advance word on the university's long-term construction plans simply by hearing the development office lobbying for applicants from families with pockets deep enough to fund the projects.[93]

The revenue that colleges derive from commercialized college sports helps ensure coaches have a say in admissions decisions involving recruited athletes, whom researchers have found to benefit from the largest admissions preference afforded any subset of applicants at most selective colleges. Athletes can easily account for 25 to 40 percent of each entering class at a selective Division III liberal arts college, and 20 to 30 percent of an entering class at an Ivy League institution.[94] Although minority students are disproportionately represented among men recruited to play football and basketball, on most teams in country club sports such as golf, tennis, and lacrosse, the recruited athletes are disproportionately white and unlikely to come from low-income backgrounds.[95]

A separate book could be written—and many have been—about the ways in which colleges' desire to enroll talented athletes compromises the integrity of their admissions processes and other aspects of the academic enterprise. In the eyes of many in higher education, the chief crime of the coaches implicated in the "Operation Varsity Blues" scandal was that they secured the admission of questionable applicants in ways that benefited only themselves. Rather than simply getting their colleges to admit applicants with lackluster academic records but impressive athletic talents that might drive revenue to the institution, as happens all the time, they duped their colleges into admitting applicants with lackluster academic records who also were mediocre athletes—or not even athletes at all. Colleges had given coaches so much leeway to strike Faustian bargains no one elsewhere in their administration even seemed to notice until the scandal broke.[96]

Admissions preferences for black and Latino students help bring both racial and socioeconomic diversity to campuses. But, while such minority students are likelier than others on campus to have been raised by low-income or working-class parents, they're much likelier to be affluent and the children or grandchildren of prosperous recent immigrants than representative members of the nation's black and Latino populations.[97]

If college faculty members and employees don't make much of a fuss over academic standards being threatened by various types of admissions preferences, it may be because they have a personal stake in the outcomes. Colleges routinely offer their employees tuition remission as a low-cost but high-value perk, and they are loath to deny admission to the children of faculty members or administrators and risk having furious employees on their hands. Most either put a big thumb on the scale when the applicant is an employee's child or route such applications through a separate admissions track that circumvents filtering points where they'd risk being sifted out.[98]

Applicants related to alumni also routinely benefit from substantial admissions preferences based on colleges' desire to maintain good relations with alumni and their belief that admitted legacies are more likely to matriculate.[99] Legacy preferences play a role not just in undergraduate admissions, but also in admissions to graduate and professional schools.[100] The 2010 book *Affirmative Action for the Rich* found that almost three-quarters of selective research universities and virtually all elite liberal arts colleges systematically afforded legacy applicants some edge.[101] A 2011 analysis of data from thirty highly selective colleges found that, all things being equal, legacy status resulted in a 23.3-percentage-point bump in the probability of admission. If the applicant was a "primary legacy," meaning that their parent attended the college as an undergraduate, the probability of admission was 45.1 percentage points above the norm.[102] Research has shown that legacies are substantially likelier than other applicants to come from the wealthiest quarter of society and that black and Latino students are about half as represented among legacies as they are in the broader applicant pool.[103]

For all of the controversy surrounding race-conscious admissions, it's the white beneficiaries of various admissions preferences who account for the largest share of students who fall below the standards that colleges claim to follow. One analysis of admissions and student data from 146 of the nation's most selective colleges determined that 15 percent of their students were white students whose presence on campus was tough to justify. Their grades, test scores, teacher recommendations, and high school extracurricular records all were well below those of other students. They were statistical outliers that could not be accounted for in analyses charting the relationship between applicants' academic qualifications and chances of acceptance. They'd been accepted because they were athletes or because of their connections to alumni, donors, college employees, or others in a position to help them get in.[104]

"When it comes to holistic review, low-income students are at a disadvantage in nearly every element of the process," Bastedo writes.[105]

Many institutions are devoting a growing share of their aid dollars to offering merit-based tuition discounts to well-off students even as they restrict their low-income enrollments by increasingly denying sufficient need-based aid to the disadvantaged. "In an era when the majority of colleges cannot come close to meeting student demand for need-based financial aid, every dollar that goes to enroll students who do not really require aid diminishes access and equity for those who have moderate and high levels of financial need," researcher Donald Hossler has noted.[106] Broader displacement effects play a role as well, as affluent students enticed by merit awards push others out of contention. A study of one hundred top colleges found that increases in the share of students who received National Merit Scholarships were associated with reductions in the share of their students receiving need-based federal Pell Grants, especially at those colleges with the largest concentrations of needy students.[107]

Public universities have been shown to increase their enrollments of nonresident students, who pay much higher out-of-state tuitions, when their state appropriations dip.[108] Increases in their share of students who are nonresident have been associated with declines in the share of their students who are low income.[109] State governments are similarly pumping a growing share of student-aid dollars into merit-based programs, often in response to pressure from upper-middle-class parents and ostensibly for the sake of keeping their states' "best and brightest" residents close to home.

If students whose families aren't affluent manage to somehow survive an admissions contest badly rigged against them, selective colleges always have the option of denying them the financial aid they'll need to actually enroll. At a student-by-student level, colleges can calibrate how much aid they offer based on their expected revenue from a student and that student's likelihood of enrolling without any aid. "Financial-aid leveraging is the enrollment manager's secret weapon," Matthew Quirk noted in *The Atlantic*, debunking colleges' claims that they're "need blind" and don't take into account students' ability to pay. "Gapping" is higher education's lingo for deliberately denying students the full amount of financial aid they'll need. "Admit-deny" refers to offering needy students a financial aid package "so rotten that you hope they get the message: 'Don't come,'" a top executive at one large enrollment-management consulting firm told the magazine.[110]

The message "you don't belong here" resonates with what many low-income and minority students hear repeatedly from selective institutions. When they apply, they face low acceptance rates; if they're accepted, they have to endure whispers of "not up to it" and "affirmative action." This broader message is enveloped in the insistence that selective colleges value inclusivity and reward merit—so students who didn't make the cut are led to believe that they have no one to blame but themselves. These students may not know how the admission machine is rigged against them, but they do know that a college education is essential to their future success. And thus they tend to abandon hopes of attending a selective college and join the majority of students seeking opportunity in an entirely different set of institutions: the underresourced, over-enrolled, nonselective public ones created to ensure that postsecondary education is broadly available to the American public. It's a decision that often carries heavy personal and social costs.

5

SEPARATE AND UNEQUAL

If you want to see the divide in American higher education, you don't have to go very far. Just travel less than two miles in New Haven, Connecticut, down the aptly named Division Street. At one end, you'll find the wealth and architectural splendor of the elite private Yale University, at the other, the utilitarian campus of the public Southern Connecticut State University. Yale has an endowment of $29 billion; Southern Connecticut's is 0.1 percent as big, at $28 million.[1] Yale spends $166,000 per year per student on instruction, academic support, and student services, while Southern Connecticut State spends $13,000.[2] And yet, they offer many of the same credentials: bachelor's degrees in art, anthropology, computer science, economics, English, biology, chemistry, and the like.

Such extremes of opulence and need define modern higher education in this country. Elsewhere around the nation, resource-starved Eastern Michigan University sits on the doorstep of the internationally renowned University of Michigan. The Boston metro area hosts the wealthiest and most famous college of all, Harvard University, and a phalanx of other well-heeled colleges, including MIT, alongside struggling small private institutions like Emmanuel College, Curry College, and the recently closed Newbury College. Working-class San Francisco State University, where more than 70 percent of undergraduates are from racial and ethnic minority groups, sits smack dab in the middle between the gilded behemoths Stanford University and the University of California at Berkeley.[3]

It wasn't supposed to be this way. The early architects of American higher education would most likely be astounded by our current system's size and complexity, and also disappointed with the reality of how it operates.

U.S. colleges and universities have grown dramatically over the past 150 years as technological advances and increased economic competition have made postsecondary education all the more necessary. The absence of centralized government control of higher education in the United States—especially in comparison with the national systems of Europe—has allowed for tremendous variation in our colleges' missions, costs, academic offerings, and administrative structures. The U.S. postsecondary system now includes about 1,500 community colleges and about 2,800 four-year colleges or universities, ranging from small technical colleges providing short-term job training to huge, prestigious research universities offering doctorates in highly specialized fields.[4]

The good news is that this huge number of options has resulted in vastly increased attendance. In 1870, only about one percent of Americans attended college.[5] Today, seven out of ten recent high school graduates go.[6] Their ranks include nearly six in ten young blacks and just over seven in ten young Latinos who recently graduated from high school—populations that had little access to higher education a half century ago.[7] Women have gone from being shut out of many colleges to accounting for more than half of students enrolled in every higher-education sector.[8]

The bad news is that America's colleges are separate and unequal in just about every sense. Our higher-education system neither provides the equal educational access championed by common-schools advocate Horace Mann nor maintains the sort of meritocracy envisioned by Thomas Jefferson.

Our colleges are highly stratified in terms of their selectivity, how much they spend per student or faculty member, and the backgrounds of the students who attend them. Elite colleges lavish huge sums of money on subsidizing the conspicuous consumption of wealthy families, who see prestigious degrees as their children's birthright. These children emerge from elite institutions with cultural capital derived from exposure to the liberal arts, up-to-date skills that make them desired employees, and rich networks of personal connections that will open doors for them throughout their careers. Meanwhile, the children of the less fortunate attend colleges that have comparatively little to spend on each student's education.

Our postsecondary institutions magnify the disadvantages built into pre-K through twelfth grade education and project them into the labor market, fueling the spiral of racial and class-based inequality.

Paradoxically, rising access to our postsecondary system has benefited all subsets of the population while also sustaining or even increasing distances between them. The children of low-income parents are much more likely to go on to college than they were a few decades ago, but they still do so at much lower rates than the children of the affluent.*[9] Black, Latino, and low-income students are disproportionately attending our nation's community colleges and less-selective four-year colleges. They often end up sidelined in our economy as a result of having attended these resource-starved postsecondary institutions.

Though color-blind and class-blind *in theory*, our higher-education system *in fact* operates at least partly as a systematic barrier to opportunity for many African Americans, Latinos, and low-income whites. Many who are qualified to attend selective colleges instead get tracked elsewhere, reducing their chances of developing their talents, graduating, and landing good jobs.

Growing Divides

We may think of Yale as the very definition of excellence in American higher education, but places like Southern Connecticut State are far

---

* For example, between 1990 and 2012, there was a huge increase in college enrollment among families from the least-affluent groups. In 1990, 43 percent of high school students from the lowest fourth of socioeconomic status went to college; by 2013, this had increased to 71 percent. That's significant growth, but its endpoint is still markedly lower than the 96 percent enrollment rate of students from the most affluent families.

closer to the definition of American higher education's mainstream. About 75 percent of U.S. college students attend public institutions, many of them at the closest institution to their home.[10] Outside the local area, many people have never heard of Southern Connecticut State, even though its undergraduate enrollment is more than 60 percent larger than Yale's.[11]

Both Yale and Southern Connecticut are doing the best by their students, but what different students they are: Yale accepts fewer than 6 percent of applicants,[12] while Southern Connecticut accepts nearly two-thirds.[13] Within six years of enrolling, 97 percent of Yale students will graduate, but only 48 percent of Southern Connecticut State students will finish their degrees.[14]

So, who should we care more about—the students at Yale, who unarguably are going to be successful no matter where they attend college, or the students of Southern Connecticut State, who may well see college as their only ticket to the middle class? When thinking about colleges, Americans are often drawn to the prestige of Yale while feeling ambivalent toward its workhorse neighbor and others like it that, in the end, produce the majority of college graduates.

Our higher-education system increasingly functions as a passive agent in the systematic reproduction of racial and class privilege across generations. The high college completion rates concentrated among white and upper-income parents help bring them higher earnings, giving them the means to pass their educational advantages on to their children. These higher earnings enable well-off parents to send their children to good private schools or to buy more expensive housing in areas with the best public schools, where their children will be surrounded by peers who help push them along. The growing economic value of education and the increased sorting of our society by housing values synergistically work in tandem to make parental education the strongest predictor of a child's educational attainment and future earnings. The outsized roles that parental education and housing expenditures play in the fates of children in the United States have helped give the country one of the lowest levels of intergenerational

educational and income mobility among the advanced economic nations.[15] High school seniors from the top socioeconomic quartile are
likelier than their peers in the lowest quartile to think that they will
attend college, to attend college right after high school, to have completed a degree within ten years, and to be in the top socioeconomic
quartile themselves as young adults.[16]

Yes, preparation for higher education matters in determining who
attends and graduates from selective colleges, but it's not the whole
story. The tiered and tracked American postsecondary system brings
unequal results even among equally qualified students.[17]

Money matters, and selective colleges have more to spend per
student to provide services that leave students more likely to earn
a degree than they would be if they'd enrolled in a less-selective
college. Future earnings from a college degree vary substantially
by field of study, but even within a specific field, degrees from elite
colleges confer greater economic rewards than those from non-elite
colleges.[18]

That we have a divided system also matters because the four-year
degree is still the gold standard: the best path to economic opportunity. There are wide differences in earnings by field of study, but in
any particular field, the combination of general and specific education
available at the four-year-degree level provides the best entrée to graduate education, to jobs that provide training and access to cutting-edge
technology, and to long-term earnings. It also fosters in students the
most adaptability in changing labor markets.[19]

The differences between races and classes in terms of access to higher-
education opportunity are becoming starker over time. Open-access
two- and four-year colleges account for the majority of enrollment
growth among black and Latino students, while white students are
becoming more concentrated in the most selective colleges.*[20] Whites
have been fleeing from open-access public colleges, where their share

* From 1994 to 2009, 82 percent of enrollment gains among white students were at the most selective
colleges, while 68 percent of enrollment gains made by blacks and 72 percent made by Latinos were
at the opposite end of the college spectrum: open-access institutions.

of enrollment has plunged in recent decades to a level below their share of the college-going population.*[21]

In many ways, our higher-education system has replicated the class-conscious academic structure once dominant at comprehensive public high schools. Just as public high schools once maintained distinct tracks for those bound for college and white-collar careers and those bound for blue-collar careers and physical labor, our higher-education system routes students into distinct tiers of its hierarchy based on assumptions about academic potential. It grooms some for leadership and trains others for specific mechanical or technical jobs. As was the case in comprehensive high schools, minority and low-income students are often tracked toward vocational training for relatively low-wage employment, while the upper tracks cater to students from privileged backgrounds, offering them pathways to professional credentials.[22]

Glaring Inequality

By educating a growing share of the population on a ramen noodle budget, we've freed up funds to treat others to the educational equivalent of caviar. As of 2009, the eighty-two most selective institutions spent almost four times as much per student annually on education and related costs as did open-access institutions.[23]

As a result of shifting funding priorities and market trends, colleges at the bottom of the four-year hierarchy are disproportionately likely to find themselves in financial trouble. A very small number have been clawing their way up into higher tiers of selectivity, but others that are floundering have consolidated, trimmed offerings, or shut down.[24] The institutions most likely to be affected by disinvestment include many classified as "minority-serving" based on their black or Latino enrollments.[25]

The gaps between higher education's tiers have widened—and the

---

* The whites' share of total enrollment at open-access colleges shrank from 63 percent to 48 percent from 2005 to 2015, while as of 2015 they accounted for 64 percent of total enrollment at selective institutions.

colleges within tiers have become more similar—in terms of resources, the composition of their enrollments, the quality of their support services, and their curriculums.

The growing similarity of colleges within tiers is driven mainly by market forces, including many colleges' desire to be more competitive in college rankings. Prestige is something that *U.S. News* and other college rankers generally confer upon institutions as a whole, rather than based on specific undergraduate programs. Similar colleges, by increasingly competing for the same narrow segments of the market, find themselves under pressure to match each other's offerings. If their competitors are establishing business majors, they'll be under pressure to offer business majors. Often they'll do that rather than sweat over the distinctiveness or strength of their various programs.

Meanwhile, the gaps between the tiers are widening due to growing differences in their market niches and financial health. Selective colleges continue to prepare students to enter the most prestigious professions, while lower-tier colleges are expanding their role in vocational training.[26]

Intense competition for prestige is leading selective colleges, as a whole, to seek to differentiate themselves further from colleges in lower tiers and to take steps that make themselves less accessible.[27] They generally compete most aggressively with those just above or below them in terms of rankings and wealth, using tuition discounting, generous expenditures on amenities, and other tactics to try to entice coveted students away from those above them in the rankings. The competition for institutional prestige pulls such institutions into a vortex of upwardly spiraling costs, their quest for positional advantage leading them to spend escalating amounts on new academic programs and professors, research facilities, and infrastructure and amenities. They peg their definition of sufficient institutional wealth not to some absolute dollar threshold, but to whatever number enables them to stay ahead of, or overtake, their closest competitors in the rankings.[28] The race for position entails constant pressure to obtain additional financial support through tuition increases and appeals to donors. The only natural constraint on their spending is the willingness and ability of successive generations of wealthy families to pay steadily more to secure advantage for their children.

By far, the largest share of our nation's college students enrolls in the least-funded institutions. Open-access public colleges, which educate 55 percent of students who attend public institutions, receive less than half as much in state appropriations as more prestigious public colleges, which educate 21 percent of students at public institutions.[29] These differences are magnified in spending gaps: selective public colleges spend almost three times as much on instructional and academic support per student as open-access public colleges.[30]

Selective colleges generally offer much bigger subsidies for each student's educational program. For example, in 2006, private research universities spent on each student $15,000 in non-tuition subsidies. Community colleges, by contrast, spent $6,500 in non-tuition subsidies per student.[31] A close look at the distribution of these subsidies shows a striking overall result: the students who are getting the worst payoff in terms of educational prestige are asked to pay the highest proportion of their educational costs. As economist Gordon C. Winston has shown, students at the most selective schools are paying roughly 20 cents for every educational dollar spent on them. In contrast, students at the least prestigious schools are paying 80 cents on the dollar.[32]

Disparities in colleges' expenditures per student translate into disparities in their spending on faculty members. About seven of ten faculty members employed by community colleges are part-time adjunct instructors, as compared to just over four of ten at private baccalaureate colleges and about three of ten at doctoral and research institutions.[33] Although they are often talented and devoted to their students, most adjunct instructors receive meager institutional support and are paid far too poorly to justify doing anything more than lecture and grade tests and assignments. They generally get little, if any, compensation for time spent helping students outside of class.[34] Many spend their days dashing from college to college to earn enough to make ends meet. For the most part, public-college leaders have quietly turned to increases in tuition and in their institutions' reliance on low-paid adjuncts to offset reductions in state support, rather than doing the difficult and politically risky task of reworking non-instructional cost structures.[35]

Throughout our higher-education system, the size of both public and private colleges' student subsidies rise or fall in tandem with institutional selectivity and the standardized test scores of admitted students.

Neglecting the Public

The decentralized governance of our colleges and universities—long regarded as a key strength—has left them without effective mechanisms to rein in institutional stratification or the de facto segregation of students by race, ethnicity, and family income.

Public higher-education systems have a responsibility to serve *all* citizens of their states. But instead of ensuring that the schools within these systems fulfill this obligation equitably, state officials perpetuate the great schisms between rich and poor and whites and minorities by adopting a public policy and public funding framework that favors each state's flagship institution and other research universities over all other public colleges in that state. For example, New Jersey appropriates three times as much per student to its selective public colleges compared to its open-access colleges. A total of fifteen states give at least twice as much per student at selective colleges as they give to those at open-access ones. The governing boards of multi-campus public-college systems of many states conceivably could halt such trends, but most have proven themselves too invested in their flagships' prestige, too indifferent to the state of the lower tiers, or too weak-willed politically to be up to the task.

Selective public colleges offer relatively lavish but reasonably priced education as a result of an elite political bargain struck between legislators, governors, the colleges themselves, and affluent families. Under its terms, such families get access to a high-quality education subsidized by the public in exchange for their willingness to pay the full tuition price, or close to it. But the tuition is a relative bargain compared to the tuition prices a family would pay for a comparable degree from an elite private college.[36]

Top-tier public flagship universities now operate much like private institutions. They have less and less to do with their states as they cope with declining financial support and compete nationally and internationally for students. Their heavy reliance on tuition revenue causes them to neglect some in-state students in favor of those from out of state or abroad, who generally pay tuitions about three times as high as those charged to in-state students.[37] Many public flagships also systematically prefer applicants who appear likely to pay the full tuition price or otherwise contribute to the bottom line, and increasingly favor the wealthy in doling out financial aid as a result of their shift from need-based awards to merit-based ones.[38]

At both the state and federal levels, the general public subsidizes college for the children of the wealthy and the middle class, through laws that exempt colleges from paying taxes, provide tax-exempt 529 plans to those who can afford to save for college, and let taxpayers deduct a share of the cost of college tuition and fees on Internal Revenue Service forms. Such tax breaks are of little use to those who earn too little to pay taxes or don't incur substantial college expenses beyond those covered by need-based financial aid.

Compounding higher education's stratification, state lawmakers and higher-education systems have shifted their focus away from ensuring access and toward heavily emphasizing the distinctions between tiers.[39] A state's higher-education budget typically ranks among the first places that governors ax in response to revenue shortfalls. As a result, selective public colleges have repeatedly found themselves under pressure to take in more money from non-public sources such as donations and tuition, while community colleges have felt pushed to increase tuition and slash expenditures per student. Low-income students are typically the ones who lose out. In the 2015–16 academic year, 52 percent of all public colleges charged their most financially needy students, from families with annual incomes of less than $30,000, a minimum of $10,000 per year to attend.[40]

Since the 1990s, nearly two-thirds of selective public universities have reduced their share of students from families with incomes in the bottom 40 percent, according to a 2017 analysis by the New America think tank. About two-thirds of these colleges have increased the share of students they enroll from the top 20 percent; at more than half of selective public universities, "the increase in affluent students came at the direct expense of low-income ones," the think tank found.[41] Students from families in the bottom fifth in terms of income accounted for only 8.1 percent of the enrollments of public colleges classified as "selective" and 4.5 percent of the enrollments of public colleges classified as "highly selective."[42]

Nonselective four-year colleges, by contrast, have enrollments that are disproportionately minority and low-income students.[43] This is especially true of the community colleges at the bottom of the prestige hierarchy.

Their efforts to serve such students are hindered by the failure of public financing of higher education to account for the breadth of their missions. In response to society's demands, community colleges fulfill a host of responsibilities. In addition to programs in the arts and sciences designed to prepare students for transfer and vocational and technical training that culminates in associate's degrees, their offerings include certificates, adult basic education, remediation, community development, employee training, and non-credit courses for personal and career development.

But our higher-education financing system, being focused on differences between tiers rather than on differentiation within them, has never really accounted for the range of community colleges' missions. Government appropriations to community colleges are generally indexed to the number of "full-time equivalent" students they serve, despite tremendous variation in the costs of the various programs in which students enroll.[44] Offering programs in technical subjects, for example, costs far more per student than offering programs in academic subjects like English and math due to the need for equipment and laboratories.[45] The need to keep their budgets balanced can deter community colleges from offering technical courses that prepare students for high-paying and high-demand jobs, and leave such institutions excessively focused on offering associate's degrees with much more uncertain economic returns.

Community colleges seem ideally suited to the democratic standards of a mass higher-education system, considering how they operate at a lower cost, are inclusive, and adapt well to changing economic and social demands. But they have too many missions and not enough money. As they continue to spread revenue across a broader segment of the postsecondary population, their spending per student becomes so watered down that additional spending at the margins brings little improvement in their completion rates.[46] Accessibility and lower prices are no substitutes for affordable quality as measured by completion rates, gainful employment, earnings, and the extent to which students end up working in their field of study.[47]

Going to the "Right" College

Application strategies can play a central role in where students end up. Disparities in how well students are prepared and encouraged to enroll in selective colleges is evident in the data on two phenomena: "undermatching," which occurs when students enroll in a college below their measured ability level, or "overmatching," which occurs when students enroll in a college well above their measured ability level.

One analysis of federal data tracking the long-term progress of students found that nearly equivalent shares had done one or the other, with about one in eight having undermatched and about one in eight having overmatched. A large share of under- or overmatches stemmed from the behavior of the students themselves—the vast majority either did not apply to well-matched colleges or were accepted to at least one well-matched college but opted instead to attend a one that was not a good match.[48]

Professional college counselors usually advise students to apply to a portfolio of colleges of various selectivity levels, including a few that are a "reach," four or more that are a "match," and at least one that is "safe." The websites of college-advising organizations urge students to take a similar approach, which puts them in the running for a big payoff while also letting them hedge their bets.[49] Overmatching can sometimes be the result of pure luck or the student's possession of some talent not easily captured by standardized test scores or other objective metrics. Often, however, it is the result of some sort of preferential treatment, such as the extra consideration that many colleges give to legacies, recruited athletes, minority members, or applicants tied to administrators, faculty members, donors, or politicians.

Huge gaps exist between various student populations in terms of their likelihood of ending up at a college that is a good match for their demonstrated academic potential.

Students who use shrewd application strategies appropriate to their levels of academic achievement are statistically more likely to live in urban areas in neighborhoods with relatively large numbers of bachelor's degree holders and attend high schools with large concentrations of high-achieving students.[50]

Despite greater access than in the past to improved elementary and secondary education, substantial numbers of students from low-income, working-class, and minority families continue to attend colleges below their tested ability levels, even though many are qualified to enroll in the most selective colleges.[51] Undermatching is especially prevalent among low-income and rural students.[52] It's also common among those whose parents lack a college degree.[53] More than half of all students who undermatch either do not enroll in postsecondary education at all or enroll at an institution below their academic qualifications, generally by attending a community or technical college or trade school when they would have done well at many four-year colleges.[54] The bottom-heavy expansion of postsecondary education has encouraged such decisions.[55]

The degree to which students can rely on financial support from their families also has a substantial impact on college choice. Having a family safety net appears to leave students more willing to risk high levels of debt in hopes of high returns on their investment. The more prestigious and expensive a higher-education institution is, the larger the share of its students who are financially supported by their parents.*[56]

"The combination of testing, rankings, financial aid availability, peer anxiety and competition, and the impact of rejection on those who had aimed high can easily create a foreboding impression of college admission and attendance, particularly to students from the lower end of the income spectrum," a team of admissions experts concluded in a report published by the University of Southern California's Center for Enrollment Research, Policy and Practice.[57]

Often, poor college-application choices reflect how less advantaged students have been left adrift by their parents' personal inexperience with college or the unavailability of guidance counselors in their high schools. They may also reflect the reality that for less advantaged students, the costs associated with applying to college can hinder their ability to cast a wide net.[58] Only about 8 percent of high-achieving low-income students use the recommended strategy of applying to "reach" and "match" schools and ignoring nonselective schools. Another 53 percent fail to apply to a "match" school and instead aim low, applying to at least one nonselective college.[59]

The remaining 39 percent employ the sorts of application strategies that cause admissions experts to shake their heads. They'll apply to a nonselective local college and then loft a Hail Mary application in the direction of a single well-known top college, such as Harvard, where their chances of admission are tiny regardless of their level of academic talent. They will sometimes apply to a single, selective private college, precluding themselves from being able to compare financial aid offers if admitted. Or they'll apply to a single selective public college with lower standards than their flagship—about half the time, this happens even though their state flagship is nearer to their home.[60]

---

* One recent study of federal student loan recipients found that more than 90 percent of those enrolled at the most selective four-year colleges had parents who listed them on their taxes as dependents, compared to 70 percent at nonselective four-year colleges, 50 percent of those at two-year colleges, and 37 percent of those at for-profit schools.

Separate Worlds

In terms of the demographic composition of their enrollments, our higher-education tiers have become segregated by race and class to an extent that statistically mirrors the racial and economic segregation of our nation's neighborhoods.[61] Just like pricey suburbs, the colleges of the upper tiers are overwhelmingly dominated by affluent people.

Selective colleges have even less socioeconomic diversity than racial or ethnic diversity. At the 146 most selective colleges, members of racial or ethnic minority groups account for 26 percent of students, while the most disadvantaged fourth in terms of parental income and education accounts for just 3 percent of the student body. At the "Ivy Plus" colleges—the eight members of the Ivy League, plus Duke, MIT, Stanford, and the University of Chicago—the children of parents in the top one percent of the income distribution account for 14.5 percent of students, making them seventy-seven times more likely to be enrolled than the children of parents in the bottom fifth. The children of the most affluent one-tenth of one percent, with annual family incomes in excess of $2.2 million, are 117 times more likely than those in the bottom fifth to attend.[62] The students in their graduating classes come from families with an average income of $723,000.[63] As of 2013, only about 15 percent of the students at these universities receive federal Pell Grants, while nationally about 39 percent of all college students receive Pell Grants.[64]

Some top colleges have woken up to the fact that they have an access problem, but most of their efforts to deal with the issue have met with little real success. A few, including Harvard and the University of Virginia, made a big splash a decade ago by announcing highly publicized efforts to provide needy students with enough financial support to ensure they graduate debt free. But as the economist Peter Sacks noted at the time, such efforts "are financially feasible because so few lower-income students are admitted." He wrote, "Even if elite colleges don't deliberately limit their numbers of low-income students, their definitions of merit and their prestige-driven enrollment-management practices produce that result."[65] Referring broadly to selective colleges, Sacks

‍‌‍‍

‌‌‍‍

said: "For all but the richest institutions, enrolling more low-income students boils down to a trade-off: Do you provide full scholarships to a limited number of low-income students who meet existing admissions criteria for grades and test scores, or do you greatly expand access but provide limited amounts of financial aid for needy students?"[66]

Although black and Latino enrollments at all public colleges rose by 54 percent—or 259,000 students—from 2005 to 2015, fewer than one in six entered selective public colleges. Blacks and Latinos account for 36 percent of the traditional college-age population but just 19 percent of freshman enrollment at the 170 most selective public institutions.[67] These separate higher-education pathways matter because resources matter: selective colleges spend anywhere from two to five times as much on instruction per student as open-access colleges.[68]

The average SAT scores, grade point averages, and records of extra-curricular activities of black and Latino applicants to selective colleges have improved substantially over time. But similar improvements in the academic profiles of white and Asian applicants, combined with most such institutions' increased reliance on SAT scores, have kept improvements in the qualifications of black and Latino applicants from translating into increases in their likelihood of enrolling at selective institutions. A similar dynamic has hindered the progress of low-income students, with substantial long-term improvements in their academic achievements being competitively offset by even stronger gains among more affluent students in terms of both academic achievements and SAT scores.[69]

Disparities exist even among students with comparably impressive academic profiles. Among students with top scores on standardized admissions tests, about a fourth of those from families in the bottom half of the income distribution end up attending the top college, while well over half of those from families in the top income quartile do so.[70]

Do High-Scoring Students Deserve More?

Underlying the strata of selectivity in higher education is a hierarchy of cumulative investments in human capital. The largest subsidies for education get routed toward students from relatively advantaged backgrounds, while the smallest ones go to the disadvantaged. This imbalance rests on the assumption that our society gets the best return on its educational investment by spending the most on those students with the highest SAT or ACT scores, the most impressive high school transcripts, and the most capacity to pay tuition.[71]

The notion that the current stratification is efficient and fair is widely assumed or asserted by policymakers, but is rarely subjected to analytical or political scrutiny. Those who do question the stratification of American higher education are up against formidable market forces in doing anything about it.

Defenders of the stratification in higher education cast themselves as tough-minded realists in arguing that such an arrangement is pragmatic. They contend that the students with the highest grades and test scores are most deserving of an elite education and are most likely to benefit.[72] In theory, such a hierarchy in higher education is economically efficient. It provides the most support to the students most likely to make contributions to society, and limits investment in high-quality learning environments for the vast majority of students whose standardized test scores suggest they'd be less able to fully benefit. Underlying such arguments is the belief that institutional quality and student quality are inseparable. Because students learn from each other, students enrolled in highly selective institutions educationally benefit from being surrounded by peers who similarly had high standardized test scores.[73]

Data limitations have made it difficult to find empirical support for any assertion that surrounding students with academically talented peers improves learning, persistence, graduation rates, and prospects of subsequent career success. Researchers focused on actual students and their peer relationships have had difficulty finding evidence of such "peer effects" in the data. It's absent in student cohorts defined as a college class, and instead shows up mainly in more intimate relationships, such as those between roommates and friends.

While some studies have found that peer effects benefit less-qualified students, their effects are negligible among more-qualified students.[74]

The researchers Stacy Berg Dale and Alan B. Krueger have concluded that campus peer effects have little bearing on the relationship between degrees from selective colleges and subsequent career earnings. Their analysis has found that the differences in colleges' resources, rather than the differences in their classes' average SAT scores, best explain the differences between them in their graduates' subsequent earnings.[75]

Whether or not the system is fair and efficient, its role in upholding intergenerational privilege is central to the funding model of selective colleges. Stanford University economist Caroline M. Hoxby holds that selective colleges depend, in part, on a "dynasty" model of financial support from alumni. The contributions of each generation of alumni help build up a historic accumulation of institutional wealth that funds part of the education of subsequent generations, allowing each generation to pay a declining share of what the college spends educating it. The desire to perpetuate this intergenerational funding mechanism gives selective colleges an incentive to ensure that students succeed enough in college and in their subsequent careers to be able to replenish and grow the endowment, thus becoming part of the dynasty themselves.[76]

While there is certainly truth to the idea that affluent families have a "dynastic" relationship with certain elite colleges, the mechanism through which those relationships promote achievement has to do with wealth rather than exposure to academically talented and driven peers. It stems mainly from a cyclical relationship between the wealth of the families and the wealth of the colleges that serve them. Simply put, with increased education comes increased income, which in turn brings higher education investments, higher educational expectations, more readiness for colleges and success, and better earnings down the road. Having access to an exclusive college helps equip each generation to ensure its children have access to that institution.

Our stratified higher-education system also results in similar stratification in terms of long-term access to various social benefits, the availability of which increases in tandem with income given our lack of a strong welfare state. Such benefits include healthcare, counseling, public safety, parks and recreation, and family supports like childcare. Whether someone has a college degree with labor-market value can make a big difference in terms of overall quality of life, and, in terms of healthcare, it can literally make the difference between life and death.

Poor Returns

The destructive impact that market forces have had on our higher-education system is bad news for free-market advocates: the tiered structure of the system makes sure that, overall, it operates inefficiently, offers poor returns on investment, and squanders the human capital badly needed for our nation's workforce.

At selective colleges, higher expenditures per student bring added institutional prestige but little in the way of commensurate gains in teaching and learning. For the privileged students who account for the lion's share of selective colleges' enrollments, college represents a means of converting the advantages they had in childhood into credentials that will justify their continued access to wealth.

At nonselective four-year colleges and community colleges, money gets spent on, and by, a lot of students who will fail to earn a degree. Without one, it is unlikely that the investments in their college education will pay off in monetary terms.

The evidence of such inefficiency becomes hard to ignore when graduation rates are broken down by race, income level, academic background, and institutional type. Eight years out of high school, 61 percent of students from the top quartile of socioeconomic status (SES) have earned a bachelor's degree or more, compared to about 14 percent of students who come from the lowest quartile of SES.[77] The leakage's impact on social mobility becomes apparent when we look at the 110,000 black or Latino students who came from the bottom half of the family income distribution and were in the top half of their high school class, yet did not complete college.[78] If they had attended one of the most selective colleges and graduated at rates similar to those of their black or Latino counterparts at these institutions, 73 percent could have earned a bachelor's degree.[79]

Many people assume that it is harder to earn a bachelor's degree at a highly selective college than at a less rigorous one, but actually the opposite holds true, mainly because selective colleges have much greater resources to support students in the face of academic challenges. Top-performing high school students, those with SAT scores above 1000, graduate from the most selective schools at rates of around 87 percent, compared to only 58 percent for those top-performing students who attend open-access institutions.[80] Students from families in the bottom half of income have a graduation rate of about 77 percent at the top five hundred colleges, but just 45 percent at open-access institutions.[81]

The choices that students make in response to the high cost of four-year colleges inadvertently hurt their chances of earning a degree. Many who see starting and completing their educations at a four-year college as too great a financial commitment instead enroll at community colleges with the intent of transferring to four-year institutions—a move encouraged by many state governments seeking to lower their own higher-education costs. Unfortunately, these students don't realize they are unlikely to follow that path: the transfer rates from two-year to four-year colleges are low, and only 11 percent of those who begin their postsecondary educations at community colleges ever end up earning a bachelor's degree.[82] Another 15 percent of community college students earn an associate's degree, and just 36 percent earn any postsecondary degree or certificate.[83]

Similarly, many students who start and end their educations at four-year colleges, especially those students from low-income backgrounds, feel compelled to enroll in the lowest-cost institutions and academic programs available to them, which generally means sacrificing educational quality and being at greater risk of dropping out.[84]

The disparities in postsecondary opportunity and success produce an equally polarized pattern in career opportunities and individual empowerment after the college years. The growing stratification of higher education is not just about money—it is also about what money buys.

The postsecondary education that best equips one for success in life combines general preparation at the baccalaureate level with postgraduate professional training. By preparing students for this combination of attainment, graduates of more-selective four-year institutions disproportionately find their ways to careers that bring high earnings and comparatively high levels of autonomy on the job and in society. As a result of attending less-selective colleges, students generally get tracked into lower-paying rank-and-file professions.[85] Most who fail to earn any postsecondary education credential, because they either dropped out or failed to go on to college at all, struggle to earn a living wage over the course of their lives.[86]

The heightened importance of postsecondary education in the economy has widened these gaps. More than 60 percent of the increase in earnings differences among Americans since 1980 is due to differences in access to postsecondary education programs with economic value.[87] That access is stratified by race and class in ways that prove it is better to be rich than talented in America. The children of the rich tend to succeed regardless of promise: a child from the top fourth of families in terms of socioeconomic status (SES) who tests in the bottom fourth of his or her kindergarten class still has a 71 percent chance of graduating from college and getting a good job by age twenty-five. The promising children of the poor tend to tumble: a child from the lowest-status fourth of families who tests in the top fourth in kindergarten has only a 31 percent chance of graduating from college and getting a good job by age twenty-five. Those who are black or Latino face even longer odds.[88]

While we like to think we have an egalitarian society in which each individual has the chance to achieve whatever is possible, the reality is that a person's path is mostly preordained by the class into which that person is born. In such a society, college is the most obvious way to alter that course, to rise from one strata to a higher one. Each person's advantages and disadvantages in later life will have a profound impact—not only on their own lives, but also on the long-term fates of their children. The wealthy and connected will still go to Yale, Princeton, Michigan, Vanderbilt, and their ilk. But is it preordained that these schools must be the provenance of pretty much only the wealthy and connected? Or, should we open the gates to a high-quality education to a wider swath of society? If we cannot reduce the role that the intergenerational transfer of wealth plays in Americans' fates, class disparities and racial injustice will shape our nation's future just as they shaped its past.

6

THE FIGHT FOR FAIRNESS

Demetrio Rodriguez wasn't going to stand for it. The school attended by his children and others from their predominantly Latino neighborhood in San Antonio, Texas, was plagued by abysmal conditions: part of the building had been condemned, the bathrooms lacked toilet paper, and some teachers did not even carry state certification. It wasn't supposed to be like this. More than a decade earlier, the *Brown vs. Board of Education* decision had overturned school segregation and promised an end to the sort of deep inequities in public schools' resources that caused such conditions.

At least that's what most people thought *Brown* would do. But that hadn't happened.

Born to a family of migrant farm workers, Rodriguez had dropped out of school after the sixth grade and was in the military before becoming a sheet metal worker. Having faced economic challenges over the years, as well as discrimination based on his Mexican American heritage, he wanted better for his five children. So, when he discovered that the elementary school his children attended in the city's Edgewood neighborhood had infrastructure and resources that were far inferior to those of nearby districts, he stepped forward as the first person to sign on to a class-action lawsuit against the Texas Board of Education.[1]

The property taxes in the Edgewood district yielded about $50 per

student, while in the nearby neighborhood of Alamo Heights, schools
had ten times more to spend per student, even with a property tax rate
half that of Edgewood. Although geographically close together, the
two districts existed worlds apart. Edgewood languished as the poorest school district within San Antonio, while Alamo Heights thrived
as the richest. Edgewood's enrollment was 90 percent Mexican American and 6 percent black, Alamo Heights' more than 80 percent white.[2]

The plaintiffs, an association of parents from the Edgewood school
district, argued that students had a fundamental right to equal educational opportunity, and that equal opportunity depended on equal
funding. Initially, they prevailed in federal district court, with their
lawsuit filed against several districts and the state of Texas. When the
U.S. Supreme Court agreed to hear the case on appeal, they expected
a judgment in their favor: a *Brown*-inspired holding that equal educational funding amounted to a constitutional right.

Instead, the majority of justices delivered a crushing blow, along
with the hard lesson that it's a mistake to count on our nation's courts
to remedy the inequality of our education system. The Supreme
Court's 5-to-4 ruling, handed down in 1973, interpreted the U.S. Constitution as lacking any reference to a fundamental right to educational equity—or, for that matter, education at all—while also finding
no evidence that Texas had systematically and deliberately discriminated against poor people. It acknowledged the need to reform state
tax systems "which may well have relied too long and too heavily on
the local property tax," but said the Constitution required that such
change must come from state legislatures, not the federal government.

For many, the *Rodriguez* decision would come to represent a turning point in the history of constitutional law—the first in a series of
post-*Brown* decisions through which the courts have placed obstacles
in front of those who want to secure educational equity. While some
of the most pivotal decisions, like *Brown* and *Rodriguez*, have focused
on educational equality in primary and secondary schools, other decisions with direct effects on postsecondary education have limited
the reach of desegregation efforts, placed strict limits on the use of
race-conscious admissions, and upheld state bans on the use of racial

preferences by public colleges. Such decisions have had chilling effects on attempts to ensure racial parity at the postsecondary level. As a result, the promise of *Brown* has never truly been realized.

Efforts to use courts to knock down barriers to educational opportunity stalled decades ago. They bumped up against a series of court rulings that limited the power of government and educational institutions to rectify past discrimination or redistribute education funds from rich to poor, rulings that enabled white families to flee integrated school systems by relocating and left intact the strong links between public school quality and community wealth.

Those legal and regulatory rules against intentional discrimination that have been put in place have proven useless as responses to unconscious biases and their significant role in perpetuating race- and class-based inequality and segregation.

On key fronts—such as the fights over college affirmative action—the tide has turned in the other direction, and advocates for the education of black and Latino students have been put on the defensive. Their struggle appears likely to only get harder as a result of President Donald Trump's recent appointments to the U.S. Supreme Court. Lawsuits challenging the race-conscious admissions policies of Harvard and the University of North Carolina appear likely to offer the court a chance to further curtail such policies or even strike them a final death blow.

Meanwhile, those fighting class-based barriers to education have barely gained a foothold in federal courts. In general, they've only made sporadic and limited progress in legal battles at the state level. Their efforts to change legislation have similarly foundered in a nation that continues to tolerate huge disparities in public school quality linked to class.

The hard truth is that formidable obstacles to educational justice are built right into the structure of our political system. The chief ideology underlying its governance and resource distribution—liberal individualism—instinctively rejects any effort by governments to redistribute resources or impose demands of equal educational access.

Adherence to that individualist ideology has left our nation with an education system that lacks cohesiveness, accountability, or anything close to consistent quality. At the elementary and secondary levels, it consists of a patchwork of public school districts governed not by the federal government but by local boards and by the states, as well as private schools that operate largely out of the reach of the government. At the college level, it consists of institutions that resist calls for change by shielding themselves behind far-reaching autonomy formally enshrined by Supreme Court rulings dealing with academic freedom. Colleges operate largely out of the government's reach when it comes to whom they admit or how they spend their funds, even though they are heavily subsidized by the public, especially if they are public institutions.

Our nation's deep faith in individualism creates a confined arena in which debates over educational access for racial and ethnic minorities and low-income students can take place. It tends to leave both sides feeling compelled to appeal to the same values—fairness and individual opportunity—while relegating other values, such as equality and civic responsibility, to the sidelines. The actions of educational institutions are judged primarily according to whether they respect individual rights, with pragmatic considerations related to efficiency and effectiveness also playing a role. Rather than seeking to further the common good, these institutions promote their respective interests— and in battles that boil down to a clash of interests, their rich and powerful stakeholders are better equipped to look out for themselves and almost always get the upper hand.

To understand how we got to where we are, it's important to look at how the history of segregation and inequality left us a long way from where we need to be, and how our nation's basic principles complicate efforts to achieve necessary education reform.

The Deep Roots of Discrimination

From the outset, equality actually has been a stated goal of American education. How we define equality, however, has changed frequently over time.[3]

In an influential 1972 essay describing the evolution of that definition, the Harvard sociologist Daniel Bell noted that among early New
England colonists, "there was an equality, but in the Puritan sense of
an equality of the elect," an equality among virtuous men who shared
religious beliefs and saw themselves as chosen by God. Later, the
founding fathers famously declared that "all men are created equal,"
but also embraced the liberal philosopher John Locke's belief in the
existence of a "hierarchy of intellect," in which some men are more
intelligent and worthy of entrusting with leadership. Throughout
the nineteenth century, Bell wrote, "the notion of equality was never
sharply defined. In its voiced assertions it came down to the sentiment
that each man was as good as another and no man was better than
anyone else. What it meant, in effect, was that no one should take on
the air of an aristocrat and lord it over other men" and that "no formal
barrier or prescribed positions" stood in the way of anyone's chances
of getting ahead.[4]

Well into the twentieth century, notions of equality covered only
one subset of the population, white men, especially when it came to
access to education and the advancement it offered. Nearly all colleges
excluded women of any race. Most states of the antebellum South out-
lawed the teaching of slaves, and northerners who sought to educate
blacks were subject to being harassed, their schools torched.[5] Antioch
College, Berea College, and Oberlin College began admitting black
students by the mid-1800s, but only twenty-eight black graduates
earned baccalaureates in the thirty years leading up to the Civil War.[6]
The decades following the Civil War did not usher in colleges' integration of races and sexes as much as the creation of separate colleges for
women or African Americans. Nineteen states that had belonged to or
bordered the Confederacy enacted laws calling for public higher education to be racially segregated into all-white or all-black institutions.

The equal protection clause of the Fourteenth Amendment, rati-
fied just after the Civil War, seemed hard to square with such racial
segregation, but the U.S. Supreme Court claimed to do just that by
declaring that black-only public accommodations could be "separate but equal" in its 1896 *Plessy v. Ferguson* decision, which involved

racially segregated rail cars. State laws requiring the racial segregation of public colleges would persist until the middle of the twentieth century, and some leading northern private colleges, including Princeton, would continue to prohibit or restrict the admission of black students nearly until then.[7] Through the 1940s, public elementary and secondary schools remained legally segregated in the South, six of its border states, and the District of Columbia. School districts had the option of maintaining segregated elementary and secondary schools in Arizona, Indiana, Kansas, and New Mexico.[8]

Other minority groups similarly suffered exclusion from education. Native Americans, for example, often found themselves denied the schools they'd been promised in treaties, and also barred by the federal government from receiving instruction in their tribes' languages. Both California and Texas operated separate schools for Mexican Americans, and California similarly put Chinese, Mongolian, and Japanese students in separate schools until the Supreme Court ended the practice in 1945.[9] As discussed in chapter 4, many of the admissions practices currently used by selective colleges—such as requirements of personal interviews and letters of recommendation—arose at Ivy League colleges as a means to limit Jewish enrollments.

Even in states that did not require the racial segregation of public education, schools often ended up segregated anyway as a result of both residential zoning ordinances and housing discrimination based on race, ethnicity, religion, or class. The suburbs that proliferated in response to the perceived ills of big cities often sought to keep out the less affluent by banning multi-family dwellings or requiring that lots be of a minimum size, rendering them unaffordable to many. Home sellers and buyers commonly entered into "restrictive land covenants" barring members of certain racial, religious, or ethnic groups from occupying the property. Although the practice was struck down by the Supreme Court in 1948, it continued to be perpetuated through unwritten "gentlemen's agreements."[10] The federal government fostered class- and race-based residential segregation by building interstate highways that gave rise to new white suburbs, destroying working-class neighborhoods to promote "urban renewal," and financing the construction of public housing complexes.[11] Stephen Richard Higley, a geographer who has extensively researched the housing patterns of the rich, has observed that our nation's laws related to property and municipal governance continue to function essentially as a formalized class system, creating "a stratified place hierarchy with profound consequences for all of society."[12] Minneapolis officials explicitly acknowledged that dark truth in 2018 by making theirs the first major city in the United States to strike down single-family zoning based on that zoning category's long ties to residential segregation.[13]

Promising Victories

For a while, in the mid-twentieth century, it seemed as though a lasting solution to desegregation would soon be within reach. African Americans gained at least some access to previously all-white public colleges in the 1930s, as a result of a series of federal and state court rulings that, applying the logic of the 1896 *Plessy* decision, required such institutions to enroll those black students for whom no other options existed.[14] The *Plessy* decision's language requiring equality in segregated public accommodations similarly played into 1940s court rulings demanding reductions in gaps in tax-dollar support for separate black and white public schools.[15]

When it comes to the racial desegregation of education, the "separate" part of "separate but equal" did not face serious legal challenge until the civil rights movement, which stirred to life in the demands for equal treatment from black veterans returning home from World War II. As part of it, the NAACP and sympathetic lawyers mounted efforts to secure black access to the same educational institutions that served whites. They scored a huge victory on June 5, 1950, when the U.S. Supreme Court struck down the segregation of public higher education in a pair of decisions involving advanced-degree programs. One case, *Sweatt v. Painter*, dealt with a separate minority law school that Texas lawmakers had established to avoid asking the University of Texas's law school to admit a single black applicant, Heman Marion Sweatt. In the other case, *McLaurin v. Oklahoma State Regents*, the

University of Oklahoma had admitted George W. McLaurin, a black student, to its doctoral program in education, but insisted that he sit separately in classrooms, the library, and the cafeteria. In both cases the high court's majorities, while not explicitly overturning the *Plessy* "separate but equal" doctrine, declared that the doctrine was inapplicable to higher education as a practical matter. Their opinions strongly suggested that providing equal higher education in the context of racially separate higher education might be an impossible task.

The Supreme Court finally overturned *Plessy* with its 1954 *Brown* decision, a case that consolidated several legal challenges to the racial segregation of several school districts. The court majority's opinion held that the separate-but-equal doctrine "has no place" in public education, reasoning that racially segregated educational facilities "are inherently unequal," especially given their detrimental effects on black children, whom they stigmatize as inferior. The following year, the court handed down a follow-up *Brown* decision calling for school systems to desegregate "with all deliberate speed."

Members of the nation's elite saw the danger of black frustration and alienation in the face of thwarted demands for change. The Cold War that raged at that time was a battle for hearts and minds, and the entrenched oppression of America's black population embarrassed the nation's leadership and undermined efforts to convince those at home and abroad that our political system represented an ideal. Former Harvard president James Bryant Conant, having spent more than a decade urging selective colleges to promote meritocracy to equip the best and brightest to fight the Cold War, fretted about how frustration with the lack of opportunity in big-city slums might undermine the patriotism of the young people living in them. In his 1961 book *Slums and Suburbs*, he asked: "What can words like 'freedom,' 'liberty' and 'equality of opportunity' mean to these young people? With what kind of zeal and dedication can we expect them to withstand the relentless pressures of communism?" [16]

In *The Chosen*, his exhaustive history of admissions policies at Harvard, Princeton, and Yale, the sociologist Jerome Karabel says internal memos that circulated within those institutions show that their

leaders regarded increasing black enrollments as necessary to culti-
vate the nation's black leadership. They believed that "a fateful struggle
for the soul of the nation's black population" was being waged between
advocates of militancy and advocates of nonviolence and integration,
and selective colleges needed to enroll enough black students to send
the message that African Americans could achieve upward social mobility and gain power through nonviolent means.[17]

Selective colleges began using affirmative action in admissions
about a decade after *Brown*, making the decision on their own as it
became apparent that simply ending Jim Crow–mandated segregation
was not enough to end racism, bring about integration, and remedy
the effects of hundreds of years of social and economic oppression
of African Americans.[18] It had dawned on such institutions, some
of which had been aggressively recruiting black students for several
years, that undertaking such efforts in tandem with race-blind admissions policies would not be enough to integrate their campuses.
The academic standards by which they judged applicants served as
a bottleneck that left them competing with one another for the same
highly qualified pool of black students, a population too small to
begin bringing about meaningful integration on all of their campuses.

Yale University's admissions office decided during the 1965–66 academic year to begin giving a second look at black applicants with SAT
scores below its usual standards. They blamed cultural deprivation—
namely a lack of exposure to the academic and social opportunities
that lead to success in predominantly white schools and professional
environments—for the consistent gaps between the typical scores
of black students and those of white applicants. Yale's black enrollment rose, inspiring other selective colleges to similarly use separate
admissions criteria or processes in weighing applications from black
students.[19]

Race-conscious admissions policies proliferated at other selective
colleges and took hold. Selective colleges characterized their efforts to
increase minority enrollments as necessary to help remedy American
society's racial injustice. Importantly, they did not speak to any need
to remedy the effects of any discrimination on their own part.[20]

As race-conscious college admissions policies became more common, the Supreme Court intensified the desegregation demands being placed on local school districts. In *Green v. County School Board of New Kent County*, a 1968 decision involving a rural Virginia school system, the high court held that simply opening public schools up to students of any race was not enough, and the district must actively desegregate and remedy discrimination "root and branch." In its 1971 *Swann v. Charlotte-Mecklenburg Board of Education* decision, the Supreme Court upheld the controversial mandatory school busing plans that lower courts had been ordering to help remedy the school segregation that had arisen in tandem with housing segregation. Although such busing plans would be shown to have educational benefits for black children, they'd infuriate many white parents, who hated seeing their children bused off to schools they regarded as dangerous and academically inferior, alleged characteristics that had not seemed as bothersome when the schools served only the children of people with darker skin.

Backlash on Multiple Fronts

The power of the courts extends only as far as the willingness of other branches of government to comply with their rulings, and many politicians and white members of the public responded to the Supreme Court's desegregation rulings in ways that tested the government's resolve.

The second *Brown* decision's call for school desegregation with "all deliberate speed" was soft enough to allow for foot-dragging in response to white resistance. Many states similarly fought the desegregation of their public colleges, with lawmakers inciting angry white mobs rather than holding them in check. The 1962 unrest surrounding efforts by James Meredith, a black man, to enroll in the University of Mississippi resulted in two deaths and 160 injuries. Congress responded to resistance to desegregation by passing the Civil Rights Act of 1964, which established within the federal government an enforcement structure capable of pressuring state and local compliance with civil rights laws. But it immediately became apparent that the act was no universal salve for the country's racial divides. In July 1964, just sixteen days after the act's passage, a New York police lieutenant shot and killed ninth-grader James Powell, triggering the first of hundreds of violent urban uprisings that would rock American cities during the middle and late 1960s.[21]

In the midst of ongoing racial tensions, the work of the enforcement structure that the Civil Rights Act established would become politicized, and its priorities and interpretation of civil rights laws would vary greatly from one administration to the next. But its existence meant that educational institutions that violated civil rights laws faced the threat of federal lawsuits or the loss of federal funds. Over the coming decades, federal agencies and the courts would repeatedly crack down on states, school districts, and colleges that engaged in discrimination, and would demand that states with formerly segregated public-college systems spend enough on historically black colleges to make them attractive options for white students. The approach, while often helping historically black institutions secure big infusions of tax-dollar support, met with mixed success in achieving meaningful racial integration.[22]

State and local efforts to integrate public education were further undermined by a bedrock reality of American politics: that the government cannot control the actions of individuals if doing so infringes on their constitutionally guaranteed freedoms. Black families' Fourteenth Amendment right to send their children to desegregated schools bumped up against the First Amendment–guaranteed freedom of white families to transfer their children into overwhelmingly white schools that were private and, in many cases, religious. Virtually all-white Christian fundamentalist schools cropped up in rural areas of the South, and the robust economic growth of many of that region's cities left a growing share of their white residents able to afford private academies.[23]

Similarly, nothing could stop white opponents of desegregation from expressing their displeasure over it in the voting booth. As a result, the tide turned against it at the federal level. Richard Nixon won the 1968 presidential election partly by opposing busing and other liberal policies that helped blacks. In doing so, he co-opted the political strategy that then third-party candidate George C. Wallace Jr. had been using to win over both southerners and blue-collar whites in the North, and helped remake the Republican Party of Abraham Lincoln into a big tent that brought together opponents of liberal social policies and advocates of big business, a coalition that continues to dominate the party today.[24]

Political opposition to colleges' use of affirmative action stirred to life in 1972, sparked by academics who were irked when the federal government threatened to withhold research dollars from universities that failed to come up with plans to hire more women to comply with Title IX, a new federal law prohibiting educational institutions that receive federal funding from engaging in discrimination based on sex. About five hundred professors formed the Committee for Academic Nondiscrimination and Integrity, a group opposed to colleges' use of affirmative action preferences. One, Harvard sociologist and emerging neoconservative leader Nathan Glazer, would write the 1975 book that served as the framework for the right's critique of affirmative action, *Affirmative Discrimination: Ethnic Inequality and Public Policy*.[25] In it he argued that the promotion of equality through affirmative action "has meant that we abandon the first principle of a liberal society," the primacy of individual rights. He warned that the outcome would be growing divisiveness as a result of minorities' growing consciousness of their group membership and growing resentment among those disfavored by affirmative action policies.[26]

Importantly, Glazer and other neoconservative critics of affirmative action did not fit the stereotype of the racist Southern reactionary blocking the schoolhouse door. For the most part, they were northern intellectuals.[27] In sharp contrast to conservatives who had opposed the civil rights movement, they cited, rather than challenged, the rejection of discrimination and unequal treatment enshrined in the Civil Rights Act of 1964 and espoused in much of the rhetoric of the civil rights movement.[28] They characterized the preferential treatment of racial and ethnic minorities as "reverse discrimination" against white people, constitutionally suspect and morally wrong in ways that distinguished it from the special treatment of veterans or people with disabilities. They would co-opt not just the rhetoric of the civil rights movement but also its tactics, forming advocacy groups that would recruit like-minded lawyers to fight their battles.[29]

Troubling Consequences

Several developments hailed as victories by advocates for colleges and for minority groups had long-term consequences that complicated efforts to provide equal access to educational opportunity.

The Supreme Court's enshrinement of academic freedom as a right protected under the First Amendment would, for example, arm colleges with a double-edged sword, distancing them enough from court intervention to protect both their efforts to increase minority enrollments and their efforts to keep in place admissions practices biased in favor of the wealthy.

The Supreme Court rulings that embraced academic freedom as a core right were a clear win for one type of campus diversity: diversity of thought. They arose from litigation challenging state laws and policies adopted in the 1950s for the sake of thwarting the spread of communist ideology via college campuses. The Supreme Court tackled the question of whether faculty speech on campus deserved constitutional protection in the case *Sweezy v. New Hampshire*, which centered around a University of New Hampshire lecturer suspected of being a communist. In a 1957 ruling that came down in favor of the lecturer, the court's majority embraced Justice Felix Frankfurter's argument that the free speech of college faculty members deserves particular constitutional protection. In a concurring opinion that would be cited by the Supreme Court in later cases involving race-conscious admissions, Justice Frankfurter held that every university has "four essential freedoms," those being "to determine for itself on academic grounds who may teach, what may be taught, how it shall be taught, and who may be admitted to study."[30] Ten years later, in holding that the State University of New York had violated the constitutional rights of faculty members fired for refusing to sign documents formally denying any involvement with the Communist Party, the Supreme Court declared academic freedom to be "a special concern of the First Amendment."

Such precedents would serve as the basis for the Supreme Court's later inclination to defer to colleges' judgments on admissions matters, factoring prominently in later legal victories for affirmative action in which the courts declined to second-guess universities' conclusions that they needed to consider applicants' race to achieve sufficient levels of diversity for educational purposes. Ironically, however, precedents that served to protect people accused of communist sympathies would serve to shield selective colleges from any court demands that they defuse much of the controversy over race-conscious admissions by abandoning their systemic favoritism toward the affluent.

The long-term impacts of civil rights victories for other subsets of the population ironically complicated efforts to increase black enrollments at selective colleges. This had the effect of greatly increasing competition from other groups in what was perceived as a zero-sum competition for the limited numbers of seats in entering classes. These victories included the opening of previously all-male colleges to women and the dramatic expansion of the nation's immigrant stream through the passage of the Immigration and Nationality Act of 1965.[31] In addition, the 1967 Supreme Court ruling that struck down state bans on interracial marriage helped give rise to an increase in the nation's biracial and multiracial population, which complicated the racial identification of students necessary to apply race-conscious admissions policies and track the educational progress of minority groups.

A number of elite colleges began admitting women in the 1960s, over opposition from some powerful alumni and board members, as part of a strategy to attract the best male applicants—a change that eventually gained the support of wealthy alumni as their daughters and granddaughters began to benefit from the decision.[32] Those colleges that hesitated were strongly nudged by the passage of Title IX in 1972. The opening of colleges' doors to women clearly was a development to be cheered, and would benefit women of all races and ethnicities. And it's worth noting that women continue to struggle to be treated equitably by many colleges, especially when it comes to their participation in athletics programs, their access to male-dominated fields such as mathematics, engineering, philosophy, and physics, and their right to be educated in a non-hostile environment where they aren't subjected to sexual assault and harassment. Today, with women now accounting for a disproportionate share of college applicants with strong academic profiles, some selective colleges actually lower the bar for male applicants to maintain gender balance.[33]

The 1965 immigration act similarly represented a huge victory for segments of the population that had suffered past oppression and came from regions of the world that had not in the decades immediately prior accounted for major shares of the nation's immigrant stream, such as Asia and Latin America. The Supreme Court would enshrine their right to access effective educational services in its 1974 *Lau v. Nichols* ruling, which held that the San Francisco school system had been violating the Civil Rights Act of 1964 by failing to provide supplemental language instruction to Chinese students with limited English proficiency. In recognition of the discrimination suffered by a wide variety of minority populations, selective colleges began widening the scope of their affirmative action programs to include Native Americans as well as Asian Americans and Latinos. Included were some recent immigrant populations without the same long history of being oppressed in the United States.[34]

Rather than expanding enough to accommodate new populations of qualified applicants, most colleges have opted to limit enrollments to maintain selectivity. As a result, the share of seats given to members of a new population is a share taken from members of old ones. Surges in the number of highly qualified Asian American applicants, some from ethnic groups that quickly ascended to the top of the economic pile, posed a threat to enrollments not just of black and Latino students, but also of the children of wealthy white families that had been selective colleges' bread and butter. Under pressure to keep generations-old constituencies happy while also maintaining racial and ethnic diversity, colleges adopted admissions criteria and policies that led them to enroll far fewer Asian American students than might be expected given such students' share of all highly qualified applicants.

Asian Americans began in the 1980s to complain that they were suffering discrimination as a result of race-conscious admissions policies. Such complaints would eventually prompt some selective colleges to admit to bias and pledge reform.[35] Most such colleges, however, would argue that Asian American underrepresentation stems not from any deliberate bias, but from such students' relative lack of certain qualities not easily measured by grades or standardized admissions test scores, such as leadership potential, or the relatively few numbers of them among "hooked" applicant populations such as legacies and athletes.[36]

Asian Americans were, and remain, deeply divided on the issue, with organizations that represent them weighing in on both sides in friend-of-the-court briefs submitted whenever the Supreme Court has taken up cases involving race-conscious college admissions policies. Those groups that support race-conscious admissions accuse conservatives of seeking to use their population for its own ends. They point out that many ethnic groups that fall under the broad "Asian American" label, such as Cambodians and Laotians, are struggling in our education system and are underrepresented at selective colleges, making them worthy beneficiaries of race-conscious admissions decisions. They note that Asian Americans overall account for much larger shares of selective colleges' enrollments than might be expected given their share of the overall college-going population.[37]

The debate over selective colleges' treatment of Asian Americans has flared up again in recent years as a result of the lawsuit mounted against Harvard in 2014 by Students for Fair Admissions, an advocacy group headed by long-time affirmative action critic Edward Blum. The suit challenged Harvard's undergraduate admissions policy based specifically on allegations of bias against Asian American applicants. Calling for all race-conscious admissions policies at the nation's colleges to be struck down by federal courts as facilitating inevitable discrimination, the suit argued that Harvard and other colleges "should not be trusted with the awesome and historically dangerous tool of racial classification," because they will use any leeway that the Supreme Court gives them "to engage in racial stereotyping, discrimination against disfavored minorities, and quota setting to advance their social-engineering agenda."[38] A federal judge decided against the plaintiffs in late 2019, but their lawyers quickly announced plans to appeal.

Lasting Damage

Advocates of equal educational opportunity learned early on that our judicial system would be reluctant to demand any remedying of disparities in school quality. In a series of decisions dating back to the early 1970s, the U.S. Supreme Court has limited the impact of its 1954 *Brown* ruling and cemented into place the inequities in public school quality rooted in our nation's history, hamstringing efforts to increase the supply of highly qualified black, Latino, and low-income students knocking on selective colleges' doors.

Civil rights lawyers' efforts to bring about the racial desegregation of public schools hit an insurmountable wall in 1974, as a result of the Supreme Court's ruling in *Milliken v. Bradley*, a case involving the Detroit school system and fifty-three neighboring districts. In the lawsuit, the NAACP called for federal courts to order the State of Michigan to carry out a desegregation plan involving schools in Detroit and its suburbs, several of which stood accused of practicing housing discrimination that fostered school segregation. In rejecting that demand, the Supreme Court held that school systems that had not themselves been found guilty of racial discrimination cannot be compelled to remedy racial segregation that was not their own doing. The ruling sharpened the Supreme Court's distinction between racial segregation that had been *de jure*, or required under law, and segregation that was *de facto*, or caused by other forces such as individual decisions. It had the effect of leaving many suburban school districts outside the reach of court-ordered metropolitan desegregation plans, and it enabled white families in big-city school districts covered by such plans to ensure their children would continue to attend overwhelmingly white schools by moving to the suburbs.[39]

Well before the Supreme Court's *Milliken* decision, selective colleges began to claim that they could not graduate more black students simply by giving extra consideration to black applicants. Yale University, which pioneered the approach of relaxing its standards for black applicants for admission in the fall of 1966, discovered that many black freshmen that year found adjusting to life at Yale difficult. More than a third were gone by their sophomore year.[40] By 1970, many leaders of selective colleges argued that their institutions had been admitting too many black students from low-income backgrounds who lacked the academic preparation to handle the demands placed on them.

Harvard's admissions dean wrote that his institution had learned "that we cannot accept the victims of social disaster however deserving of promise they might have been, or however romantically or emotionally an advocate (or a society) might plead for them." The share of Harvard's black students who come from low-income families dropped from nearly 40 percent in 1969 to less than 25 percent by 1973. Other selective colleges similarly retreated from recruiting low-income black students from big cities, opting instead to compete with each other for the smaller pool of middle-class black students, whose relative advantages had left them better prepared.[41]

This pullback by Harvard, Yale, and other elite institutions predated the realization that less-prepared students require substantial academic support to succeed. It planted the seeds, however, for the belief that minority students are "mismatched" at elite colleges, a canard that found its way into arguments by Supreme Court justices Clarence Thomas and Antonin Scalia. In his dissent to the 2003 decision in *Grutter v. Bollinger*, Thomas wrote: "The Law School tantalizes unprepared students with the promise of a University of Michigan degree and all of the opportunities that it offers. These overmatched students take the bait, only to find that they cannot succeed in the cauldron of competition."[42]

The data shows, however, that such students, rather than being intimidated by not being able to meet the standards of their peers, welcome the challenge and graduate at rates comparable to their peers. This applies to black and Latino students as well as white ones. The chances of graduating improve as students move up in tiers of selectivity: for example, students with SAT scores between 1000 and 1100 have a 45 percent graduation rate at open-access institutions, but a 73 percent graduation rate at the five hundred most selective schools in the country. Black and Latino students who score above 1000 on the SAT have a graduation rate more than 30 percentage points higher at the top five hundred schools in the country than at open-access colleges.[43]

But in adopting race-conscious admissions beginning in the late 1960s, elite colleges ignored this fact. Rather than creating pathways for minority students to succeed, the selective colleges retreated en masse, and settled for trying to find black students with qualifications as close as possible to their white students. Many enticed black students away from less-prestigious colleges and historically black institutions in what one top College Board official described as the dawning of "an all-out recruiting war."[44]

When middle-class minority students struggled, some higher education leaders blamed the students' perceived inability to overcome discrimination rather than acknowledging the college's lack of support for them.[45] A shifting of selective colleges' minority recruitment efforts to focus almost solely on race and ethnicity, independent of class, has caused their minority enrollments to skew wealthier, to the point of being nearly as affluent as their enrollments of white students.[46]

Later Supreme Court decisions further curtailed the racial desegregation of public education. They included a 1991 ruling, involving the Oklahoma City schools, holding that school systems need only eliminate vestiges of past segregation "to the extent practicable," signaling that desegregation plans had an ending point short of what many black families might see as the ideal.[47] In a 1992 decision dealing with the DeKalb County, Georgia, school district, the court let school systems that seemed to have racially balanced their schools off the hook for remedying subsequent segregation resulting from changed housing patterns.[48] In a 1995 ruling involving the Kansas City, Missouri, public schools, the court held that remediating past segregation does not require closing gaps in teacher salaries or student achievement.[49]

In 2007, the court struck a blow to voluntary integration efforts by holding that the school systems of Seattle and metropolitan Louisville, Kentucky, had violated the equal-protection rights of students by using race-based school assignments to promote racial integration in the absence of any court order to desegregate. Writing for the court's majority, Chief Justice John G. Roberts Jr. said, "The way to stop discrimination on the basis of race is to stop discriminating on the basis of race."[50]

Efforts to desegregate state public-college systems did not experience the same sort of Supreme Court setbacks, but leaders of historically black public colleges often have complained that a lack of federal enforcement left their institutions inadequately funded and vulnerable to having their integration efforts undermined by competitive moves by historically white institutions.[51] People who sought to file federal lawsuits accusing states of discriminating against black students had a major hurdle placed in front of them by the Supreme Court's 2001 ruling in *Alexander v. Sandoval*, which held that their lawyers must show that such discrimination was intentional, and cannot hang their arguments solely on findings that state actions had a "disparate impact" on minorities.[52]

The Assault on Affirmative Action

The first major legal challenge to race-conscious admissions policies came in 1971, when a white student, Marco DeFunis, sued the University of Washington's law school for rejecting him through an admissions process with a separate track for minority applicants. The Supreme Court took up his case in 1974 but ducked deciding it by declaring it moot.[53] (A lower court had ordered the law school to admit DeFunis while the case was pending, and his graduation was just months away.) That same year, another white student, Allan Bakke, filed a lawsuit challenging his rejection by the medical school at the University of California at Davis. In deciding that dispute in 1978, the Supreme Court established a legal rationale for such policies that caught much of higher education off guard, and would limit the scale of race-conscious admissions policies in the decades to come.[54]

Even before the Supreme Court took up the *Bakke* case, colleges had been overhauling their race-conscious admissions policies to try to make them more legally defensible. Many, following the advice of a national advisory panel, the Carnegie Council on Policy Studies in Higher Education, had established a two-stage admissions process intended to shield them from accusations of holding minority students to lower standards. In the first stage, they'd require that all applicants meet absolute minimum academic standards set "no higher than is necessary"—typically at a level calibrated to screen out those who would be unable to graduate. Consideration of applicants' race and ethnicity would factor into the second stage, in choosing among applicants who'd gotten past the first cut.[55]

Among those filing briefs that urged the Supreme Court to rule in favor of Bakke were groups representing white ethnic populations— Jews, Poles, Italians, Greeks, and Ukrainians—who complained that they should not be called upon to make sacrifices to remedy discrimination because they'd historically been its victims rather than its perpetrators.[56]

The Davis medical school stood as a singularly unlikely example of a higher education institution that might be accused of discrimination. It had opened in 1966 and, from the start, reserved set numbers of seats for minority applicants. In defending the school's admissions policies in lower courts, the University of California's lawyers had not pinned their case on the educational benefits of diversity, instead characterizing the school's quotas as necessary to provide minority students educational opportunities that they otherwise might be denied as a result of societal discrimination. Some minority groups had seen the medical school's policy as so difficult to justify that they'd urged the University of California to accept a defeat in the state's highest court rather than giving the U.S. Supreme Court a chance to rule on the dispute.[57]

Justice Lewis F. Powell Jr. ended up as the key swing vote among the nine justices who heard the Bakke case. Although he agreed with the court's four-member conservative faction that the medical school's quota system was too heavy-handed to pass constitutional muster, he hesitated to cause upheaval in higher education by going along with them in rejecting any consideration of race by colleges not under desegregation orders. At the same time, he refused to embrace the four-member liberal faction's defense of race-conscious admissions as necessary to remedy broader societal discrimination, based on his conviction that our government should not be in the business of trying to sort through which segments of American history owed debts to others for past oppression.[58]

Justice Powell ultimately found a path to upholding race-conscious admissions policies without accepting the liberals' social-justice rationale. It came via a friend-of-the-court brief submitted by Columbia, Harvard, Stanford, and the University of Pennsylvania. They jointly argued that race-conscious admissions policies should be preserved because diversity "makes the university a better learning environment," and that many faculty members reported "that the insights provided by the participation of minority students enrich the curriculum, broaden the teachers' scholarly interests, and protect them from insensitivity to minority perspectives." Praising the brief, Powell articulated a rationale for race-conscious admissions that had not even been on the table. His opinion said colleges were justified in giving some modest consideration to applicants' race given the educational benefits of enrolling students with diverse experiences and perspectives.[59]

With the court so divided that its nine members issued six different opinions, Powell ended up playing the tie-breaker role and issuing the controlling opinion of the court. It allowed colleges to consider applicants' race as a "plus factor" to promote diversity in enrollments, but it rejected the use of outright racial quotas. It replaced an affirmative action rationale grounded in history with one grounded in educational theory, and established "diversity" as both a buzzword and goal in higher education and beyond. While affirming the value of diversity, the opinion had unintended consequences: Colleges cited Powell's rationale in extending affirmative action to applicants from minority groups without long histories of suffering serious oppression on American soil. Business groups talked about the need to have workforces that reflect the diversity of society instead of doing the hard work of righting historical wrongs. Advocates for minority students lamented that the decision diverted attention from the pursuit of racial equality and social justice.[60]

Several subsequent Supreme Court decisions, in cases not directly involving colleges, weakened the legal underpinnings of race-conscious admissions policies and emboldened those hoping to challenge them. They included a 1986 employment law–related decision that rejected the idea that public agencies can take adverse actions against white workers to remedy broader societal discrimination, and a 1989 ruling that looked askance at public agencies' favoritism of minority contractors in the absence of any remedial need.[61] Most crucially, in its 1995 decision in *Adarand Constructors v. Peña*, involving federal minority contracting requirements, the court held that any consideration of race by state or federal agencies must pass a three-pronged "strict scrutiny" test established under decades-old court precedents: it must seek to fulfill a compelling government interest, it must be narrowly tailored to consider race no more than is necessary to fulfill that interest, and it must exist in the absence of any "less drastic means" of fulfilling that interest.[62]

On the higher-education front, the Supreme Court essentially pinned a bullseye on college scholarships or programs reserved for minority students. It let stand a 1994 federal circuit court decision that, in striking down a University of Maryland scholarship program reserved for black students, held that racially exclusive programs cannot pass strict scrutiny.[63] In the coming years, conservative advocacy groups and federal civil rights officials under Republican administrations would pressure more than one hundred colleges to open race-exclusive scholarships or programs up to students of any race.[64] At least a few colleges opted to shut down the programs rather than continue them with diluted missions.[65] Corporations and philanthropies that had generously funded race-exclusive programs that groomed minority students for the workforce were less inclined to support programs also open to socioeconomically disadvantaged white students.[66]

Relentless Attack

The legal battle over race-conscious admissions flared up again in the early 1990s, when a libertarian legal advocacy group, the Center for Individual Rights, took up a lawsuit brought against the University of Texas's law school by a rejected white applicant, Barbara Hopwood.

In a ruling that sent shockwaves through higher education, the U.S. Court of Appeals for the Fifth Circuit ruled in Hopwood's favor in 1996. Its decision cited the Supreme Court's recent precedents dealing with affirmative action in other contexts in repudiating the *Bakke* diversity rationale as insufficient justification for any discrimination against white applicants.[67] With Texas's public colleges blocked from considering applicants' race, state lawmakers there tried a new strategy, passing a measure effectively guaranteeing Texas students in the top 10 percent of their high school class admission to the public college of their choice.

The year 1996 marked the opening of an entirely new front in the battle against the use of affirmative action in admissions: the ballot box. That November, California voters approved Proposition 209, a ballot initiative that amended the state's constitution to ban public colleges and other public agencies from using racial, ethnic, or gender preferences in admissions, hiring, or contracting. Among the leaders of that effort was Ward Connerly, who, a year before, as a member of the University of California's Board of Regents, had helped persuade fellow Republicans who dominated the board to pass a resolution banning the use of such preferences throughout the university system.[68] In an effort to prevent sharp declines in minority enrollment, the University of California adopted an admission guarantee for students in the top 4 percent of their classes, similar to the Texas 10-percent plan.[69]

Along with legally buttressing the university board's resolution, the success of the California ballot measure demonstrated the viability of a new populist strategy for attacking such preferences: circumventing lawmakers who had supported them or shown a reluctance to take a stand against them by letting the voting public decide the matter. In contrast to politicians, whose public opposition to affirmative action preferences was likely to get them accused of racism or alienate business interests concerned with workforce diversification, citizens in the privacy of voting booths could act to eliminate such preferences without fear of backlash. Again and again over the following decades, the race-conscious admissions policies of public colleges would be abolished nearly every time voters were given a chance to weigh in on them.

It's often assumed that voter opposition to affirmative action is rooted in conscious or unconscious racism or bias. That's partly, but not completely, true. Some critics of affirmative action have argued persuasively that the use of race- or gender-based preferences in hiring or admission tramples individual rights, sows division, stigmatizes beneficiaries, undermines meritocracy and individual striving, and diverts attention from the broader societal problems that create the perceived need for such preferences in the first place.[70] Others oppose such preferences based on an uncompromising and highly idealized allegiance to individualism and merit-based principles, which they see as trumping any consideration of the status of minority groups or the general egalitarian health of the nation.[71] Researchers have found that a relatively high proportion of those who oppose affirmative action policies have a personality type that favors hierarchy and order and fears the instability that some see as the inevitable consequence of aggressive attempts to create equality.[72]

The success of the challenges to affirmative action in California and Texas inspired a new wave of assaults. Without waiting for a court ruling or popular vote compelling it to take such action, the governing board of Florida's state university system voted in early 2000 to end the use of race-conscious admissions by the system's campuses and replace them with a policy guaranteeing a seat on some system campuses to Florida students in the top 20 percent of their high school class. It took the action at the behest of Florida governor Jeb Bush, whose brother, George W. Bush, a fellow Republican, was running for president that year and was believed to have wanted to head off a possible affirmative action referendum that would mobilize black voters that fall.[73]

In 2001, a federal circuit court embraced the *Hopwood* decision's reasoning in striking down the race-conscious admissions policy at the University of Georgia, a development that prompted the public university to end its admission preferences for legacies.[74] One powerful and prominent libertarian advocacy group, the Center for Individual Rights, headed up lawsuits challenging the race-conscious admissions policies used by the law school at the University of Washington, the law school at the University of Michigan, and the chief undergraduate program at Michigan. Federal circuit courts ruled in the universities' favor in the two law-school cases.[75] With the federal circuits split, the Supreme Court decided to take up the Michigan cases.

Even the colleges that did not fall in the federal circuits that had rejected the use of race-conscious admissions took note of the defeats their peers had suffered and responded by modifying their practices to reduce the risk of running afoul of federal civil rights offices or suffering expensive defeats in the courts.[76] Surveys of colleges showed that the legal pressure on them had taken a toll, and fewer gave special treatment to minority applicants than had been the case twenty years earlier.[77] As of 2003, the year when the Supreme Court ruled on the Michigan cases, about a third of colleges considered race and ethnicity in weighing applicants. More than two-fifths continued, however, to operate programs intended to help ensure that minority students graduated, nearly half employed a multicultural recruitment staff, two-thirds had incorporated commitments to racial and ethnic diversity in their mission statements, and nearly three-fourths engaged in recruitment activities intended to increase minority enrollments.[78] While retreating on some fronts, they'd hardly surrendered.

In its rulings in the two Michigan cases, the Supreme Court upheld the ability of colleges to consider applicants' race and ethnicity but imposed new limits on the practice. The majority opinion in the law-school case, *Grutter v. Bollinger*, embraced the diversity rationale that Justice Powell had used in *Bakke*, putting to rest a long-running debate among judges and legal scholars over whether Powell's opinion had truly represented the holding of the court. In refusing to second-guess the law school's judgment regarding the viability of race-neutral alternatives to its policy or how much minority representation it needed, the majority invoked Justice Frankfurter's 1957 opinion declaring autonomy over admissions decisions to be one of universities' essential academic freedoms under the First Amendment. In its ruling in the undergraduate case, *Gratz v. Bollinger*, the court struck down the policy at issue—a point-based applicant-scoring system that conferred a substantial bonus to minority applicants—concluding that such a mechanistic system transgressed the narrow-tailoring requirement. Taken together, the rulings reiterated the court's view that race-conscious admissions policies serve a compelling interest, but made clear that race can be considered only as part of a holistic evaluation process.[79]

Ten years later, in requiring lower courts to reconsider *Fisher v. University of Texas at Austin*, a lawsuit challenging that institution's undergraduate admissions practices, the Supreme Court emphasized that strict scrutiny requires that race-conscious admissions policies undergo close examination.[80] Three years after that, however, the Supreme Court revisited the case and, in ruling in Texas's favor, emphasized that courts should give substantial deference to colleges' judgments on matters such as whether the policies were needed.[81]

More unambiguously devastating to affected public colleges' consideration of race have been the most recent state ballot initiatives banning their use of racial and ethnic preferences. Such measures are now law in Arizona, Michigan, Nebraska, Oklahoma, and Washington State, reversing the gains that public colleges in Michigan and Washington had made in court battles. In a 2014 ruling, the U.S. Supreme Court upheld a ban on racial preferences established by Michigan voters, rejecting the argument that such bans discriminate against minorities.[82]

As a result of such measures, as well as of the action taken by Florida's board and a 2011 vote by New Hampshire lawmakers to bar public colleges' use of race-conscious admissions policies, more than two out of five of the nation's Latino residents and nearly one in five of its black residents now live in a state that prohibits public colleges from considering applicants' race.[83]

Missing the Point?

The class rank–based admission practices adopted in many states amount to an acknowledgment that they won't have the sorts of integrated public schools envisioned in the Supreme Court's landmark *Brown* ruling any time soon. Such strategies accept that public high schools are stratified by class and race, and use that fact to diversify enrollment. They assume that a college that skims the top of the graduating class of *every* high school in a state is highly likely to get a student body that is as diverse as that state's population.

More broadly, public colleges barred from using race-conscious admissions have sought to bolster minority enrollments by stepping up recruitment efforts, offering more financial aid, expanding outreach to high schools with large minority populations, seeking to improve teacher preparation, experimenting with class-based affirmative action, pushing states to expand access to college preparatory courses, and reconsidering their use of preferences for legacies and other subsets of the applicant population that tend to be disproportionately white. All such developments are positive, but the efficacy of such alternatives to race-conscious admissions has been hotly debated before the Supreme Court. In its most recent *Fisher* ruling, the court stressed its reluctance to second-guess colleges' judgments on such matters, effectively giving those not covered by state bans on race-conscious admissions leeway to give a little consideration to alternatives. It also, however, expressed doubts that "percent plans" that draw the top students from overwhelmingly white, black, or Latino public schools are in any meaningful way "race-neutral," in a sense its own admission that the promise of *Brown* never has been realized.

Higher education has yet to come up with an alternative to race-conscious admissions that will maintain current levels of diversity without lowering test scores, although research has shown that a Texas-like 10-percent model implemented nationally can move the needle substantially on race.[84] With liberals invested in promoting the idea that race-conscious admissions remain the only viable means of achieving our society's interest in racially diverse college enrollments, and conservatives generally opposed to any government remediation of inequities that they attribute to individual competition, neither side of the battle over race-conscious admissions has demonstrated much desire to broadly challenge admissions policies that favor the wealthy and well connected.

Factoring heavily into both the legal and the political battles over race-conscious admissions are debates over the policies' educational benefits, effects on underrepresented minority students, and necessity. Many conservatives argue that the race-conscious admissions policies hurt selective colleges' educational environment by eroding academic standards. Liberal supporters of the policies argue that diversity has educational benefits even within individual classrooms where students are learning subjects, such as mathematics, where matters related to race virtually never come up. Careful educational research paints a more nuanced picture, suggesting that diversity has educational benefits if it is not brought about through heavy-handed preferences that stigmatize their beneficiaries, and if educators actively take steps to ensure students learn from it.[85]

The debate over the effects of race-conscious admissions policies on underrepresented minority students includes the question of whether students admitted through such policies are harmed by being "mismatched" to highly challenging academic environments. As with the debate over diversity's benefits, the educational research paints a nuanced picture. It suggests that students admitted through selective colleges' race-conscious admissions policies generally do fine, ending up with prestigious degrees that open doors, unless they're poorly prepared for college and try to major in fields, such as mathematics or science, where knowledge is cumulative and falling behind early can spell long-term academic trouble.[86] Less settled is the question of whether race-conscious admissions policies set students up for failure in fields such as medicine or law where they must pass rigorous tests in order to earn professional degrees and eventually practice.[87]

Race was being considered in admissions by about 60 percent of the 338 public or private four-year colleges whose admissions or enrollment-management officers responded to a 2014–15 academic year survey on their practices. Among admissions strategies intended to bolster minority enrollments, race-conscious admissions ranked below targeted recruitment and outreach and the encouragement of student transfer, but well above reduced emphasis on legacy preferences, test-optional policies, or percentage plans, in terms of the share of institutions using them.[88]

Critics assert that while colleges pay lip service to affirmative action, they are hiding their real motives. Harvard law professor and civil rights theorist Lani Guinier characterized the diversity that race-conscious policies bring as "a fig leaf to camouflage privilege."[89]

In her book *The Tyranny of the Meritocracy*, Guinier says:

> If affirmative action has failed, it's not because it has admitted unmeritorious students of color at the expense of whites, or that it has failed to propel us into a postracial, color-blind society. Rather, affirmative action's weakness and vulnerability cooperate with, and perhaps unnecessarily legitimate, a meritocracy that privileges test scores over other indicators of student potential in the first place. Affirmative action has fed into the societal vision we have of our citizens belonging to their place in a pyramid— some further up, some further down—our positions based to some degree on where we were born or how successfully we have clawed our way up over others.[90]

Rather than challenging our faith in meritocracy, affirmative action seeks to hide meritocracy's shortcomings enough to legitimize it in the eyes of those on the bottom of the pile. It circumvents or interferes with mechanisms of the sorting machine rather than overhauling the machine itself. True equality of educational opportunity will require much more ambitious change, change that is unlikely in the foreseeable future to come from the courts. A good start is to take a hard look at the machine's inner workings and ask whether they're doing what we need them to do.

7

BUILT TO COLLAPSE

A huge gathering of college leaders promised to give its attendees insights on how to improve the admissions process. Instead, it offered example after example of how badly the college admissions game has gone awry and how much it sets the nation up for disaster.

More than seven thousand people had shown up for the 2018 annual conference of the National Association for College Admission Counseling, or NACAC, a testament to the vast size of the field and the related industries it has spawned. Along with college admissions officers, the gathering included high school counselors, policy experts, and salespeople bent on making a buck off colleges' frenzied competition for students and off students' frenzied competition for seats in desired colleges' entering classes.

Some conference sessions focused on token efforts to provide more college access to the disadvantaged, but the real action involved reinforcing the pipeline from affluent communities to selective institutions. High school counselors and admissions officers sat through PowerPoint presentations offering tips on how to better meet one another's needs, traded notes in bars and restaurants, and schmoozed with each other at catered after-hours receptions. Representatives of expensive private prep schools that spend generously on their counseling staffs spoke of devoting long hours to polishing students' application essays. Those from working-class high schools or ordinary, nonselective colleges confided that they felt like they'd jumped into shark-infested water by being there.[1]

In theory, college counseling should help all students succeed, but success is defined differently along the education food chain. At affluent high schools, the experienced and savvy counselors are a conduit to elite colleges. At less affluent and rural high schools, the poorly financed and understaffed counseling programs have limited connections with elite colleges and thus limited ability to advise students on how to get into them.

In the convention center's exhibit hall stood row upon row of slick booths offering to sell either colleges or students a competitive edge. Tech firms peddled software or online platforms that let colleges link prospective students with current ones or keep helicopter parents in the loop throughout their child's application process. Consulting firms handed out brochures describing how they can improve colleges' marketing and recruitment efforts, monitor references to colleges on social media, design more effective campus tours, or hone admissions criteria to ensure colleges enroll the right mix of students.

The Independent Educational Consultants Association, which represents freelance counselors, boasted of having more than 1,800 members who, for a price, will guide individual families and their children through the application process. They provide an average of eighteen hours of counseling to each of their clients, a figure that dwarfs the roughly thirty minutes of individualized counseling received by students at the average public high school.[2] Other companies offered, at prices well beyond the reach of most American families, to provide intensive one-on-one SAT tutoring, help students to produce brief "elevator pitch" videos of themselves, or arrange for high schoolers to spend several weeks of their summer on the campus of an elite college.

In the meeting rooms, it was tough to miss the strain that frenzied competition has placed on colleges, parents, and students. College admissions officers complained of being so deluged with applications that they routinely needed to work past midnight or on weekends and holidays. They expressed fears of their colleges suffering a decline in application numbers in a few years due to a projected dip in the number of students graduating from the nation's high schools.[3]

High school counselors talked about families obsessed over colleges' *U.S. News* rankings and expressed concern about the mental and physical health of students they see actually weeping over rejection letters. Colleges sometimes are inexcusably at fault: Roderick Rose, associate director of admissions for the University of Denver, said that more than half of the eighty colleges in a survey admitted to urging borderline high school students to apply even though they had no chance of acceptance, the goal being to boast of high rejection rates as a sign of their "quality."

Perhaps the conference's most telling moment came during a panel discussion of Harvard Graduate School of Education's Making Caring Common project, an effort to promote ethical and respectful behavior among children and teens partly by rewarding it in college admissions decisions. Richard Weissbourd, a psychologist who runs the project, lamented a survey that had found that high school students place far more value on achievement than on caring for others or being happy. The kicker came when he got to the report's recommendation that colleges ask prospective students questions designed to measure character and give those who demonstrated a strong sense of ethics the same extra consideration given those tied to a significant donor. Asked about the irony of a college equally favoring both applicants who seem ethical and applicants hoping to benefit from bribery, Weissbourd said that the idea of curtailing preferences for donor-connected or legacy applicants had come up but proved to be "a nonstarter" among college representatives involved in the project.[4]

Weissbourd's response betrayed how necessary higher-education reforms often get stymied by those with power. Reformers know what must be done to make higher education more open, equitable, and transparent, but feel powerless to bring needed changes about. They're thwarted by how much cost has emerged as the chief force driving what happens in higher education. Students and their families are consumed by questions of who can afford to go where against what odds. Colleges grapple with the question of how to sustain a business model that is precarious, at best, rather than questioning whether their business model needs to be abandoned and replaced.

Many Americans cling to the ideal that colleges provide opportunity while ignoring the reality that they're widening the gap between rich and poor. The nation, by way of rhetoric and public policies, promotes an ideal of meritocracy while meting out access to a good education primarily to the already-privileged. The consequence is deep social tension, an undercurrent that threatens to erode the entire system if access to opportunity is not extended more equitably.

At the heart of the problem is an industry built around the fetish of elite colleges, driven by the unquenchable thirst of families to send their children to them, and the self-interests of those who are helping families accomplish just that. This industry keeps alive the belief that all is possible in life if you just get into the right college.

Highly selective public and private colleges, which collectively educate no more than 18 percent of the college-going high school class, admit 52 percent of the most affluent students with the highest scores on standardized tests.[5] For many of those students, price is no object—the only natural limit on what elite colleges can charge them is their families' willingness to pay. The prestige of the colleges is the point. The more prestigious a college becomes, the harder it is to get into. The harder it is to get into, the more prestigious it becomes. Both families and colleges play roles in upholding this codependent relationship, and both sometimes behave as though the ecosystem of college selectivity must be preserved at all costs.

Are we doomed to a bifurcated system, where the elites go to top colleges and form a ruling aristocracy, and everyone else can hope, at best, to attend a lower-status college and earn a degree that is practical but lacks distinction? What about the colleges that sit between these two extremes: the small, selective, private liberal arts institutions that are struggling to attract the students they need to keep themselves afloat financially, and the middle-tier state colleges suffering from inadequate public support?

Already, nearly a fifth of private colleges are offering tuition discounts of at least 60 percent to incoming students.[6] Two major bond-rating agencies, Moody's Investors Service and Fitch Ratings, have been bleak in recent years about the finances of higher education. Moody's downgraded its outlook on the sector from "stable" to "negative" in 2017, citing financial strain for both public and private colleges.[7] Fitch adjusted its outlook to "negative" in 2018. Moody's has upgraded its outlook back to "stable," citing revenue growth at large comprehensive universities, even as it acknowledged that smaller public and private colleges have slower revenue growth. But Fitch has maintained its negative outlook, citing concerns about the slowing growth in the traditional college-age population and the "widening credit gap" between prestigious colleges with strong finances and struggling colleges that are reliant on tuition revenue.[8] What will happen to the system as a whole if the middle dwindles as a consequence of the race for prestige? Are we doomed to face an ever-widening gap between the haves and have-nots?

The Failures of Meritocracy

The NACAC conference, in short, was a gathering of people in denial. These are the hard facts: the current structure and policies of our higher-education system cause institutions to spend money inefficiently and waste academic talent, while skewing the educational priorities of elementary and secondary schools. The result is continued inequities in educational outcomes, economic opportunity, and intergenerational mobility. Too many colleges themselves appear headed for disaster as they compete by engaging in behavior that is financially unsustainable and erodes their public support.

At the conference, exhortations to stop obsessing over rankings seemed naïve given how much the resources of selective colleges—and, arguably, their very survival—hinge on their prestige. Calls to increase selective colleges' enrollments of students from disadvantaged backgrounds rang hollow in an environment where representatives of top colleges and expensive prep schools greeted each other as old chums.

While no one challenged assertions that our education system needs to do more to promote social mobility, a huge share of NACAC attendees had jobs that required they be actively engaged in the perpetuation of inequality from one generation to the next.

As our higher-education system has evolved into a vertical edifice that teeters on the brink of collapse, it's worth asking how we got here.

Our collective support of a system that breeds inequality is perversely rooted in our nation's deep faith that people's skills and hard work fairly determine how high they rise or how low they fall. That belief can be used to justify the fact that most high school graduates end up shut out of the selective colleges that represent the surest path to graduate and professional education and to high-paying, high-status careers. It helps us accept that the most selectively educated wield disproportionate power.[9]

"Many countries like the sound of meritocracy. But only in America is equality of opportunity a virtual national religion, reconciling individual liberty—the freedom to get ahead and 'make something of yourself'—with societal equality," Richard Reeves of the Brookings Institution argues in *Dream Hoarders*. He observes that "Americans are more tolerant of income inequality than the citizens of other countries, in part because of this faith that in each generation the poor run a fair race against the rich, and the brightest succeed."[10]

The problem with assuming that opportunity is based on merit is that the world doesn't work that way, and never has. Everyone does not start out on equal footing. As the sociologist Daniel Bell observed back in 1972: "There can never be a pure meritocracy because high-status parents will invariably seek to pass on their positions, either through the use of influence or simply by the cultural advantages their children inevitably possess. Thus after one generation a meritocracy simply becomes an enclaved class."[11]

Equally problematic is how these dynamics can be unseen, or at least unacknowledged, by the very people they most benefit. In a confessional essay published in 2017, Jason England, former assistant dean of admissions at Wesleyan University, said, "It is fascinating to observe people's attitudes about who deserves what, and why. The truth is that the bulk of incoming classes at top liberal-arts colleges are interchangeable. It's never really clear which candidates are more qualified, better fits, sharper thinkers. Even less clear is who *deserves* a spot in the class, and how anyone could comfortably determine such a thing. The bulk of those credentialed enough to be seriously considered for acceptance are in that position because of circumstance and wealth."[12]

"But," England added, "try to get someone who has benefited from circumstance to sincerely accept their interchangeability, and you'll meet with a resistance that can border on violent. Acknowledging the luck of birth undermines the key cog of the American Dream machine: the myth of the self, which reduces the built-in advantages of children of the wealthy to irrelevant biographical footnotes, while transforming the disadvantages of everyone else to personal faults."[13]

In a meritocracy, people claim to have earned their successes through talent and hard work alone, even after using their cash or connections to cheat or circumvent the selection process. Colleges reward and incentivize such bad behavior by ushering in applicants who are legacies or have ties to donors, politicians, or their own employees. They so commonly reward applicants willing to wield their privilege that the primary surprise of 2019's "Operation Varsity Blues" scandal was that parents involved felt the need to break the law to cash in on their status. Through their standard admissions practices, colleges screen out many people who are committed to playing fair and offer entry into our nation's leadership class to obvious cutthroats. Although many of the beneficiaries of string-pulling are fully qualified, their admission contributes to insider dominance of selective colleges' enrollments and stifles social mobility. Meanwhile, those who rely solely on fair recognition of their talent and hard work to get them in the door often end up at a distinct disadvantage.

Also questionable is the basic assumption underlying the vertical structure of our higher-education system, that colleges can specialize in educating students at specific levels of general aptitude. That assumption makes sense only if such a thing as general aptitude actually exists, as the Stanford economist Caroline Hoxby argues.[14] We neither know for certain that general aptitude exists nor have any precise means to measure it. The closest we come to measuring general aptitude is through administration of SAT and ACT tests. As chapter 4 explains, these tests only loosely predict long-term college performance, and are far more closely tied to family wealth.[15] There are multiple forms of aptitude that the SAT or ACT don't measure that can lead to great success in certain fields.

Yet colleges rely on these metrics well beyond their predictive validity, and they use them to justify the distribution of resources within the higher-education system in a way that steers the most money toward the education of students who came out on top in the competition for college seats. The system's defenders make a tough-minded, realist argument that this distribution is both fair and efficient—fair because the best students are most deserving of elite education; efficient because such students have the greatest ability to benefit from an elite education.[16] Such claims don't hold up to close scrutiny.

The SAT and ACT scores that the system relies on to measure students' ability are highly correlated with racial, ethnic, and socioeconomic disparities. They serve as mechanisms for legitimizing illegitimate differences in children's prior and future opportunities to learn.[17] As for the quest for efficiency, allocating resources based on the prestige and reputation of colleges concentrates money where it is least needed. It subsidizes conspicuous consumption and gives us the worst possible system-wide investment return as measured by access, quality, completion, and upward mobility.

Perhaps worst of all, the act of sorting students into college by selectivity presumes that ability is fixed and innate rather than flexible and developed. We are assuming we already know all we need to about students' potential before they have even reached adulthood. Otherwise, why do we suppose that the student who scores 1000 on the SAT cannot learn as much as a student who scored 1200, especially in a selective college with the best available teaching resources?

Such presumptions cynically undercut the real value of education. College should enhance students' knowledge, skills, and abilities, preparing them to find good jobs and contribute to society—not just further codify their existing prestige. It should offer equal opportunity to all students, not serve as a mechanism for sorting a privileged leadership class from a class of promising but chronically underserved potential talent.

Increasing Stratification

If we intend to offer more access to high-quality college learning and raise completion rates—the goals that make the most sense in light of the demands of our current economy—we should be spending much more public money on less-selective public four-year colleges and community colleges. This is where nearly 60 percent of the students in higher education are.[18] It's also where the biggest losses occur—and not necessarily because of any flaws in the students enrolled. All too many highly qualified students drop out for want of support or resources, not because of a lack of talent. Increases in financial support to these less-selective schools have the potential to dramatically raise their low graduation rates, which average 49 percent in open-access two- and four-year schools.[19]

Focusing on where the students are can have a big impact on the lives of the low-income and minority students concentrated at such institutions. Well-financed selective colleges already have graduation rates above 80 percent, and therefore don't have as much room for improvement in their productivity as the less-selective colleges.[20] Improving graduation rates at selective schools could require big investments with little relative payoff. These colleges could effectively graduate more students by increasing their capacity, but they have historically resisted that solution, because it might threaten the cachet they acquire through high rejection rates.

In addition, it is not at all clear that differences in institutional prestige—as opposed simply to gross differences in institutional spending—account for the advantages that selective colleges offer students in terms of their learning and future earnings. Prestige is an intangible and insatiable target for postsecondary investments. It is mostly attached to institutions, not curricula, and has no documented relationship with the quality of teaching.[21] In the higher-education market, like the markets for housing, apparel, and automobiles,

demand at the high end of the market distorts investments and reduces returns on them. College students who pay tuition of $60,000
per year do not receive twice the amount or quality of postsecondary
education as students who pay $30,000 per year.

Merit Aid: Welfare for the Rich

An expensive college education represents what economists call a "positional good." Like a pricey designer handbag or a luxury car, its value
stems partly from its price, artificially inflated by the inability of most
people to afford it. The additional money spent on it signals wealth and
status as much as any measurable additional quality. People are welcome, of course, to engage in conspicuous consumption, such as the
purchase of Gucci purses or Lamborghini roadsters, with their own
money. But their purchase of elite postsecondary education shouldn't
be subsidized if all it amounts to is a positional good. All public and
not-for-profit colleges are publicly subsidized through measures like
federal grants, tax-deductible donations, and not-for-profit tax breaks.
We all have a stake in them, regardless of whether or not we have children who attend them or might do so down the road.

Meanwhile, the colleges in the lower tiers of the higher-education
system wither from thirst for attention and students. Recruitment
costs have surged: as of 2017, the median cost of recruiting a single
undergraduate student had risen to nearly $2,400 at private colleges
and more than $500 at public ones, according to the results of a survey
of colleges by the consulting firm Ruffalo Noel Levitz.[22]

The higher-education policy experts Donald Hossler and David
Kalsbeek say colleges' operational costs have surged partly because
"many institutions have invested heavily in larger admissions staffs,
expensive customer relationship management products, expansive
recruitment marketing efforts to drive application volume, and, of
course, the costs of institutional aid, especially for colleges and universities that are heavily invested in the merit aid game." To keep rising tuitions from driving prospective students away, colleges are using

merit aid to offer tuition discounts "over what were already rates that at many institutions economists believe were unsustainable."[23]

A NACAC-commissioned report by admissions experts concluded: "While more applications and fewer acceptances may help establish positions in the *U.S. News & World Report*'s annual rankings of best colleges, these trends may indicate inefficiencies and excess expenditures in college admission. In tough economic times it is reasonable to question this use of scarce resources when we should be improving the quality of educational experiences and increasing graduation rates."[24]

Many middle-tier selective colleges must offer large discounts off their tuition in order to compete for students. The idea is that more students produce more revenue, but when discounts get too large, the resulting revenue increases are marginal. A 2017 study of data from 450 small baccalaureate colleges found that after tuition discounts, tuition revenue only increased by 2.3 percent per year.[25] At that level of growth, colleges are hard-pressed to invest in new faculty, technology, or buildings, among other priorities. Huge tuition discounts could be a sign that a college is in financial trouble. At many small colleges, more than 90 percent of the student body is getting at least some discount. The enrollment at these colleges can be very volatile if a primary reason that many students are there is because their cost is low.[26]

Dwindling resources are a threat to the very existence of these middle-tier selective institutions. Some regional public colleges in this boat have reacted by severely cutting back the number of majors they offer.[27] Among privates, Goucher College, a liberal arts institution near Baltimore, has moved to eliminate a number of majors, more than half of them in the liberal arts, in what it termed an "academic revitalization."[28] Earlham College, a nationally known Quaker-affiliated liberal arts college in Indiana with a $400 million endowment, has been struggling through years of financial decline. It charges more than $45,000 for tuition, but nets only about $12,000 in tuition revenue per student. Attendance is continuing to decline, and the college has accumulated $47 million in budget deficits over the last several years.[29]

Who's to Blame?

Our stratified higher-education system wastes human potential. It does a poor job of serving highly capable students from all kinds of backgrounds. Arguably, students with ACT or SAT scores in the top fourth of all test-takers should be able to handle the work at a four-year college. Yet, among students in the top fourth on standardized tests, a two-year college is the destination of 14 percent of those from the most affluent fourth of families, and 20 to 24 percent of those from the lower three socioeconomic quartiles.[30] Each year, about 500,000 students in the top half of their high school class essentially disappear from the postsecondary radar.[31] They never earn a degree or certificate at all. Yet we know that these students would have stood a very good chance of graduating from a four-year college, especially if they went to a selective one.

Poor academic preparation in many elementary and secondary schools deserves a share of the blame for disappointing college enrollments and graduation rates. Yet, it's wrong to scapegoat K–12 education for higher education's problems. Admission to college should signal a college's belief that an admitted student is adequately prepared to succeed at that institution, and should indicate a commitment to helping ensure that the student can graduate. When colleges and universities fail to uphold their end of the bargain and provide inadequate academic support based on a student's demonstrated levels of preparation at the point of enrollment, they risk further eroding the public's trust in higher education.

The fact is that increasing disparities in public funding for colleges play a major role in graduation rate gaps. Ironically, even as our nation has pursued a goal of college for all as one way to undo the damage done by tracking in high schools, it has constructed within higher education a similar tracking system, with inequitably apportioned resources.

As our higher-education system has become more stratified, the gaps between the educational offerings of its various tiers have widened. Increasingly, it steers students in one of two directions: toward

a pricey, full-service, brand-name college that pretty much assures
graduation and entry into graduate schools and good jobs, or toward some unexceptional alternative, where they'll struggle to earn
a credential. Affordable quality, which should be the core offering of
a mass education system in a democratic society, has become harder
and harder to find.

The Benefits of a Degree

Since 1970, the wage advantage that a bachelor's degree recipient
holds over someone whose education ended with a high school diploma has risen from 36 percent to 66 percent,[32] or to about $1 million
in earnings over a working lifetime.[33] Those figures are much higher
for those who go to graduate school. Since the early 1980s, it has become increasingly difficult for anyone who has not attended college
to secure a good job that provides a real shot at a middle-class existence. The number of Americans with four or more years of college
education has surged from 22 million in 1980 to 74 million in 2017.[34]
The middle class has been dispersing into either the upwardly mobile
college-haves or the downwardly mobile college-have-nots. People
with bachelor's degrees have been rising out of the middle class into
the highest-earning 30 percent. People with no more education than
a high school diploma have been dropping from the middle class into
the bottom 30 percent.[35]

The wages of college-educated workers have increased both in absolute terms and relative to those of other workers largely as a result of
structural changes in the workforce. Since the mid-twentieth century,
industries that favor workers with at least some college learning—such
as financial services, education, government, and healthcare—have
grown from less than 30 percent to almost half of the workforce. At
the same time, industries with relatively low levels of postsecondary
attainment, including construction and manufacturing, have shrunk
from nearly half to less than 20 percent of the workforce.[36]

The upshot of these changes is that educational attainment and
educational prestige are rewarded handsomely in the labor market.

Employers tend to hire those fresh out of college, using speculative judgments of potential workplace performance based on the applicants' highest level of education, their educational attainment, and the selectivity of the institutions and programs that awarded their credentials. Those with the most impressive academic credentials have the greatest choice of employers, and they tend to enter careers that offer the most learning on the job.

The economy now rewards the kind of education often associated with prestigious four-year colleges, including the richest mixes of general cognitive competencies such as problem-solving and critical thinking and soft competencies such as teamwork and communications. High-octane combinations of general and occupation-specific competencies maximize learning and adaptability at work as well as access to flexible technology on the job—and students are most likely to have the time and opportunity to develop those skill combinations at four-year schools. Those with specific sub-baccalaureate certificates, certifications, and degrees do achieve middle-class wages, but careers and career ladders leading to top pay, personal autonomy, or the institutional power primarily enjoyed by professionals and managers remain out of their reach.

Wider education-linked gaps in income beget more intense class segregation, larger disparities in local property-tax bases and the quality of elementary and secondary schools, and higher barriers between the tracks routing advantaged children toward educational opportunity and disadvantaged children away from it. The wealthiest segment of society seems intent on insulating its cocoon. Within the ranks of our nation's elites, the higher one looks, the more concentrated power becomes: a 2002 analysis by political scientist Thomas R. Dye found that 54 percent of America's corporate leaders and 42 percent of its governmental leaders are graduates of just twelve institutions.[37]

In addition, whites are padding their advantage in the workplace. Having benefited from decades of discrimination in hiring and promotion in the workforce, they now seize upon a disproportionate share of bachelor's degrees as their tickets to good jobs in the modern knowledge-based economy. Between 1991 and 2016, overall white employment increased by only 1.9 million, but their number of bachelor's degrees increased by 13 million, and the number of good jobs held by white workers increased by 7.5 million. At the end of this fifteen-year period, white workers held 77 percent of good jobs, markedly higher than their 69-percent share of the U.S. workforce. Black workers held 10 percent of good jobs, less than their 13-percent overall share of the U.S. workforce. Latino workers' share of good jobs amounted to 13 percent, below their 18-percent share of the U.S. workforce. As a group, white workers with good jobs earned $554 billion more in 2016 than they would have earned if their number of good jobs and their good jobs earnings were proportional to their share of employment. Meanwhile, in 2016, Latino workers earned $352 billion less, and black workers $202 billion less, than they would have if their number of good jobs and earnings from those jobs had been proportional to their percentage of the workforce.[38] These sorts of structural advantages, once established, take decades if not centuries to overcome.

The American sociologist Willard Waller observed, in *The Sociology of Teaching*, that parents and educators are natural enemies because educators look out for all children while parents are concerned only with their own.[39] Fear of their children suffering downward mobility inspires affluent parents to fight school reforms that threaten their advantages as aggressively as bears defend their cubs. High school students devote time that they could spend learning subject matter that interests them to padding their applications and learning how to game standardized tests. Admissions experts have said this obsession with getting into the best possible college "distorts students' relationship with learning, causing them to regard the high school years as an Olympic training season demanding ever-greater feats of accomplishment in order to qualify for admissions to a selective university or college."[40]

Neglecting the Needs of Society

Much of the precarious state of American higher education arises from the pressure we've placed on our educational system to ensure individual opportunity in a capitalist democracy. The built-in tension between postsecondary selectivity and upward mobility is far more acute in the United States than in Europe. Europeans rely on the welfare state's direct redistribution of wealth, and on narrow wage bands, to enable citizenship and markets to coexist. Americans, by contrast, rely much more on education, and the economic opportunity that it affords, to reconcile the equality implicit in citizenship with the inequality implicit in markets. American higher education's stratification, however, has made it harder for people raised here in humble circumstances to rise.

In the United States, race-conscious admissions policies lift up some members of minority groups, but they benefit a relatively small share of students. These policies ensure a presence of black and Latino students at most selective colleges, but they mask the effects of broader racial and economic stratification rather than doing much to remedy it.

For the most part, the education gap between blacks, Latinos, and whites has widened since the 1980s, not closed as hoped. Only 19 percent of high-scoring blacks and Latinos go to selective institutions, compared to 31 percent of whites with similar scores.[41] Admissions preferences based on race or ethnicity are, and are likely to remain, legally and politically on the defensive as a result of the broader backlash against identity politics and the redistributive government policies that arose partly in response to them.

In addition, tensions have risen over the large share of black beneficiaries of such admissions policies who are not descended from American slaves. At the most selective colleges, affirmative action increasingly benefits West Indian or African immigrants or their children—populations that often encounter the same racism as other black Americans but do not have the same history of cumulative economic and cultural oppression on U.S. soil.[42] The African American and Latino enrollments at selective colleges are marginally more socioeconomically diverse than their enrollments of white students, but still largely drawn from middle-class and upper-class families.[43] Selective colleges create a volatile mix in saddling minority students with suspicions of being preference beneficiaries in an environment dominated by white students from privileged, overwhelmingly white communities and schools. Ugly racist incidents are common on college campuses, as are controversies over colleges' often clumsy efforts to promote civility or curtail racist speech.[44]

A landmark study published in 2017 drove home just how much damage is being done to social mobility by the selectivity-based stratification of higher education. Conducted by the Equality of Opportunity Project, it examined both the number of low-income students admitted by various colleges and the share of those students who ended up substantially wealthier than their parents. It assigned colleges "Mobility Report Cards" based on how well they are helping students from humble circumstances achieve the American dream.[45]

Past studies dealing with class and college access have focused on the share of students at colleges who receive need-based federal Pell Grants and largely ignored considerations of how they fared financially later in life. Also, counting Pell Grant recipients can overstate how much socioeconomic diversity exists at a college because the eligibility criteria for such grants encompass a lot of students whose families are at or above the middle-class income threshold. The Equality of Opportunity Project used detailed federal income and tax data to better define the poor, as well as other specific income groups. It covered thirty million college students who were born between 1980 and 1991 and entered college from 1999 to 2013, collecting data on their earnings as adults.[46]

Much of the study focuses on the share of colleges' students who come from the bottom fifth of society in economic terms and later end up in the top fifth. It found the lowest social mobility rates at nonselective colleges, whose low-income students almost never went on to become affluent. At some community colleges in North Carolina, students from low-income families actually went on to earn less annually as adults than low-income peers who had never gone on to college. The most social mobility occurred at middle-tier colleges that were both accessible to low-income students and adept at preparing students to earn a good living.

The study found that elite colleges had not substantially increased their low-income enrollments since 2000, despite having undertaken much-ballyhooed efforts to help cover the education costs of students whose families were below certain income thresholds. The far worse news yielded by the study was that enrollments of low-income students had plunged at the institutions that had been bright spots: accessible mid-tier public colleges with high social mobility rates. Much of the blame fell on deep cuts in the institutions' state support, which generally had left them with less money for financial aid and more need to enroll students who could pay full tuition.[47]

"Colleges, once seen as beacons of egalitarian hope, are becoming bastions of wealth and privilege that perpetuate inequality," writes the economist and social critic Peter Sacks. The share of children from low-income American families who earn a bachelor's degree by age twenty-four has not budged above 6 percent since 1970, he says, but "political and educational leaders have been slow to respond. The rich and powerful of both the left and the right seem to have convinced them that confronting that divide comes at their peril. Members of America's ruling class have too much at stake, including family legacies, for their children not to follow in their footsteps to Harvard, Yale, or Michigan."[48]

A Cycle of Lasting Damage

The stratification of higher education weakens academic quality and integrity, too, by discouraging improvements in teaching and learning outcomes. Instead of rewarding colleges for educating students well, the highest rankings and greatest prestige go to colleges that admit students who have higher levels of baseline preparation. In other words, our current system for sorting colleges differentiates among institutions based on differences in inputs—such as the number of students with high test scores—and is not based on outcomes such as graduation rates and measures of teaching, learning, and career success. The focus on ranking also inhibits colleges from crafting and pursuing distinct missions, programs, and teaching methods, thereby inhibiting diversity in the system at large. Institutions don't compete by specializing, but by increasing the scope of their marketable course offerings and programs so they can cast the net wider among students shopping for colleges on the basis of selectivity and prestige.

With so many people shut out of selective colleges or poorly served by nonselective ones, it's no wonder that public support for higher education has declined over time. Americans may still look to higher education as the clearest pathway to opportunity, but only about 14 percent express a great deal of confidence in the higher-education sector to deliver on that promise. Such confidence levels are exceptionally low among people classified as extremely conservative and exceptionally high among the extremely liberal.[49]

Overall, the United States treats public higher education as a private good to be financed by private sources. In half of the states, students now pay a larger share of their public-college costs than state governments do.[50] Along with reducing tax-dollar support for public higher education, state lawmakers have taken a narrower view of its mission, with many pressuring colleges to focus on job training. In 2015, then Governor Scott Walker of Wisconsin tried to replace language in state law holding that the University of Wisconsin exists "to provide public service and improve the human condition" with language saying its mission is to "meet the state's workforce needs."[51]

In *The University in a Corporate Culture*, Eric Gould, a University of Denver English professor, argues that the culture wars at colleges boil down to a struggle between those who think colleges should be focused on workforce and economic development and those who think colleges should strive to impart much broader knowledge, dealing with culture, ethics, and values, that helps people be better thinkers and live fuller lives.[52] There is, of course, a third possible view, embraced by some college leaders: that these two goals are not mutually exclusive and in fact can be reciprocally reinforcing. That idea may have little traction with corporate leaders and politicians who strongly influence how public colleges seek to meet workforce needs, however. According to Gordon Lafer, an associate professor at the Labor Education and Research Center at the University of Oregon, corporate leaders have come to view mass higher education as "an expensive and unnecessary luxury" and argue that colleges could better meet companies' staffing needs "by targeting funding to specific programs."[53]

Mark G. Yudof, then the president of the University of Minnesota, lamented in 2002 that the previous twenty-five years had brought about the withering of "an extraordinary compact" between state governments and public research universities. That compact had assured public universities taxpayer support in return for keeping tuition low, providing access to students from a full range of economic backgrounds, conducting groundbreaking research, promoting arts and culture, and otherwise helping the community. More recently, however, state governments had cast such universities into "a purgatory of insufficient resources and declining competitiveness."[54] As a result of flat or declining state support, universities have become less accessible to those from modest backgrounds and more financially dependent on private sources of revenue, including donors and students who can pay full fare.

The rising tuitions and low graduation rates at many poorly financed community colleges and nonselective four-year colleges fuel the nation's student loan crisis. People who attend college on borrowed money and then fail to earn a credential that qualifies them for a decent job end up struggling to pay off their loans. Student loan debt has nearly tripled over the past decade and now stands at almost $1.5 trillion.[55] More than one in ten borrowers of student loans ends up defaulting.[56] As of 2016, about eight million borrowers had ceased paying more than $137 million in debt.[57] Most of the growth in default rates is among students who attended community colleges, nonselective four-year colleges, or for-profit schools. Students who enroll in selective four-year colleges tend to graduate with more debt but a much greater likelihood of paying it off.[58]

All these trends in access and affordability have stark consequences for the nation. The United States is losing its edge in terms of educational attainment. It ranks eighth among Organisation for Economic Co-operation and Development nations in terms of bachelor's degree attainment, eleventh in educational attainment at the pre-baccalaureate

level, and eleventh in terms of high school graduation rates.[59] The rate
of increase in our nation's supply of college-educated workers has
not kept up with demand.[60] While we were once the world's leader in
terms of educational attainment, we now face competition from other
developed and developing countries that have made great strides in
creating a highly educated workforce.[61]

It's worrisome to see the United States sinking in terms of relative
educational attainment. But it's downright alarming to see how narrow the pathways to such attainment are, and how deeply stratified
they are by race and class. In upholding the use of race-conscious
admissions by the University of Michigan law school in 2003, U.S.
Supreme Court Justice Sandra Day O'Connor said: "In order to cul-
tivate a set of leaders with legitimacy in the eyes of the citizenry, it is
necessary that the path to leadership be visibly open to talented and
qualified individuals of every race and ethnicity. All members of our
heterogeneous society must have confidence in the openness and integrity of the educational institutions that provide this training."[62]

There's little reason for such confidence anymore. Instead of creating such a diverse leadership class, the current stratification of society
and lack of social mobility are fanning a politics of resentment that
threatens American institutions.

Changing Course Before It's Too Late

"Elite failure and the distrust it has spawned is the most powerful and
least understood aspect of current politics and society," MSNBC host
Christopher Hayes argues in *Twilight of the Elites*. He says, "Across
the ideological divide you find a deep sense of alienation, anger, and
betrayal directed at the elites who run the country," and "it's clear that
we're in the midst of something far grander and more perilous than
just a crisis of government or a crisis of capitalism. We are in the midst
of a broad and devastating crisis of authority."[63]

We might have seen this coming if we had been paying attention.
In embracing meritocracy as a goal, we seemed to have ignored how
the British writer who coined the term—a mashup of Latin and

Greek—characterized meritocracy as a path to ruin. In his futuristic 1958 novel *The Rise of the Meritocracy, 1870–2033*, the sociologist and politician Michael Young depicted a meritocratic Great Britain as a dystopia. In his fictional society, where people's IQ dictated their station in life, the gaps between the haves and have-nots widened as those deemed as having the most "merit" worked to ensure their children would have a similar edge. Those on top felt too entitled to their elevated status to care much about inequality and the misfortune of others, and eventually the downtrodden and supposedly dim rebelled.[64]

Although intended primarily as a satiric critique of the British educational system of Young's time, the book proved prescient in foreshadowing the flaws of the meritocracy that America codifies and promotes today. Our competitive admissions process "feeds a sense of inflated self-esteem and superiority in many students who succeed in gaining admission to highly selective institutions—an attitude that hinders the capacity for empathy and widens the separation between the most and least privileged in society," a 2011 report by admissions experts concluded.[65] "Given that over half of those who attain leadership positions in our society are graduates of the nation's most selective universities and colleges, one effect of this sorting is to diminish the likelihood of those in the most powerful positions having significant interaction with capable people who have emerged from educational or cultural backgrounds different from their own."[66]

That widening gap is apparent in the elite's psychological separation from the poor, affirmed by research such as an experimental study in which students at an elite law school—an institution where ethics are proclaimed to reign supreme—were more likely than the public at large to disregard considerations of fairness and focus on selfish gain in distributing goods.[67] In other experiments, students randomly assigned power within a group proved prone to seize upon negative stereotypes of subordinates as an apparent means of reassuring themselves of their own worthiness.[68] Students and professionals who displayed a social-dominance orientation—or a general, nonegalitarian

preference for the dominance of certain social groups over others—
were less likely to perceive unethical behaviors as such.[69]

This psychosocial gap is also evident in signs of distress among the
economically and socially disenfranchised. In modern America, the
politics of class is closely tied to education as the surest route to economic stability as well as social and economic capital. Ours is a society
based on work: those unable to get or keep jobs for extended periods
are excluded from full participation in American life and disappear
from the mainstream economy, culture, and political system. Jobless-
ness is tied to homelessness, hunger, and poorer health for individuals and their families. In the worst cases, people turn to alternative
economies, cultures, and even extremist ideologies that breed hate
and violence.

Globalization has added an additional stressor to this dynamic mix.
Historically, cultural tensions have existed in the United States between people with cosmopolitan orientations and people with locally
oriented identities.[70] Globalization seems to have given cosmopolitans the upper hand by unleashing technology and trade that threaten
jobs tied to local labor markets while creating new jobs in national
and global labor markets. The new class of managers and professionals that benefits most from this change tends to come from the elite
four-year college system and the research universities, while those
who have depended on the declining local labor market tend to have
less prestigious college degrees or no degree at all. The economic and
political interests of these two groups have diverged, adding a new
dimension to the politics of resentment.

For its part, higher education aims to prepare students for the
stresses of globalization by advancing the intellectual skepticism,
tolerance, civic engagement, and increased secularization that are
defining values of Western academic culture. Universities seek to act
as a training ground, preparing students to carry these practices into
their professional and civic lives.[71] The greater income and financial
security associated with increased educational attainment can serve
as a shield against racism, xenophobia, or other feelings of animosity

toward members of groups perceived as one's economic competitors.[72] People who learned at college how to deal with the various forces that affect them through adulthood feel more in control of their lives. They are less likely to perceive diversity as a threat to their personal autonomy, and therefore are more likely to extend the social and political tolerance that is the hallmark of a functioning democracy.[73] It's perhaps unsurprising, then, that a highly educated populace is highly correlated with democratic governance across the world.[74]

Education has become the foundation of American democracy, but educational inequality is destabilizing the framework and crumbling the façade. As our nation's lack of equal educational opportunity and the resulting loss of social mobility become more evident, it will become increasingly difficult to maintain public belief in the foundational American idea that individualism and equality can be reconciled. The splitting of Americans into distinct individualist or egalitarian camps will bring new, destructive levels of political instability.

In *Why Liberalism Failed*, Patrick J. Deneen said colleges and universities convened a multitude of panels on the 2008 economic collapse, but "one searches in vain for a university president or college leader—especially at the elite echelon—acknowledging that there was deep culpability on the part of their own institutions for our failure and our students' as well." After all, he said, "graduates of the elite colleges led the financial and political institutions responsible for precipitating the economic crisis." Noting that colleges' leaders "readily take credit for Rhodes and Fulbright scholars," he asked: "What of those graduates who helped foster an environment of avarice and schemes of the get-rich-quick? Are we so assured that they did not learn exceedingly well the lessons that they learned in college?"[75]

We had early warning signs that wealth would corrupt colleges' ability to identify and educate a "natural aristocracy" even at the outset, at Jefferson's beloved University of Virginia. Far from being the virtuous, talented gifts from nature to mankind that Jefferson hoped to see educated, the young men who enrolled there during its first two decades often were "the spoiled, self-indulgent scions of Southern plantation owners or prosperous merchants," and many gravitated

there "to lark and laze," according to university records. They gam-
bled, rioted, and even buried a hatchet in the door of the Rotunda.
In what he would call "the most painful event" of his life, an eighty-
two-year-old Jefferson summoned the university's students together
to try to beseech them to behave properly, and then found himself too
choked up to speak.[76]

If American higher education continues where it is headed now, the
outcome is likely to be even more racial and economic segregation,
less social mobility, starker divides between the classes, growing political polarization and extremism, and the continued decline of higher
education and its capacity to bring about needed change. The veritable
religion we've created around merit, with its false notions of equal opportunity, misleads us and blocks the path to progress.

Change begins with taking responsibility. We need to embark on a
new course.

8

COLLEGE FOR ALL

Our higher education system serves this nation poorly at a time when we need an effective system more than ever. Our colleges waste human potential and enormous sums of money. They perpetuate segregation through stratification based on race and class. Our system fails to ensure that people are prepared to earn a living wage in a rapidly changing economy. The situation appears likely to get worse before it gets any better. Financially, higher education is headed for a cliff.

Market forces have led our higher-education system to abandon its historic mission of providing the opportunity that balances our nation's dual commitments to individualism and egalitarianism. The system has tilted toward promoting individualistic competition for wealth, status, and power instead.

To return our higher-education system to its rightful place, we must pull it back from its focus on private interests and compel it to focus more squarely on the common good.

This struggle will be about more than toppling the fetish of selectivity—it will require top-to-bottom reconstruction. Higher education has become far too important in preparing young people for the workforce and for life to allow it to remain structured as a feudal kingdom in which the self-interests of selective institutions drive allocation of resources across the entire system. Other economic sectors have been moving toward outcomes-based standards that focus on quality, value, and transparency to produce efficiencies since the early eighties.[1] That revolution is coming to higher education in the form of demands for transparency and outcomes-based accountability. It is urgently needed: when people choose to go to college, they are making one of the biggest investments of their lives.

As a society, we have largely had a hands-off attitude toward higher education, and we have suffered for it. Weak regulation on the outside and skewed priorities on the inside have resulted in a tiered system of colleges, with rarified educational options more available to the wealthy and connected than to everyone else. The current dysfunction in higher education has been developing for a long time, the result of competing interests that unerringly favor the whims of the few at the expense of the many. Left to their own devices, elite colleges will simply continue to act in their narrow self-interest, and the rest of the system will have no choice but to follow their lead. Higher-education reform should be based on what is best for society, including what is needed to meet the structural needs of our workforce.

In a landmark 1997 essay, the sociologist David F. Labaree described American education as having three goals:

1. *social mobility*, or the preparation of individuals to compete for private material advantages
2. *democratic equality*, or preparation for citizenship
3. *social efficiency*, or training for active participation in the economy

Two of the goals—democratic equality and social efficiency—are based on the idea that education is a public good. The third goal, social mobility, stems from the idea that education represents a private good. "From the perspective of democratic equality, schools should make republicans; from the perspective of social efficiency, they should make workers; but from the perspective of social mobility, they should make winners," Labaree wrote.[2]

Tension between these goals can cause elements of the educational system to work against each other, undermining its effectiveness. For example, those interested mainly in workforce preparation perceive a waste of resources in colleges' awarding of advanced degrees in liberal arts fields that are not in high demand among employers, even if those degrees advance knowledge and forms of human expression. The never-ending race for social status encourages sharp-elbowed competition for unequal educational opportunities rather than ensuring we're meeting the needs of the broader economy or teaching concern for the common good.

Advocates of democratic equality often reject the idea that education's chief purpose should be to prepare people for work or to determine who will rise to positions of wealth and power.[3] Rather than acting as a further sifting device, they argue, higher education ought to benefit all of society, not just part of it.

Education is uniquely suited to mend divisions in society because education is our social glue. There exists near-consensus across the political spectrum that learning is valuable. Red, blue, and purple voters typically agree that education effectively equips people to deal with economic change and represents the fairest way to allocate opportunity and encourage upward mobility. This faith in education rests firmly on our individualistic cultural biases. We rely on education as the arbiter of economic opportunity because, in theory, education allows us to expand merit-based opportunity without surrendering individual responsibility.

Education *seems* fair. After all, each of us has to do our own homework to achieve the grades and test scores that get us into college and in line for good jobs. The education consensus complements other key aspects of American life, such as an open economy and limited government intervention in personal freedoms. It has become the nation's preferred way to cope with the economic instability that comes with runaway world markets while minimizing the risk of the individual dependency of the welfare state.

More than that, Americans treat education as a fundamental right, even though the U.S. Supreme Court has declared that there is no constitutional right to education.[4] Most state constitutions mention education as an obligation that the state holds toward its residents.[5] Every state requires students to attend some form of school, usually until at least age sixteen.[6]

But we are squandering that consensus in a race-to-the-bottom struggle that treats higher education primarily as a consumer good that confers social advantage. The perceived meritocracy that arose to facilitate social mobility has elevated the pursuit of credentials over the acquisition of knowledge.[7] In reality, we have a higher-education system that pays lip service to social mobility and meritocracy but does not offer much of either.

It doesn't have to be that way—but systemic change will require systemic reform.

Reform at the Top

For necessary changes to be adopted—and for them to stick—we'll need a leadership class less dominated by those who have lived lives of privilege and more attuned to the needs of society as a whole. Creating that leadership class will require us to put pressure to reform on the selective colleges that function as the system's gatekeepers.

It's widely believed that the most selective colleges take the best of the best, without regard to privilege, and give these students a straight shot to the top. In fact, that's the story that these colleges tell us about themselves. But it isn't true—more than half of the students attending the country's most selective colleges were not among the top scorers on the SAT. The students who got in despite their lesser credentials were disproportionately affluent.[8] So, privilege begets privilege. Given that selective colleges historically produce a large share of this nation's leadership class, this country's leaders won't look like America unless we ensure that elite institutions admit students from all racial, ethnic, and economic backgrounds.

Selectivity has been the keystone that locks in the race- and class-based disparities throughout our higher-education system—and beyond. The fact that 60 percent of the students in the top two hundred colleges come from the top quartile of family socioeconomic status (SES) stands as clear evidence of that.[9] And it's not just about preparation: among graduating high school students who scored above 1250 on the SAT, 52 percent of those who are affluent go on to attend a selective college, compared to 38 percent of those from the bottom three socioeconomic quartiles.[10]

We currently set aside seats in the top colleges for students who already have the most advantages—the equivalent of reserving beds in the best hospitals for the healthiest people. As a result, access to college is increasingly concentrated among families with college-educated parents and high wages, and higher education has become a passive participant in a system that reproduces economic and cultural elites.

Fortunately, we have access to policy levers that can affect the operation of these colleges. Worth considering are proposals to tax wealthy colleges' endowments or limit public investments in higher education to educational purposes that serve all of society, which will force colleges to seek to honor their broader commitments.

Using such policy levers, we need to reform how selective colleges admit students to ensure that they are enrolling enough young people from modest backgrounds—those who have been shown by research to derive much more benefit from attending such institutions than the children of wealthy families.[11] Essentially, we need to change who we define as deserving, qualified, and having potential. Looking more favorably upon striving students who have overcome disadvantage would be a natural step for a culture interested not just in academic rank but also in how far people have traveled to get where they are.

A separate admissions practice, colleges' recruitment of applicants known to have virtually no chance of acceptance, inarguably needs to end. This practice artificially inflates the number of applicants that colleges reject so those colleges appear to be more selective. It's a sham that violates consumer trust every bit as much as a counterfeit good or a rigged lottery. The damage extends well beyond wasted time and application fees. "Raising the hopes of students only to exploit them in this way does a disservice to students beyond the initial disappointment of being denied admission; for some it could create a sense of alienation that inhibits the inspiration to attend any university or college," says a report arising from a 2011 meeting of admissions experts at the University of Southern California.[12]

Ending these practices would be important advances. Even so, while reforms at elite colleges would have a trickle-down effect likely to influence all of higher education, the elite colleges cannot be the sole focus of reform efforts. The impulse to tear down elites and their hierarches, a factor in American politics since our nation's founding, only goes so far. Focusing solely on who gets into top-tier colleges distracts attention from huge problems throughout higher education and risks validating and encouraging the obsession with elite status that has created much of the mess we're in. There isn't enough capacity or money in elite higher education to change the entire postsecondary system. Besides, ordinary colleges with low graduation rates have a lot more room for improvement than selective colleges, where graduation rates already stand above 80 percent.[13]

If we want to increase access, quality, completion, and upward mobility in higher education, we'll get a lot more bang for our buck with greater investments in community colleges and nonselective four-year colleges. After all, such institutions serve about eight out of every ten students, operate efficiently out of necessity, and don't waste money chasing prestige.[14]

A Broader Reform Agenda

Our educational institutions, economic institutions, and government all are part of a larger system. That system functions organically, like the human body, rather than mechanistically, like a car engine. Each part depends on the others, and a change to one part eventually gets rejected if it does not bring change to the whole. Any effort to reform higher education must be based on a realistic assessment of what our culture, political system, and economy need. Ultimately, we need to improve efficiency across the entire education system if we are going to render racial and economic justice affordable.

As the economic importance of a college education has grown, so too has the competition for seats. Most of the historic rise in economic inequality since the early 1980s can be traced to differences in access to postsecondary programs with labor-market value.[15] Our failure to update the interconnections between our education system, our economy, and our government lies at the heart of racial and class-based inequalities in higher education.

We will need to make changes to the overall system, and we can get started by identifying the components that most need to be fixed or replaced. For example, we need to place more emphasis on programs of study rather than on colleges; link K–12 education, higher education, and the workforce; and revamp college and career counseling to ease the transition from youth dependency to independent adulthood. We should make fourteen years of schooling the universal standard, rather than the present twelve.[16]

At the same time, treating education as a panacea would be a mistake. Our increasing reliance on education in America sometimes borders on fundamentalism—the tiresome notion that the remedy for every economic and social problem lies in the mantra: education, education, education! Such a belief allows the nation's elites to offer education bromides instead of real remedies on hard issues like trade, unemployment, access to pensions and healthcare, immigration, race, and income dispersion. There exists a huge vacuum in the nation's economic and social policy that education alone cannot fill.

Moreover, we need to come to terms with the fact that most of the costs of our educational failures are absorbed by those with the fewest opportunities. We always invest our next education dollar in those who are already ahead in the education race, and that practice overwhelmingly favors people who are white and affluent. The American system sorts aggressively from cradle to grave, with the largest investments in human capital going to those who already have the most resources throughout the life cycle. The relationship between American education and labor markets is brutally unforgiving and unfair, and it's a key driver in the American inequality machine. In a society in which people start out unequal, attainment among students at the elementary and secondary levels, as measured by test scores and grades, has become a dodge, a means of avoiding the pressing need to face racial and class inequality.

Balancing Equality and Choice

The American postsecondary system increasingly has become a dual system of economically and racially separate and unequal tracks that perpetuate the intergenerational reproduction of privilege.[17] Polarization by class and race in the top tiers of the nation's selective colleges has become the capstone for parallel inequality in the K–12 system and the complex economic and social mechanisms that create it. The postsecondary system mimics and magnifies the inequality it inherits from the K–12 system and then projects this inequality into labor markets. Disproportionate labor-market successes allow advantaged college graduates to buy the right house in the right neighborhood with the right K–12 schools that lead to the right colleges, beginning the self-sustaining intergenerational process anew.

Separate and unequal pathways in higher education matter because money matters. The 468 most selective colleges spend anywhere from two to nearly five times as much per student as open-access colleges. Higher spending by the most selective colleges leads to higher graduation rates, greater access to graduate and professional schools, and better economic outcomes in the labor market. The completion rate for the most-selective four-year colleges is 82 percent, compared with 49 percent for two- and four-year open-access colleges. These financially starved open-access two- and four-year colleges account for virtually all of the increase in both college dropout rates and the exorbitant time students spend in college earning a degree.[18]

While outcomes need to be more equal across higher education, higher education should not assume a one-size-fits-all approach. Students should have more, not fewer, choices, as long as economic outcomes are transparent and there are no dead ends or barriers to further education. There's value to both certificates in automotive repair and doctorates in history. The problem is that too many people

end up stuck in programs that don't match their potential and interests, through a lack of sufficient guidance or through bias on the part
of those handling placement decisions. We can help students find
their way to the right educational path by making it easier for them
to transfer between academic programs or colleges. That will take
slashing red tape. In addition, we need to discourage colleges from
arbitrarily imposing demands for prerequisites and refusing to honor
credits earned elsewhere.

Tracking within higher education has intensified in recent decades
as a result of political neglect. Underlying the development have been
two assumptions: that students' academic potential is determined by
innate ability as measured by standardized tests, and that public investments in higher education pay off most when routed toward those
with the highest test scores. We must reject both assumptions to have
a higher-education system that sustains our economy and our democratic form of government.

In order to achieve a higher-education system that comes closer to
this vision, we make several recommendations.

End Our Obsessive Love Affair with the SAT and ACT

The majority of selective colleges give far more weight to standardized
admissions test scores than is justified. For students, small variances
in SAT or ACT scores can mean the difference between getting admitted or being rejected by their school of choice. For colleges, small
fluctuations in their entering students' SAT or ACT scores can mean
climbing or falling in the rankings. Neither outcome reflects what we
know about the accuracy and reliability of the tests.

In a cutting 2014 essay, Leon Botstein, the president of Bard College, characterized the SAT not as an objective measure of students'
ability to succeed, but simply as an easy means for selective colleges to
sort through and reject applicants. "The victim in this unholy alliance
between the College Board (a profit-making business masquerading
as a not-for-profit educational institution serving the public good)

and our elite institutions of higher education are students and our nation's educational standards," he wrote. "The elite institutions have willingly supported an alliance with the College Board to make their own lives easier, and we Americans seem to have accepted this owing to our misplaced love affair with standardized testing and rankings as the proper means to ensure educational excellence."[19]

Among students in the upper half of the SAT or ACT test score distribution, minor score variations matter little when it comes to predicting graduation rates or career success. Students at selective colleges with an SAT score of 1000–1099 have a 79 percent graduation rate, only 6 percentage points lower than that for the 85 percent of students with an SAT score of 1200 or above.[20] The failure of anyone who scores above average on the SAT or ACT is unacceptable, and colleges have tremendous control over whether such students do actually drop out.

A Georgetown University Center on Education and the Workforce preliminary analysis of the data examining the link between standardized admission test scores and career success shows that, in the upper half of the score distribution, SAT score differentials of 100 or even 200 points do little to predict differences in later earnings or access to occupations.[21] At the end of the day, among these qualified students, enrollment in a selective institution has more bearing on their graduation rates than does variation in their admissions test scores.

Colleges' reliance on SAT and ACT scores hinders efforts to improve elementary and secondary schools because the tests have no connection with teaching and learning in the K–12 systems. Tests should be used as diagnostic tools to enhance access to good teaching and learning, not as racial and class-based barriers to entry.

The standards-based K–12 education reform movement emphasizes the development of core academic knowledge throughout the population, not the identification of innate aptitude among a select few. A stronger reliance on achievement tests than on tests that supposedly measure general aptitude would clarify the connection between college and K–12 standards-based teaching and learning, representing a step toward a comprehensive K–16 accountability system. College admissions testing would no longer be a high-stakes game of spotting trick questions in the SAT or ACT while beating the clock. The time that students spend on preparing for the SAT and ACT would be better spent on meaningful academic activities, and the money parents spend on test prep could go toward other needs, like paying college tuition.[22] Although grading standards differ across high schools, students' cumulative grade point averages in academic subjects have repeatedly been proven by researchers to be the best overall predictor of student performance in college.[23]

Colleges consider SAT and ACT scores not just in admissions, but also in recruitment, and here even minor shifts in which test they rely upon will help them identify more diamonds in the rough. A 2010 study found that high-ability, low-income high school students are disproportionately concentrated in several Midwestern states, where most students take the ACT. Yet many selective colleges continue to focus their recruitment efforts on students in their own region who have high SAT scores, and therefore end up scrapping over the same small coastal pools of low-income students who score well.[24]

Halt Legacy Admissions

We must work to deter selective colleges from relying on admissions criteria that measure privilege more than true potential, and from compounding the effects of past advantage by favoring applicants who are legacies—the offspring of alumni—or the children of administrators or faculty members, or tied to rich donors and powerful politicians.[25] Transparency, integrity, and fairness should be the guiding principles of selective colleges' admissions processes, which would mean eradicating admissions practices that are secretive, dishonest, and biased.

To be sure, when it comes to legacy admissions, there are good arguments on both sides of the debate. Defenders of legacy admissions can point to the "bonds of community" that are forged when multiple generations of the same family are affiliated with a school.[26] But on balance, the costs outweigh the gains. Likewise, there is no good reason to favor the children of donors. Current practice allows wealthy people to make large payments to a college to obtain something of value—the admission of an applicant with borderline qualifications—and then write off the money exchanged as a charitable donation. Private nonprofit colleges and universities should be expected to undergo reviews of their tax-exempt status similar to the reviews that nonprofit hospitals undergo every three years.[27] They should be expected to document the benefits they provide to the community, report how many of their students are low-income or members of other disadvantaged groups, and fully describe what institutional support such students receive.

Preferences for legacy applicants are worth challenging because they hinder efforts to remedy the effects of past racial discrimination, result in the admission of less-qualified students, and enable certain families to dominate colleges to which the broader public expects fair access.[28] The chief institutional rationale for legacy preferences—that they result in increased alumni giving—has been challenged by research showing that they actually produce little overall gain in contributions. The perceived connection between such preferences and alumni giving stems mainly from how they enable colleges to over-select the children of wealthy parents.[29] As Richard Kahlenberg, a senior fellow at the Century Foundation, has noted, Internal Revenue Service regulations put colleges that use legacy preferences in a Catch-22: "Either donations are not linked to legacy preferences, in which case the fundamental rationale for ancestry discrimination is flawed; or giving is linked to legacy preferences, in which case donations should not be tax deductible."[30]

Blatant preferences for applicants based solely on power and money trigger huge controversies, and almost always end up being abandoned whenever they are exposed. Preferences for recruited athletes are a subject worthy of an entire book, but abuses in this area—as well as others mentioned here—can be minimized through the establishment of firewalls that protect admissions offices from interference from other administrative units, including those in charge of athletics, development and fundraising, alumni relations, government relations, and employee relations. After the University of Illinois at Urbana-Champaign was busted in 2009 for operating a "shadow admissions system" favoring applicants connected to state politicians and its own trustees, the university adopted a policy requiring admissions officials to track all inquiries by anyone other than an applicant, parent or guardian, or high school counselor.[31]

New ethics rules would fly in the face of recent developments in the admissions profession, whose primary association deleted parts of its ethics code in 2019 in response to various court decisions indicating that practices that suppress competition for students violate antitrust laws.[32] But in the end, the widespread adoption of stricter ethics policies would help expose interference in admissions decisions and be a good start to reforming admissions practices.

Admittedly, eliminating legacy preferences would result in only small changes in the overall composition of student bodies at selective institutions. Nonetheless, it would be a significant symbolic victory for advocates of social mobility, and would help rebuild trust in higher education among the general populace.[33]

Require Colleges to Admit a Minimum Percentage of Low-Income Students

While it is unrealistic to expect elite nonprofit colleges and universities to educate all low-income and disadvantaged students, they can certainly do more than what they are currently doing. There are 240,000 high-achieving low-income high school graduates who could succeed in a selective college or university, but the majority of them do not get the chance to attend selective institutions.[34] Focusing on low-income high achievers would help elite colleges balance recognizing merit with providing students an opportunity for upward mobility.

Encouraging race and class diversity by mandating that every college enroll at least 20 percent Pell Grant recipients would leave the prestige queue in place but would give 72,000 additional Pell students a chance to attend a high-spending selective college.[35] More than one-third of undergraduates receive federal Pell Grants, which help low-income students pay for tuition and other college costs.[36] But these students are unequally distributed across higher education. At more than half of all colleges and universities, more than 50 percent of all undergraduates receive Pell Grants. These colleges are primarily community colleges, for-profit colleges, and regional public universities. Meanwhile, at about one-third of the nation's five hundred most selective colleges, less than 20 percent of students receive Pell Grants. Some colleges have student bodies in which less than 7 percent of students are Pell Grant recipients. Allowing more Pell Grant recipients into selective colleges would make these colleges more diverse not only by class, but also by race. More than half of Pell Grant recipients are non-white.[37]

Elite private colleges have pushed back against such ideas by saying that Pell Grant recipients are less likely to be qualified to meet their stringent admissions requirements. However, there are more than enough Pell Grant recipients who scored above the median on the SAT for all students at selective colleges (1120 or higher) to increase their presence at those colleges without any decrease in student quality. Moreover, these private colleges can easily afford to meet the financial aid needs of these low-income students. While colleges claim they can't afford to give full scholarships to low-income students, the "most competitive" have an average endowment of $1.2 billion and an average annual budget surplus of $139 million.[38] Elite colleges have the means to make change, they just lack the will.

Redirect Financial Aid

Far too large a share of overall spending on student financial assistance is squandered on "merit-based" aid intended to entice affluent students to attend public colleges in their own state or sweeten the deal for affluent families considering a private college.

There's no good reason for the federal government and the states to allow public dollars to be channeled toward students who don't need the money. It would be far more productive to offer more need-based financial aid so that disadvantaged students are better able to afford the colleges that admit them. A policy of offering publicly financed assistance only to the students who need it would use public dollars for a public good: higher graduation rates among students who are not affluent.

Compared to public colleges, private colleges are less dependent on public funds and therefore would retain more freedom to choose how they spend their financial aid dollars. We can make appeals to their morality and concern for the common good, but the reality is that only the wealthiest private colleges, with long histories and huge endowments, can afford to be much more generous in their awards of need-based aid. The rest feel pressure to enroll enough tuition-paying students to finance their operations. It is only after meeting the bottom line that they grapple with whether to award full scholarships to low-income students.[39]

It's worth noting, however, that much of this scarcity is artificial, the result of colleges using merit aid and other forms of tuition discounts to try to outbid each other for affluent students. As the education researchers Donald Hossler and David Kalsbeek have noted, higher-education associations have been "increasingly calling for reductions in the so-called merit aid arms race," and senior enrollment officials are increasingly realizing that competing via merit aid becomes costlier and less effective when colleges counter each other's offers.[40] To the extent that they can do so without violating antitrust laws, colleges should call off the bidding wars and free up financial aid for students who can't enroll without it. Requiring greater transparency from colleges about the socioeconomic backgrounds of their students and the distribution of their aid dollars will empower foundations and individuals who philanthropically support higher education to make more-informed decisions about which institutions are worthy of their contributions.[41]

Because selective colleges simply lack enough seats to serve all of the deserving less-advantaged students they currently exclude, we need to bring more quality programs, and the money to pay for them, to the community colleges and less-selective four-year colleges where the least-advantaged American postsecondary students are currently enrolled. We need an "all-hands-on-deck" effort to improve quality that acknowledges the hard work already being done at these institutions and that significantly expands efforts that yield demonstrable improvements. Community colleges and less-selective four-year colleges are truly underresourced, and larger investments will be required to improve the work they do for students at the margins.

Elementary and secondary education must be part of this discussion. The age of eighteen is awfully late in the game to take stock of a person's preparation for college. At the same time, it is too early for most students to commit to a lifetime career track. Higher education needs to take a greater interest in quality and equity in education from preschool onward, overhauling teacher training and promoting public awareness of what success in college requires. High school leaders continue to claim to make students "college and career ready," but there is no direct relationship between the basics learned in high school and careers, and almost half of high school sophomores don't go on to earn a degree or certificate by the age of twenty-six.[42] Federal and state officials need to be doing more to ensure universal access to a college preparatory curriculum—for example, by requiring and financing the coursework needed for college entry.

To be clear, we are not arguing for a centralized, European-style system. It's apparent, however, that we've moved into a period in which our laissez-faire, market-driven system has gone from an advantage to a mixed blessing.

Reward "Strivers"

American folklore and family lore is replete with inspiring stories of people who work hard and succeed despite long odds. Their stories are all variations on the American Dream: that if you work hard and take advantage of opportunities—presumed to be available to everyone—you can succeed.

Every college applicant pool includes young people who have overcome obstacles to have much better academic profiles than might be expected given their circumstances. Let's say a young person who grew up disadvantaged in just about every respect, who generally might be expected to have an SAT score of about 550 out of 1600, instead submits a score of 1050. Education researchers call these people "strivers," and have found that the traits that have enabled them to beat the odds, such as resilience and strong work ethic, tend to serve them well in the face of challenges at college.[43] But at most selective colleges, a student with a score of 1050 would be quickly dismissed from consideration for admission.

Selective colleges and universities can reward character and promote upward mobility by considering the differences between an applicant's grades, test scores, and other qualifications and the qualifications expected of those with their background. They should look for information shedding light on any obstacles faced by applicants, and consider it in assessing applicants' merits. A 2014 experiment in which admissions officers considered fictitious applicants found that those who had been given rich background information about fictitious applicants' high schools were more willing to recommend the admission of students from low-income backgrounds. The problem is that colleges seldom systemically gather such information.[44]

Personal qualities can predict college success.[45] Increasing enrollments of disadvantaged students who have beaten the odds represents one of the easiest ways to increase diversity at selective colleges.

Strike the Right Balance Between Class- and Race-Based Affirmative Action

The most controversial form of affirmative action in higher education—the granting of extra consideration and a degree of preference to applicants who are black, Latino, or Native American—has been deeply divisive and been used as a wedge issue to pit poor and working-class whites against members of racial and ethnic minority groups. Supporters of such admissions policies are correct to point toward continuing racial biases and the general benefits of diversity, but they tend to overstate the benefits as presently practiced in higher education and, in many cases, to feel threatened by and seek to squelch discussions of worthy alternatives.[46]

The civil rights theorist Lani Guinier has said that such policies primarily benefit the children of immigrants or upper-middle-class parents, and produce "cosmetic diversity" that enables higher-education institutions to dodge discussions of deeper systemic problems.[47] More than two out of five of the nation's Latino residents and nearly one in five of its black residents live in states where voters or lawmakers have banned public colleges from granting preference to applicants based on race or ethnicity.[48] Shifts in the ideological composition of the U.S. Supreme Court under President Donald Trump have made it much likelier that those who have long sought a ruling striking down the use of such preferences as discriminatory will finally prevail.

The diversity produced by race- and ethnicity-conscious admissions policies papers over huge systemic problems such as the overheated competition for seats at selective public colleges. Dealing with such problems will require systemic responses, such as demanding that such colleges pull back from their efforts to one-up each other in terms of their entering classes' average SAT scores.[49]

On the whole, getting the enrollments of selective colleges to better reflect the nation's population will require a major overhaul of college admissions policies and a drastic reduction of inequities in our nation's public schools. In the meantime, there's no getting around the fact that admission test scores reflect gaps associated with race and ethnicity. In part, that's because of racial differences in socioeconomic status. Largely as a result of historic oppression that has hindered African Americans from accumulating property and passing it on to their children, median household wealth for African Americans is one-tenth the median household wealth for whites.[50] At the same time, the disadvantages associated with racial disparities persist even as African American incomes rise: racial gaps in SAT scores are evident at every level of family income, and test scores correlate more closely to family income for black students than they do for white students.[51] It is almost impossible to overcome deeply entrenched racial advantages without admissions policies that specifically consider race.

Race-conscious admissions policies actually can be seen as an element of systemic change. After all, the black and Latino students who attend selective colleges have a graduation rate of 81 percent, nearly as high as the 86 percent graduation rate for such institutions' white students.[52] While pulling highly qualified minority and low-income students up from open-access colleges into selective public colleges may marginally reduce graduation rates at the selective publics, it can be expected to substantially increase system-wide graduation rates because disadvantaged students graduate at higher rates at selective colleges than they do at nonselective schools.[53]

It's important to keep in mind that "affirmative action" extends well beyond preferences based on race and ethnicity, and covers a wide array of policies that are much less controversial. Selective colleges can substantially increase minority enrollments by offering admission to students at the top of their class in heavily minority high schools, by simultaneously expanding and focusing their efforts to recruit minority students through the use of computer-assisted analysis of neighborhood and school demographics, by expanding outreach to underserved schools with the help of their alumni networks, and by awarding a greater share of their financial aid based on need rather than merit.

Class-based affirmative action stands relatively immune to the sorts of legal challenges based on federal anti-discrimination laws that have bedeviled affirmative action based on ethnicity or race. Moreover, it's popular. In a 2016 Gallup poll, 61 percent of respondents indicated that "family economic circumstances" should play a role in admissions decisions, and 83 percent of respondents to a 2018 survey by the public broadcasting station WGBH said that "overcoming hardships such as poverty or health problems" should be a consideration in admissions.[54] However, our top colleges are better at focusing on race-based rather than class-based diversity. Most reserve their preferential treatment based on low socioeconomic status largely for minority students.[55]

If the Supreme Court ultimately strikes down college admissions offices' use of admissions preferences based on race or ethnicity, class-based affirmative action preferences won't suffice to replace them. But class-based admissions preferences would reduce the need to engage in more controversial admissions practices. And it would remedy the much starker underrepresentation of low-income students on selective colleges' campuses.[56]

Measure College Outcomes Rather Than Inputs

Across industries, the new networks of production and service delivery tend to be driven by measured performance standards more focused on outcomes than on inputs or reputational value. Everything from baseball players' performance to what people learn and earn based on their college major can be measured by effect. But in higher education, we are a long way from applying such outcomes-based measures to organization and governance.

The obsession with rankings and prestige has rendered Americans far too focused on the inputs of higher-education institutions, such as the academic profiles of entering classes and how much colleges pay faculty members or spend per student. Colleges can easily inflate supposed measures of their quality simply by catering to the wealthy and becoming more exclusive. Our current accountability system relies on the demonstrably flawed self-regulating mechanism of accreditation, which has been designed to set structural and process standards for colleges and provide feedback on how well colleges are meeting them. Accreditation does little more than rubber stamp institutions' eligibility for federal funding, and does little to inform students and their families about educational quality.[57]

We can begin changing the system by measuring the output of higher education in terms of value and quality: how much colleges teach, how well their students learn, and the value colleges add in terms of their students' knowledge, critical thinking skills, likelihood of graduating, and ability to land a good job.[58] The measurement of outcomes in themselves helps us identify weak and underfinanced parts of the system. The measurement of outcomes defined in added-value terms, on the other hand, recognizes that colleges do not have the same resources and helps us identify effective programs. If we wish to push colleges to effectively educate all of their students, we must hold them accountable based on outcome measures that take into account a student's expected graduation and earnings compared to what actually happens.[59] A move toward this type of transparency focused on outcomes would compel us to do more to help the many qualified but disadvantaged students who never make it through college or stop their educations with a degree well below their potential.

Shifting the Focus from Institutions to Programs

We need to pressure colleges to make information about student outcomes publicly available so that students and their families can make informed decisions. It should be broken down not just by institutions but by programs. The programs that students study are increasingly the fundamental vehicles that transmit economic value, and students' majors have been shown to play a much greater role than the college attended in determining their future success and earnings.[60] Colleges should not be allowed to blow smoke by claiming that specific programs offer students value based solely on the average labor-market performance of all graduates (as the original College Scorecard did) or based on the broad benefits of college education in general.

Higher education has traditionally resisted the kind of outcomes-based testing that is common in K–12, but such testing would be a game-changer. Only when we shift from prestige based on college inputs to objective measures of college outcomes will we have a better sense of the changes we need to make in how colleges are governed, financed, and held accountable.

In structuring our higher-education system as a tower with ascending levels of prestige, we have become fixated on institutions as key to success. But this is a myopic approach. More earnings variation now occurs within degrees than across education levels.[61] That's why, ultimately, outcomes-based evaluation of higher education needs to be driven down to the level of programs and fields of study. Currently, our focus remains on institutions, not on what students are actually studying. At the undergraduate level, students apply to colleges, not necessarily to college programs. Our most closely followed ranking systems evaluate the best colleges in America and, only rarely, the very best programs in certain fields. On the whole, we have only a vague sense of what goes into making a good college education. We hope for the best and write a big check.

In order to move the system forward, we need to set learning and earning standards at the program level, based on what students need to know to succeed in a postindustrial and globalized economy, culture, and political system. That will involve setting standards for job training, and also for broadening liberal arts curriculums that prepare people for full inclusion in the culture and polity.[62] Striking the right balance between general education and career-specific education is crucial. Students cannot fully flourish if they do not attain economic self-sufficiency in our capitalist economy—it's hard to be involved in the life of the republic while living under a bridge.[63] At the same time, the best evidence indicates that the classic liberal arts education is one of our most effective tools for encouraging republican values and discouraging intolerance and authoritarianism.[64]

Students should be made aware that they will likely do better in the labor market if they combine what they learn in general education courses with study in specific fields designed toward labor-market outcomes. Such an approach will not mean the end of the humanities and the liberal arts, but may change the way we think about them. Degrees in the liberal arts were once the most common on college campuses, but they now constitute only 9 percent of all awarded bachelor's degrees.[65] Nonetheless, the humanities and liberal arts play an important role in teaching students critical thinking, self-reflection, creativity, empathy, tolerance, and communications skills—qualities that are useful in the full spectrum of one's life, including professional, personal, and civic pursuits.[66] Courses in such fields should remain a major part of general education, and students should remain free to place one foot in them through a double major, or to major solely in them if they're confident they'll pursue graduate education.

In order to motivate change, we need to ask who benefits from current practice. The institution-based method for sorting higher education is very convenient for admissions decisions, fundraising, motivating alumni, selling sweatshirts, and, especially, ginning up interest in intercollegiate athletics. But it speaks very little to the main reason most people go to college: to get a degree that will help them get a job. The careers people hope to attain by attending college begin with what they major in, not so much with where they earn their degrees. Too often, elite colleges ignore this.

Program-level information is vital to increasing the transparency of higher education, and it will help consumers make better decisions about their postsecondary pathways.

This new approach is needed for a number of reasons:

- **Most college students already regret their choices.** If they could do it all over again, 51 percent would change their degree type, institution, or major, according to the results of a 2017 Gallup Poll.[67] These regrets were influenced by a number of factors, but one was lack of information about a degree and the careers it would lead to.

- **Investing in a college degree is not as straightforward as it seems.** Many one-year technical certificates and even non-credit programs outperform a substantial share of four-year degrees, at least when it comes to completers' earnings. Almost a third of associate's degree holders make more than the average bachelor's degree recipient.[68] Major makes a difference, too: a person with a bachelor of science degree in petroleum engineering will make $3.3 million more in a lifetime than the holder of a bachelor of arts in elementary education (despite society's protestations that this reality reflects skewed priorities).[69] And more than 40 percent of bachelor's degree holders will outperform the average graduate degree holder in earnings.[70] All of this attests to the importance of field of study. But, to complicate matters even further, many people with degrees don't end up working in their field of study anyway. In some degreed fields—for example, education, psychology, and

many of the humanities—it's best financially to work out of
field, especially if you don't go to graduate school. Nevertheless, within the majority of fields, a higher degree will outperform a lower-level award. If you find this confusing, imagine
how it must strike the majority of students entering college
at eighteen years old with no credible information or decent
counseling to guide their decisions.[71]

- **The variety of postsecondary programs and credentials
  has become too vast for consumers to comprehend and
  evaluate.** Postsecondary programs of study more than quin-
  tupled from 1985 to 2010, from 410 to 2,260. Since 1950, the
  number of colleges and universities has more than doubled,
  the number of college students has increased tenfold, and the
  number of occupations recognized in government statistics
  has tripled to more than 800.[72] The Credential Engine, a nonprofit clearinghouse of information about credentials and
  employer requirements, estimates that there are more than
  730,000 unique program, institution, and award combinations in the United States.[73] Colleges are offering a blizzard
  of degrees, certificates, licenses, certifications, badges, and
  other micro-credentials, all of which purport to qualify the
  recipients to enter an occupation. But who really knows what
  they all mean?

- **Shifting transparency and accountability to the program
  level will trigger longer-term market-based reforms of
  institutional finances.** Program-level information would
  unbundle institutional spending, tighten the connection between learning and earning, encourage competition among
  program providers, and foster specialization. These dynamic
  market forces would move us away from the current cafeteria
  system, in which every college has to offer every program to be
  competitive. Accreditation based on economic outcomes can
  rejuvenate current practices gone stale. Finally, program-level
  information on employment and earnings, aggregated and
  made available to the public, would encourage competition

among providers to develop counseling tools for institutions
and families.

Treat High School, College, and Careers as One System

The 1983 release of *A Nation at Risk* marked recognition that our
K–12 education system was having trouble keeping up with changes
in the economy. The real need for younger Americans is not K–12
reform by itself, or higher education reform by itself, or more access
to middle-class careers by itself. Instead, it's the need to prepare for
the key rite of passage in front of them—the transition from youth
dependency to adult independence. And that transition has become
longer. While young adults once attained median earnings at an average age of twenty-six, they now reach that milestone well beyond the
age of thirty.[74] As the path to adult independence has been drawn out,
traveling it has become more and more expensive and difficult.

Supporting this transition from youth dependency to adult
independence—an obvious task of our education system—requires
that we take on the challenge of connecting education to careers. This
means bringing together the isolated silos of American education,
government, and employers. We need to take an all-one-system perspective, focusing especially on students' journey from middle school
through college and then into early careers.

Sadly, it is not clear that the current system of educational governance, financing, and policy is up to the task. For its part, we suggest
that higher-education management take inspiration from modern
systems of industrial organization that disregard institutional silos
and make connections through information systems directly accessible to consumers. These networked information systems could help
colleges and universities show students the way, with exits and on-
ramps marked by clear outcome standards along personalized education and career pathways with no dead ends. The ultimate goal in
building education and career pathways is to constantly facilitate the
transparent and free flow of students, financial support, educational

programs, internships, and measured performance across institutional boundaries.[75]

Make 14 the New 12

Throughout our nation's history, we've repeatedly raised the bar in defining how much education Americans need. Students are no longer assured a living wage with just a high school education. The nation needs to face the fact that people now need at least two years of college to have access to economic opportunity in a complex modern society. It's time to make the leap and think of two years of college the same way we once thought about four years of high school: as the minimum amount of education that all Americans should receive at government expense. We need to embark on a reform drive with the slogan "14 is the new 12."

As a political argument, "14 is the new 12" represents a middle ground. It's the political sweet spot between the abandoned practice of offering a vocational track in public high schools and the recent calls for free access to four years of college, which essentially ask less-advantaged segments of the population with less access to four-year colleges to subsidize the college educations of children of the upper-middle class. It eliminates the scourge of tracking because the high school degree no longer represents the final destination, and it provides an on-ramp to the bachelor's degree. A K–14 system would make it likelier that a clear majority of Americans would be college or career ready.

This suggested policy change honors the spirit of several state-court decisions requiring public schools to provide an "adequate" education, defined as the minimum necessary to prepare students for employment and citizenship at that point in time. At least seventeen states now offer tuition-free access to two-year college programs to at least some of their residents. Some municipalities have implemented similar plans.[76] Many of these programs, however, exclude part-time or returning adult students, as well as those who cannot meet minimum academic requirements or have family incomes above a certain level.[77]

Meanwhile, every year at least 500,000 American students graduate in the top half of their high school class without ever going on to earn a postsecondary credential. The nation misses out on a total of $400 billion in annual income that these students would have earned with a college education, representing tremendous lost potential for our economy and society.[78] Getting policymakers to regard two years of college as essential will inspire efforts to patch the holes in our talent pipeline.

Train and Empower Counselors

An empowered professional cadre of education and career counselors, equipped with a modern information system, remains the missing link between high schools, college, and careers. Ultimately, these counselors will need to become equipped with emerging program-level and student-level data, the kernel of which is already built into the nation's new network of State Longitudinal Data Systems, many of which track students from high school and college into jobs and careers. The counseling system, and the dedicated professionals who run it, is the logical choice for translating the emerging transparency in program-level value to students' parents and to regulators.

But these professionals will need to be empowered externally to play this role. That's because if counselors play their role well, they will be a threat to the existing power structure within and between both secondary and postsecondary institutions by putting students' needs over the sometimes conflicting needs of institutions. Unless counselors have the power to promote the interests of the students over the priorities set by the academic deans and the institutional leadership, student interests will continue to be sublimated to institutional and faculty interests. New entities outside the existing institutional structures may be needed to empower counseling professionals if they are to enable a free flow of students, financial aid, and information along program-level education and career pathways.

At present, there is no natural home for the necessary counseling function. High school counseling is very thin on the ground and focused largely on those who are already college-bound. Any attempts to connect students' individual knowledge, skills, abilities, values, interests, or personality traits to programs of study or careers have been primitive at best.[79] Nor do high school counselors have any access to widely available comparative data on the relationship between programs at particular colleges and career outcomes. And, of course, high schools have no formal stake in their graduates' college and career success.

Counseling attached to program-level data can be even more disruptive for colleges and their programs because it threatens unflattering comparisons of outcomes across different programs within institutions as well as unflattering comparisons of similar programs across institutions. As a result, the development of true program-level networks attached to outcome standards would have to afford protections for transparency in counseling both within individual postsecondary institutions and outside of them.

Change vs. Stasis

Improving awareness of the problems of our higher-education system—as this book seeks to do—will raise awareness of the need to strike a new balance between our educational goals. But to move awareness to action, we'll need something more: leadership styles that, much like the uneasy marriage between contrasting American ideals, find balance in tension. Contradictions that cannot be resolved in theory can be mixed variously to mutual advantage in practice. As T.H. Marshall put it in 1949, "social behavior is not governed by logic, and . . . a human society can make a square meal out of a stew of paradox without getting indigestion."[80]

In *Twilight of the Elites*, MSNBC host Christopher Hayes astutely observes that when it comes to bringing about needed systemic change, distinctions between left and right are less salient than distinctions between two camps he calls *insurrectionists* and *institutionalists*. Where one falls "comes down to just how rotten you think our current pillar institutions and ruling class are." Insurrectionists have largely given up on our current institutions and "see the plummeting of trust in public institutions as a good thing if it can act as a spur for needed upheaval and change." Institutionalists, whose ranks include virtually all college presidents, argue that people in power "are doing a better job than they're given credit for" and "see the erosion of authority and declining public trust as a terrifying trend." They're concerned with strengthening institutions, not tearing them down. Hayes writes: "What divides the institutionalist from the insurrectionist is a disagreement over whether the greatest threat we face is distrust—a dark and nihilistic tendency that will produce a society bankrupted of norms and order—or whether the greater threat is the actual malfeasance and corruption of the pillar institutions themselves."[81]

Great insurrectionists can be lousy leaders of a new order due to a lack of an appreciation of how institutions work. Institutionalists' instinct is to deal with pressure to change by making small tweaks that serve their institutions'—and their own—self-interests. The tension between approaches often results in incremental or temporary changes, if change happens at all.

We've seen this pattern repeatedly in higher education as colleges have adopted token reforms—such as an abandonment of early-decision policies that favor students from advantaged backgrounds—only to scrap them over fears of losing money or being at a competitive disadvantage. Bringing necessary reform to higher education may require inspiring and empowering insurrectionists to demand it, as well as persuading institutionalists to carry it out to keep insurrectionists at bay.

Higher-education reform will go nowhere without a populist narrative to carry it to the general public and into the halls of power. The deference paid to postsecondary institutions by the courts, legislatures, and citizenry will only be justified when the higher-education community—especially the leadership of selective colleges and universities—takes greater responsibility for providing opportunity to all. We're in an era in which higher-education leaders would be wise to heed the admonition popularized by Ralph Waldo Emerson: "March without the people, and you march into the night."[82]

Bringing needed change to American higher education won't be easy. The population that holds the most power in our society has a vested interest in preserving the intergenerational transmission of wealth and status.

Consider, for a moment, that having entering first-year classes that proportionately reflect the makeup of American society would require selective colleges to shed more than 159,000 students from the top socioeconomic quartile.[83] That population will not relinquish its grip on elite higher education quietly and, in fact, can be expected to mobilize effectively against even marginal threats to their children's access. Veterans of debates over access in K–12 education can attest to what formidable foes such families can be, particularly when they are among the most affluent. One study of an affluent northeastern school district's efforts to redraw school boundaries to promote equity recalls school administrators being confronted "not just by disgruntled parents but by pediatricians, urban planners, public relations specialists and psychologists." Outraged affluent parents solicited the help of local politicians, presented school officials "with two-inch-thick binders full of copies of peer-reviewed studies," and burned about three-fourths of the superintendent's time over several months.[84] Selective colleges—especially public ones—can expect to encounter similarly sophisticated and fierce resistance to any curtailment of access for the rich. As public-policy scholar Robert Putnam writes, one of the most well-established findings of scholars of political behavior is that "more educated and affluent citizens participate more actively in public affairs, and have more political knowledge and civic skills than their impoverished, ill-educated fellow citizens."[85]

Also looming as major obstacles to higher-education reform are ideological debates over several key issues: affirmative action, the appropriate use of the SAT and ACT, and who should pay for college—and how. As a result of the debate over affirmative action, for example, many liberals react with suspicion to any calls to experiment with alternatives to race-based admissions preferences, while many conservatives fight any perceived dilution of test-based meritocracy. On the pro–affirmative action side, those who want special treatment of applicants who are black, Latino, Asian, or Native American rarely issue public critiques of the practice of giving favorable treatment to the wealthy and well connected. Rather than attacking preferences that secure greater access for affluent institutionalists, they maintain an uneasily united front against those who, lacking an admission "hook," challenge the status quo. Conservatives, meanwhile, have shown little appetite for challenging admissions preferences that benefit the wealthy, even as they wave the flag of meritocracy in attacking admissions preferences for minority students and remain divided over preferences for the economically disadvantaged.[86]

Public opposition hardly represents the only risk involved in pushing for higher-education reform. We need always to be mindful of the Law of Unintended Consequences and the ways in which people in power can cynically hijack or divert reform efforts.

How colleges have dealt with pressure to improve graduation rates serves as a cautionary tale. It was hoped that they'd respond by improving teaching, offering students more support services, and shoring up financial aid packages to spare any student from dropping out over a lack of money. But if the goal is simply raising a number—the share of entering freshmen who end up clutching a sheepskin within four or six years—it's cheaper and easier to get there by watering down the curriculum, inflating grades, and denying admission to the disadvantaged. As Colin Diver, then Reed College's president, observed in a 2005 essay, "Rewarding high retention and graduation rates encourages schools to focus on pleasing students rather than on pushing them."[87]

Lawmakers have signed on to the idea that everyone needs at least some postsecondary education, but they also argue that meeting this goal is financially prohibitive without increases in "affordability" rendered through draconian cuts to programs. However, more sensible cost-cutting, along with innovations in instructional technology, can give us more wiggle room to create more access. Every university doesn't need a graduate school in every department, four-year colleges sometimes spend too little on teaching and too much on research, not every college needs to be residential, and it's become easier to offer courses online.

But tuition revenues already cover only a fraction of the actual costs of educating college students. The notion that we can reach our access and completion goals mainly by cutting costs does not square with the facts on the ground.

The question of how to improve access and completion strategies is inextricably entangled with questions of fairness. Access for whom? Access to what? Much of the dialogue on reforms to increase access has been mute on both questions.

The challenges ahead are considerable, but we should not shy away from confronting them. If we continue down the path we've been following, we will only deepen the divisions currently fracturing us, between the educational haves and the educational have-nots, between the rich and the poor, between those with racial privilege and those fighting for opportunity in the long shadow of racism, between those who put their trust in merit and those who argue that the scales should be evenly weighted to ensure equal opportunity. Educational equity is our best hope for finding a new route forward as a country—one that will secure the health of our economy and democracy while ensuring dignity, opportunity, and political participation for our nation's people.

If we don't become a republic of education—where schools and colleges promote the common good in ways that justify faith in our system of government and in our institutions—we risk ceasing to be a republic at all.

ACKNOWLEDGMENTS

This book is an outgrowth of the research we are doing at the Center on Education and the Workforce at Georgetown University. We started the center in 2008 to examine the relationship between learning and earning, providing critical information that would allow practitioners and policymakers to better align education and training with workforce demands. But our work rapidly grew to include projections of jobs and the educational credentials that will be required to obtain them, the earnings associated with college credentials, and historical analysis of how our workforce increasingly requires a lifelong commitment to schooling and upskilling. As part of this body of work, we have taken a critical look at how colleges operate, questioning whether they are committed to equity and educating students from all racial groups and social strata.

We want to first thank Georgetown University for supporting the Center. We could not have pursued this agenda or written this book without the constant support of the Bill & Melinda Gates Foundation and Lumina Foundation. More recently, we have also enjoyed support from the Joyce Foundation, JPMorgan Chase & Co., and the Annie E. Casey Foundation. The work and resources required to write this book were generously supported by the Kresge Foundation. We have worked with many program officers and leaders of these organizations through the years, but we would like to thank in particular Jamie Merisotis, Holly Zanville, Susan D. Johnson, Daniel Greenstein, Patrick

Methvin, Jamey Rorison, Sameer Gadkaree, Bob Giloth, Allison Gerber, Sarah Steinberg, Wendy Sedlak, and Bill Moses.

We are grateful to our talented colleagues at the Center who played a key role in reviewing drafts, giving additional perspective on American higher education, and helping us hone the narrative, particularly Kathryn Peltier Campbell and Martin Van Der Werf. We thank Artem Gulish for his help with fact-checking, sourcing of data and key figures, and background research that informed our discussion of public policy. Michael C. Quinn and Megan L. Fasules also deserve our thanks for further ensuring the accuracy of data and the narrative, and we thank Tanya I. Garcia for contributing background research. Any errors that remain are our own. We could not have completed this project without Coral Castro's dedicated administrative support. We also wish to thank Tara Grove of The New Press, who doggedly pursued us to write this book—and finally convinced us.

On a more personal level, Tony and Jeff thank their spouses, Ellen Carnevale and Elena Bardasi, for their support, understanding, and patience throughout this and every research and writing process. Jeff also thanks his mom for a lifetime of support and his son, Luca, for keeping up the humor. Peter would also like to acknowledge the debt he owes to his parents, Mary Lou and Jim Schmidt, for teaching him the value of education. He also would like to thank the many friends who have provided encouragement and moral support through his own period of economic dislocation due to the decline of advertiser-financed journalism. He would especially like to thank Serena Davis, who has offered immeasurable support along this path, and the late Ellen Leonard, the grandmother who helped instill in Serena the resilience necessary to beat tough odds and the compassion that leads her to foster resilience in others.

NOTES

Introduction

1. Peter Schmidt, "Charlottesville Violence Sparks New Worries About Safety During Campus Protests," *Chronicle of Higher Education*, August 15, 2017; Nell Gluckman, "At UVa, in the Wake of a Nightmare, a Reckoning Begins," *Chronicle of Higher Education*, August 23, 2017; Jack Stripling, "Did UVa Miss Signs of Looming Violence?" *Chronicle of Higher Education*, August 14, 2017.

2. Mark Bray, "Who Are the Antifa?" *Washington Post*, August 16, 2017.

3. Jonah Engel Bromwich and Alan Blinder, "What We Know About James Alex Fields, Driver Charged in Charlottesville Killing," *New York Times*, August 13, 2017.

4. Dan Bauman, "After the 2016 Election, Campus Hate Crimes Seemed to Jump. Here's What the Data Tell Us," *Chronicle of Higher Education*, February 16, 2018.

5. Anthony P. Carnevale, Nicole Smith, and Jeff Strohl, *Recovery: Job Growth and Education Requirements through 2020* (Washington, DC: Georgetown University Center on Education and the Workforce, 2013).

6. Anthony P. Carnevale, Megan L. Fasules, Michael C. Quinn, and Kathryn Peltier Campbell, *Born to Win, Schooled to Lose: Why Equally Talented Students Don't Get Equal Chances to Be All They Can Be* (Washington, DC: Georgetown University Center on Education and the Workforce, 2019).

7. Alejandra Reyes-Verlade and Richard Winton, "College Admissions Scandal: Here Is Everyone Charged in the Case," *Los Angeles Times*, March 12, 2019; Jack Stripling, "It's an Aristocracy: What the Admissions-Bribery Scandal Has Exposed About Class on Campus," *Chronicle of Higher Education*, April 17, 2019.

8. Eric Hoover, "Bribery Scandal Reveals 'Weak Spots' in the Admissions System. Don't Look So Shocked," *Chronicle of Higher Education*, March 13, 2019; Eric Hoover, "Admissions Officers Didn't Cause the Scandal. But They Helped Shape the Culture That Spawned It," *Chronicle of Higher Education*, March 13, 2019.

9. Georgetown University Center on Education and the Workforce analysis of data from Raj Chetty, John Friedman, Emmanuel Saez, Nicholas Turner, and Danny Yagan, "Mobility Report Cards: The Role of Colleges in Intergenerational Mobility," NBER Working Paper No. 23618, July 2017 (data set available at http://www.equality-of-opportunity.org/data/).

10. Jeremy Bauer-Wolf, "Feeling Like Imposters," *Inside Higher Ed*, April 6, 2017.

11. Georgetown University Center on Education and the Workforce analysis of data from Chetty et al., "Mobility Report Cards."

12. Georgetown University Center on Education and the Workforce analysis of data from Educational Longitudinal Study of 2002.

13. Stripling, "'It's an Aristocracy.'"

14. Claudia Goldin and Lawrence F. Katz, *The Race Between Education and Technology* (Cambridge, MA: Harvard University Press, 2008).

15. Georgetown University Center on Education and the Workforce calculations using table 341 from *Digest of Education Statistics 2011* (nces.ed.gov/programs/digest/d11/tables/dt11_341.asp).

16. Socioeconomic status is defined according to household income, educational attainment, and occupational prestige.

17. Carnevale et al., *Born to Win, Schooled to Lose*. The most affluent fourth refers to the top quartile of socioeconomic status.

18. Peter Olson, "Little-Loved by Scholars, Trump Also Gets Little of Their Cash," *Chronicle of Higher Education*, November 7, 2016.

19. Jack Stripling, "A Humbling of Higher Education," *Chronicle of Higher Education*, November 11, 2016.

20. David R. Johnson and Jared L. Peifer, "How Public Confidence in Higher Education Varies by Social Context," *Journal of Higher Education*, April 4, 2017, http://dx.doi.org/10.1080/00221546.2017.1291256.

21. Pew Research Center, "Public Trust in Government: 1958–2017," December 14, 2017, http://www.people-press.org/2017/12/14/public-trust-in-government-1958-2017/.

22. Christopher Hayes, *Twilight of the Elites: America After Meritocracy* (New York: Crown Publishers, 2012), 2–13.

23. J.D. Vance, *Hillbilly Elegy: A Memoir of a Family and Culture in Crisis* (New York: HarperCollins, 2016), 193.

24. Steve Brill, *Tailspin: The People and Forces Behind America's Fifty-Year Fall—and Those Fighting to Reverse It* (New York: Alfred A. Knopf, 2018).

25. Robert D. Putnam, *Our Kids: The American Dream in Crisis* (New York: Simon & Schuster, 2015).

26. Bill Bishop, *The Big Sort: Why the Clustering of Like-Minded America is Tearing Us Apart* (New York: Houghton Mifflin, 2008).

27. Richard V. Reeves, *Dream Hoarders: How the American Upper Middle Class Is Leaving Everyone Else in the Dust, Why That Is a Problem, and What You Can Do About It* (Washington, DC: Brookings Institution Press, 2017).

28. Letter from Thomas Jefferson to John Adams, October 28, 1813, in *The Portable Thomas Jefferson*, ed. Merrill D. Peterson (New York:

Penguin, 1975), 533–39, http://press-pubs.uchicago.edu/founders/docu ments/v1ch15s61.html.

29. Letter from John Adams to Thomas Jefferson, November 15, 1813, in *The Founders' Constitution*, Vol. 1, http://press-pubs.uchicago.edu/founders /documents/v1ch15s62.html.

30. Anthony P. Carnevale and Jeff Strohl, *Separate & Unequal: How Higher Education Reinforces the Intergenerational Reproduction of White Racial Privilege* (Washington, DC: Georgetown University Center on Education and the Workforce, 2013).

31. John Bound, Michael F. Lovenheim, and Sarah Turner, "Why Have College Completion Rates Declined? An Analysis of Changing Student Preparation and Collegiate Resources," *American Economic Journal: Applied Economics* 2, no. 3 (2010): 129–57.

32. Jesse Rothstein, "College Performance Predictions and the SAT," *Journal of Econometrics* 121, no. 1–2 (2004): 297–317.

33. For instance, a study of SAT validity at the University of California system shows that high school GPA explains 17 percent of GPA in college, while the SAT explains 13.8 percent; in combination, these two metrics explain 23 percent. See Saul Geiser and Roger Studley, "UC and the SAT: Predictive Validity and Differential Impact of the SAT I and SAT II at the University of California," *Educational Assessment* 8, no. 1 (2002): 1–26. More recent work by Herman Aguinis, reported by *Inside Higher Ed*, demonstrates that the oft-cited purpose of the SAT in predicting freshman GPA does not hold water, because of extensive differences in specific college grading policies. See Scott Jaschik, "Faulty Predictions?," *Inside Higher Ed*, January 26, 2016.

34. Anthony P. Carnevale, Stephen J. Rose, and Jeff Strohl, "Achieving Racial and Economic Diversity," in *The Future of Affirmative Action: New Paths to Higher Education Diversity After Fisher v. University of Texas*, ed. Richard D. Kahlenberg (New York: The Century Foundation, 2014).

35. Daniel Golden, *The Price of Admission: How America's Ruling Class Buys Its Way Into Elite Colleges and Who Gets Left Outside the Gates* (New York: Three Rivers Press, 2006).

36. Stephen Burd, *Undermining Pell: How Colleges Compete for Wealthy Students and Leave the Low-Income Behind* (Washington, DC: New America Foundation, 2013).

37. Caroline Hoxby, "The Changing Selectivity of American Colleges," 2009, NBER Working Paper 15446. See also Gordon C. Winston, "Subsidies, Hierarchy and Peers: Awkward Economics of Higher Education," *Journal of Economic Perspectives* 13, no. 1 (Winter 1999): 13–36.

38. Lani Guinier, *The Tyranny of the Meritocracy: Democratizing Higher Education in America* (Boston: Beacon Press, 2015), 24–25.

39. Hayes, *Twilight of the Elites*, 57.

40. Daniel Markovits, "A New Aristocracy," Yale Law School Commencement Address, May 2015, https://law.yale.edu/system/files/area/department /studentaffairs/document/markovitscommencementrev.pdf.

41. Jennifer M. Morton, "The False Promise of Elite Education," *Chronicle of Higher Education*, March 29, 2019.

42. James Bryant Conant, *Slums and Suburbs: A Commentary on Schools in Metropolitan Areas* (New York: McGraw-Hill, 1961).

43. National Commission on Excellence in Education, *A Nation at Risk: The Imperative for Educational Reform*, Washington, DC, 1983.

44. Anthony P. Carnevale, Nicole Smith, and Michael C. Quinn, *The Future of Work and Education Requirements: 2017–2027* (Washington, DC: Georgetown University Center on Education and the Workforce, 2020).

45. James G. Hershberg, *James B. Conant: Harvard to Hiroshima and the Making of the Nuclear Age* (Palo Alto, CA: Stanford University Press, 1993); Anthony Carnevale, Artem Gulish, and Jeff Strohl, *Educational Adequacy in the Twenty-First Century* (Washington, DC: The Century Foundation and Georgetown University Center on Education and the Workforce, 2018).

46. Likhitha Butchireddygari, "Historic Rise of College-Educated Women in Labor Force Changes Workplace," *Wall Street Journal*, August 20, 2019.

47. Susan Snyder, "Franklin and Marshall Program Offers a Window into Colleges' Bid to Attract Low-Income Students," *The Inquirer*, August 4, 2017.

48. Richard D. Kahlenberg, "Anthony Marx's Legacy at Amherst," *Chronicle of Higher Education*, October 14, 2010.

49. Kerry Hannon, "At Vassar, a Focus on Diversity and Affordability in Higher Education," *New York Times*, June 22, 2016.

50. David Leonhardt, "Princeton—Yes, Princeton—Takes On the Class Divide," *New York Times*, May 30, 2017.

51. Beth McMurtrie, "Georgia State U. Made Its Graduation Rate Jump. How?," *Chronicle of Higher Education*, May 25, 2018, https://www.chronicle.com/article/Georgia-State-U-Made-Its/243514.

52. This figure reflects attendance at the 531 most selective institutions, using pooled twelve-month enrollment numbers from academic years 2013–14 through 2015–16; Georgetown University Center on Education and the Workforce analysis of data from the Integrated Postsecondary Education Data System (IPEDS) and the NCES-Barron's Admissions Competitiveness Index Data Files: 1972, 1982, 1992, 2004, 2008, 2014.

53. Anthony Carnevale, "Higher Education and Democratic Capitalism," *Educause Review*, October 17, 2016; and Anthony P. Carnevale, Nicole Smith, Lenka Dražanová, Artem Gulish, and Kathryn Peltier Campbell, *The Role of Education in Taming Authoritarian Attitudes* (Washington, DC: Georgetown University Center on Education and the Workforce, forthcoming).

54. Richard Weiss, *The American Myth of Success: From Horatio Alger to Norman Vincent Peale* (Urbana and Chicago: University of Illinois Press, 1988), 7.

Chapter 1: What the Nation Needs

1. The exceptions to this are America's enduring original sins: the "peculiar institution" of southern slavery and the genocidal treatment of Native Americans.

2. Louis Hartz, *The Liberal Tradition in America: An Interpretation of American Political Thought Since the Revolution* (New York: Harcourt, Brace, 1955).

3. For a seminal discussion of the Protestant work ethic's role in capitalist economies, see Max Weber, *The Protestant Ethic and the Spirit of Capitalism* (New York: Penguin Books, 2002), first published in German as a series of essays in 1904 and 1905.

4. Daniel Bell, "On Meritocracy and Equality," *The Public Interest* 29 (1972): 29–68.

5. Weber, *The Protestant Ethic and the Spirit of Capitalism*.

6. At the core of individualism is liberalism, an Enlightenment-era political philosophy holding that governments should protect individual rights and freedoms and should not interfere with the individual exercise of personal choice. While liberalism has come to be associated with the views of the American political left, it is in fact central to the American system of government and all liberal democracies. Republicanism is a political philosophy that emphasizes public virtue and the responsibilities associated with citizenship. It, too, is central to the American system of government, not just the views of the political right or the modern-day Republican party.

7. John Locke, *Second Treatise of Government: An Essay Concerning the True Original Extent and End of Civil Government*, ed. Richard H. Cox (Wheeling, IL: Harlan Davidson, Inc., 1982).

8. Patrick Deneen, *Why Liberalism Failed* (New Haven, CT: Yale University Press, 2018).

9. Plato, *The Republic*, ed. G.R.F. Ferrari (Cambridge, UK: Cambridge University Press, 2000).

10. Deneen, *Why Liberalism Failed*, 52.

11. Anatole France, *The Red Lily* (New York, NY: John Lane Company, 1910).

12. Lester J. Cappon, *The Adams-Jefferson Letters: The Complete Correspondence Between Thomas Jefferson and Abigail and John Adams* (Chapel Hill: University of North Carolina Press, 2012).

13. Bell, "On Meritocracy and Equality," 29.

14. The literary historian Stephen Greenblatt has noted that Thomas Jefferson owned at least five Latin copies of Lucretius's didactic Epicurean poem *On the Nature of Things*; see Stephen Greenblatt, "The Answer Man: An Ancient Poem Was Rediscovered—and the World Swerved," *New Yorker*, August 1, 2011, https://www.newyorker.com/magazine/2011/08/08/the-answer-man -stephen-greenblatt. For more on how Epicureanism influenced Jefferson's views, see Alexander Zubia, "Jefferson's 'Master Epicures' and the American Regime," *Public Discourse*, January 3, 2018.

15. David M. Potter, *People of Plenty* (Chicago, IL: University of Chicago Press, 1954).

16. Adam Smith, *An Inquiry into the Nature and Causes of the Wealth of Nations* (Chicago, IL: University of Chicago Press, 1976).

17. Alexis de Tocqueville, *Democracy in America*, Volume I, trans. Henry Reeve (Malvern, PA: Penn State University Press, 2002), 770.

18. Paul A. Rahe, *Republics Ancient and Modern, Vol. III: Inventions of Prudence: Constituting the American Regime* (Chapel Hill: University of North Carolina Press, 1994).

19. Rahe, *Republics Ancient and Modern*.

20. Michael J. Sandel, *Democracy's Discontent: America in Search of a Public Philosophy* (Cambridge, MA: Belknap Press, 1996), 5–6.

21. The revival of the historical importance of republicanism in American history has been led by Bernard Bailyn, *The Ideological Origins of the American Revolution* (1967), and Gordon S. Wood, *The Creation of the American Republic 1776–1787* (1969). See Rahe, *Republics Ancient and Modern*.

22. Anthony P. Carnevale, Artem Gulish, and Jeff Strohl, *Educational Adequacy in the Twenty-First Century* (Washington, DC: The Century Foundation and Georgetown University Center on Education and the Workforce, 2018); Horace Mann, *The Republic and the School: Horace Mann on the Education of Free Men*, ed. Lawrence A. Cremin (New York: Teachers College Press, Columbia University, 1957).

23. Anthony P. Carnevale and Stephen J. Rose, *The Economy Goes to College: The Hidden Promise of Higher Education in the Post-Industrial Service Economy* (Washington, DC: Georgetown University Center on Education and the Workforce, 2015).

24. Anthony P. Carnevale, Nicole Smith, Lenka Dražanová, Artem Gulish, and Kathryn Peltier Campbell, *The Role of Education in Taming Authoritarian Attitudes* (Washington, DC: Georgetown University Center on Education and the Workforce, forthcoming); Karen Stenner, *The Authoritarian Dynamic* (New York: Cambridge University Press, 2005); Lenka Dražanová, *Education and Tolerance: A Comparative Quantitative Analysis of the Educational Effect on Tolerance* (New York: Peter Lang, 2017); Edward L. Glaeser, Giacomo A.M. Ponzetto, and Andrei Schleifer, "Why Does Democracy Need Education?," *Journal of Economic Growth* 12, no. 2 (May 2007): 77–99, 79.

25. Anthony P. Carnevale, Megan L. Fasules, Michael C. Quinn, and Kathryn Peltier Campbell, *Born to Win, Schooled to Lose: Why Equally Talented Students Don't Get Equal Chances to Be All They Can Be* (Washington, DC: Georgetown University Center on Education and the Workforce, 2019).

26. Anthony P. Carnevale and Jeff Strohl, *Separate & Unequal: How Higher Education Reinforces the Intergenerational Reproduction of White Racial Privilege* (Washington, DC: Georgetown University Center on Education and the Workforce, 2013); Anthony P. Carnevale, Martin Van Der Werf, Michael C. Quinn, Jeff Strohl, and Dmitri Repnikov, *Our Separate & Unequal Public Colleges: How Public Colleges Reinforce White Racial Privilege and Marginalize Black and Latino Students* (Washington, DC: Georgetown University Center on Education and the Workforce, 2018).

27. For a thoughtful review of these questions, see Amy Guttman, *Democratic Education* (Princeton, NJ: Princeton University Press, 1999); in particular, see "Discretion in Work and Participation in Politics," pp. 282–87; "Compensatory College Education," pp. 218–22; "Distributing Higher Education," pp. 194–231; and "The Purposes of Higher Education," pp. 172–93.

28. Robert J. Steinfeld, *The Invention of Free Labor: The Employment Relation in English & American Law and Culture, 1350–1870* (Chapel Hill: University of North Carolina Press, 1991).

29. Greg Badsher, *How the West Was Settled: The 150-Year-Old Homestead Act Lured Americans Looking for New Life and New Opportunities* (Washington, DC: The U.S. National Archives and Records Administration, 2012).

30. Robert Wiebe, *Self-Rule: A Cultural History of American Democracy* (Chicago, IL: University of Chicago Press, 1995), 20; Elliot A. Krause, *Death of the Guilds: Professions, States, and the Advantage of Capitalism, 1930 to the Present* (New Haven, CT: Yale University Press, 1999).

31. Wiebe, *Self-Rule*, 67.

32. See Arthur Schlesinger Jr., *The Age of Jackson* (Boston, MA: Little, Brown and Company, 1945).

33. Wiebe, *Self-Rule*.

34. Harold W. Stanley and Richard G. Niemi, *Vital Statistics on American Politics 2015–16* (Washington, DC: CQ Press, 2015).

35. Mann, *The Republic and the School*.

36. Eric Foner, *Reconstruction: America's Unfinished Revolution, 1863–1877* (New York, NY: Harper Collins Publishers, 1988).

37. Charles Darwin, *On the Origin of Species* (New York: PF Collier & Son Company, 1909).

38. Richard Hofstadter, *Social Darwinism in American Thought* (Boston, MA: Beacon Press, 1983).

39. Natalie Oveyssi, "Eugenics, Love, and the Marriage Problem," *Psychology Today*, July 30, 2015, https://www.psychologytoday.com/us/blog/genetic-crossroads/201507/eugenics-love-and-the-marriage-problem.

40. Frederick Jackson Turner, *The Frontier in American History* (New York: Henry Holt and Company, 1920). Downloaded from Project Gutenberg at http://www.gutenberg.org/files/22994/22994-h/22994-h.htm.

41. Matthew Josephson, *The Robber Barons: The Classic Account of the Influential Capitalists Who Transformed America's Future* (New York: Harcourt, 1934).

42. Richard J. Evan, *The Pursuit of Power: Europe 1815–1914* (London: Penguin UK, 2016).

43. Fernando F. Padró, *Statistical Handbook on the Social Safety Net* (Westport, CT: Greenwood Press, 2004).

44. Thomas Humphrey Marshall and Tom Bottomore, *Citizenship and Social Class* (London: Pluto Press, 1992).

45. Alfred Marshall, as quoted in Marshall and Bottomore, *Citizenship and Social Class*, 4–5.

46. Samuel P. Hays, *The Response to Industrialism: 1885–1914* (Chicago, IL: University of Chicago Press, 1995).

47. Stanley and Niemi, *Vital Statistics on American Politics*.

48. John Shattuck, Aaron Huang, and Elisabeth Thoreson-Green, *The War on Voting Rights*, CCDP 2019-003 (Cambridge, MA: Carr Center for Human Rights, Harvard University Kennedy School of Public Policy, 2019)

49. Drew Desilver, "U.S. Trails Most Developed Countries in Voter Turn-out," *FactTank* (Washington, DC: Pew Research Center, 2018).

50. Allan J. Lichtman, *The Embattled Vote in America: From the Founding to the Present* (Cambridge, MA: President and Fellows of Harvard College, 2018).

51. Andrew Delbanco, *The Real American Dream* (Cambridge, MA: President and Fellows of Harvard College, 1999); Richard Weiss, *The American Myth of Success: From Horatio Alger to Norman Vincent Pale* (Champaign, IL: University of Illinois Press, 1988).

52. Anthony Carnevale, *We Need a New Deal Between Higher Education and Democratic Capitalism* (Washington, DC: Georgetown University Center on Education and the Workforce, 2016).

53. A. Lawrence Lowell, *Public Opinion and Popular Government* (New York: Longmans, Green, and Company, 1913).

54. Walter Lippmann, *Public Opinion: A Classic in Political and Social Thought* (Feather Trail Press, 2010); Walter Lippmann, *The Phantom Public* (New York: Taylor & Francis, 1993).

55. Richard Hofstadter, *Anti-intellectualism in American Life* (New York: Vintage Books, 1963); Richard Hofstadter, *The Paranoid Style in American Politics* (New York: Vintage Books, 1965); Richard Hofstadter, *The Age of Reform* (New York: Vintage Books, 1955).

56. For more on the dynamics of authoritarianism, see Theodor Adorno, *The Authoritarian Personality* (New York: Harper & Row, 1950); Erich Fromm, *Escape from Freedom* (New York: Henry Holt Company, LLC, 1969); Arthur Schlesinger, *The Vital Center: The Politics of Freedom* (Boston, MA: Da Capo Press, 1949); Karen Stenner, *The Authoritarian Dynamic* (New York: Cambridge University Press, 2005).

57. Christopher H. Achen and Larry M. Bartels, *Democracy for Realists: Why Elections Do Not Produce Responsive Governments* (Princeton, NJ: Princeton University Press, 2016).

58. Shawn Rosenberg, "Unfit for Democracy? Irrational, Rationalizing, and Biologically Predisposed Citizens," *Critical Review* 29, no. 3 (2017): 362–87; Rick Shenkman, *Political Animals: How Our Stone-Age Brain Gets in the Way of Smart Politics* (New York: Basic Books, 2016).

59. David Truman, *The Governmental Process: Political Interests and Public Opinion* (New York: Knopf, 1951).

60. Smith Hughes National Vocational Education Act, 64 CHS 113, 114, 1917.

61. James Truslow Adams, *The Epic of America* (New York: Taylor & Francis Group, 1931), 214–15.

62. President's Commission on Higher Education, *Higher Education for American Democracy* (Washington, DC: Government Printing Office, December 1947); Greg Schuckman, "Truman Commission's Report Has Lessons for Today," *Chronicle of Higher Education*, July 15, 2019; Nicholas Strohl, "A Good Idea, Not a New One," *Inside Higher Ed*, February 19, 2015; John Dale Russell, "Basic Conclusions and Recommendations of the President's Commission on Higher Education," *Journal of Educational Sociology* 22, no. 8: 493–508.

63. Peter Schmidt, *Color and Money: How Rich White Kids Are Winning the War Over College Affirmative Action* (New York: Palgrave Macmillan, 2007), 24; Nicholas Lemann, *The Big Test: The Secret History of the American Meritocracy* (New York: Farrar, Straus and Giroux, 1999).

64. Schmidt, *Color and Money*; Lemann, *The Big Test*; David Owen and Marilyn Doerr, *None of the Above: The Truth Behind the SATs* (New York: Rowman and Littlefield, 1999).

65. T.H. Marshall, "Citizenship and Social Class," in *Contemporary Political Philosophy: An Anthology*, ed. Robert E. Goodin and Philip Pettit (Oxford: Blackwell, 1997), 311.

66. T.H. Marshall, as quoted in Bryan S. Turner and Peter Hamilton, eds., *Citizenship: Critical Concepts, Volume 2* (London: Routledge, 1994), 33–35.

67. Scott Carlson, "When College Was a Public Good: As the Population Has Grown More Diverse, Support Has Dwindled for Grand Efforts, Like the GI Bill, to Open Doors to Higher Education. Coincidence?" *Chronicle of Higher Education*, November 27, 2016; Alberto Alesina, Edward Glaeser, and Bruce Sacerdote, "Why Doesn't the US Have a European-Style Welfare State?," Harvard Institute of Economic Research, Discussion Paper Number 1933 (Cambridge, MA: Harvard University, 2001).

68. Georgetown University Center on Education and the Workforce analysis of Current Population Survey, 1983, 2018.

69. Anthony P. Carnevale and Stephen J. Rose, *The Undereducated American* (Washington, DC: Georgetown University Center on Education and the Workforce, 2011); Carnevale and Rose, *The Economy Goes to College*; Anthony P. Carnevale, Tanya I. Garcia, and Kathryn Peltier Campbell, "All One System: The Future of Education and Career Preparation," in *Taking Action: Positioning Low-Income Workers to Succeed in a Changing Economy* (Bethesda, MD: The Hatcher Group, 2019).

70. Anthony P. Carnevale, Jeff Strohl, Artem Gulish, Martin Van Der Werf, and Kathryn Peltier Campbell, *The Unequal Race for Good Jobs: How Whites Made Outsized Gains in Education and Good Jobs Compared to Blacks and Latinos* (Washington, DC: Georgetown University Center on Education and the Workforce, 2019).

Chapter 2: The Rise of the Sorting Machine

1. Martin Van Der Werf, "Researcher Offers Unusually Candid Description of University's Effort to Rise in Rankings," *Chronicle of Higher Education*, June 3, 2009.

2. Martin Van Der Werf, "Clemson Assails Allegations That It Manipulates 'U.S. News' Rankings," *Chronicle of Higher Education*, June 4, 2009.

3. Van Der Werf, "Clemson Assails Allegations."

4. Van Der Werf, "Researcher Offers Unusually Candid Description."

5. Richard Pérez-Peña, "Best, Brightest and Rejected: Elite Colleges Turn Away up to 95%," *New York Times*, April 8, 2014.

6. Robert Morse, Eric Brooks, and Matt Mason, "How U.S. News Calculated

the 2020 Best Colleges Rankings," *U.S. News & World Report*, September 8, 2019.

7. Robert Morse and Eric Brooks, "What's New in the 2019 U.S. News Best Colleges Rankings," *U.S. News & World Report*, September 10, 2018.

8. Stacy Dale and Alan B. Krueger, "Estimating the Return to College Selectivity Over the Career Using Administrative Earnings Data," NBER Working Paper No. 17159, National Bureau of Economic Research, 2011.

9. Raj Chetty, John N. Friedman, Emmanuel Saez, Nicholas Turner, and Danny Yugan, "Mobility Report Cards: The Role of Colleges in Intergenerational Mobility," NBER Working Paper No. 23618, July 2017, http://www.equality-of-opportunity.org/papers/coll_mrc_paper.pdf.

10. This figure reflects attendance at the top three tiers of private selective colleges, using pooled twelve-month enrollment numbers from academic years 2013–14 through 2015–16; Georgetown University Center on Education and the Workforce analysis of data from the Integrated Postsecondary Education Data System (IPEDS) and the NCES-Barron's Admissions Competitiveness Index Data Files: 1972, 1982, 1992, 2004, 2008, 2014.

11. National Center for Education Statistics, *Digest of Education Statistics* tables, 2015.

12. Anthony P. Carnevale and Jeff Strohl, *Separate & Unequal: How Higher Education Reinforces the Intergenerational Reproduction of White Racial Privilege* (Washington, DC: Georgetown University Center on Education and the Workforce, 2013), 25.

13. Jeffrey Selingo, "The Disappearing State in Public Higher Education," *Chronicle of Higher Education*, February 23, 2008; Peter Schmidt, "State Spending on College Construction Does Not Track Economy, Study Finds," *Chronicle of Higher Education*, November 17, 2010.

14. Jerome Karabel, *The Chosen: The Hidden History of Admission and Exclusion at Harvard, Yale, and Princeton* (New York: Houghton Mifflin, 2005), 23, 39–76, as summarized in Peter Schmidt, *Color and Money: How Rich White Kids Are Winning the War Over College Affirmative Action* (New York: Palgrave Macmillan, 2007), 22.

15. Claude M. Fuess, *The College Board: Its First Fifty Years* (New York: College Entrance Examination Board, 1967).

16. Nicholas Lemann, *The Big Test: The Secret History of the American Meritocracy* (New York: Farrar, Straus and Giroux, 1999); David Owen and Marilyn Doerr, *None of the Above: The Truth Behind the SATs* (Lanham, MD: Rowman and Littlefield, 1999).

17. James G. Hershberg, *James B. Conant: Harvard to Hiroshima and the Making of the Nuclear Age* (Palo Alto, CA: Stanford University Press, 1993).

18. Hershberg, *James B. Conant.*

19. U.S. Department of Education, National Center for Education Statistics, *Digest of Education Statistics 1996*, NCES 96-133, Table 168. Washington, DC: U.S. Government Printing Office.

20. Karabel, *The Chosen,* 159, 174.

21. Lemann, *The Big Test.*

22. Lemann, *The Big Test*; Owen and Doerr, *None of the Above*.

23. Karabel, *The Chosen*, 4, 262–93; William G. Bowen and Sarah A. Levin, *Reclaiming the Game: College Sports and Educational Values* (Princeton, NJ: Princeton University Press, 2003), 59–60.

24. Hershberg, *James B. Conant*.

25. Hershberg, *James B. Conant*.

26. Hershberg, *James B. Conant*.

27. Hershberg, *James B. Conant*, 11.

28. David Wechsler, *The Measurement and Appraisal of Adult Intelligence*, 4th ed. (Baltimore, MD: The Williams and Wilkins Company, 1958).

29. Thomas D. Snyder, ed., *120 Years of American Education: A Statistical Portrait* (Washington, DC: U.S. Department of Education, National Center for Education Statistics, 1993).

30. Richard J. Coley, *The American Community College Turns 100: A Look at Its Students, Programs, and Prospects* (Princeton, NJ: Educational Testing Service, March 2000).

31. John Aubrey Douglass, *The California Idea and American Higher Education: 1850 to the 1960 master plan*, Vol. 1 (Palo Alto, CA: Stanford University Press, 2000).

32. Scott Carlson, "When College Was a Public Good," *Chronicle of Higher Education*, November 17, 2016; *A Master Plan for Higher Education in California, 1960–1975* (Sacramento, CA: California State Department of Education, 1960).

33. U.S. Department of Education, National Center for Education Statistics, Digest of Education tables, table 317.10, 2018.

34. National Association of Independent Colleges and Universities, "Quick Facts About Private Colleges," http://member.naicu.edu/about/page/quick-facts-about-private-colleges.

35. Gordon C. Winston, "Subsidies, Hierarchy and Peers: The Awkward Economics of Higher Education," *Journal of Economic Perspectives* 13, no. 1 (Winter 1999): 13–36.

36. Winston, "Subsidies, Hierarchy and Peers."

37. Winston, "Subsidies, Hierarchy and Peers."

38. Winston, "Subsidies, Hierarchy and Peers," 22–23, 31.

39. Joel Brown, "BU Admissions More Selective Than Ever," *BU Today*, March 28, 2017.

40. Schmidt, *Color and Money*, 26.

41. Peter Sacks, "How Colleges Perpetuate Inequality," *Chronicle of Higher Education*, January 12, 2007.

42. See, for example, Christopher Shea, "Annual College Rankings Roil but Also Gain in Influence," *Chronicle of Higher Education*, September 22, 1995; Colin Diver, "Is There Life After Rankings?," *The Atlantic*, November 2005; Michele Tolela Myers, "The Cost of Bucking College Rankings," *Washington Post*, March 11, 2007.

43. Sacks, "How Colleges Perpetuate Inequality."

44. James M. Summer, "Faked Figures Make Fools of Us," in *College*

Unranked: Ending the College Admissions Frenzy, ed. Lloyd Thacker (Cambridge, MA: Harvard University Press, 2005), 68–71.

45. Schmidt, *Color and Money*, 27–28.

46. Eric Hoover, "Application Inflation," *Chronicle of Higher Education*, November 5, 2010; Ivy Coach College Admissions Blog, "Recruiting Unqualified College Applicants," May 14, 2013; Jon Boeckenstedt, "Let's Bring Clarity to Undergraduate Admissions," *Chronicle of Higher Education*, May 13, 2013; Amanda Graves, "Dear Elite Colleges, Please Stop Recruiting Students Like Me if You Know We Won't Get In," *Washington Post*, November 17, 2014; The College Solution, "Please Apply So We Can Reject You," September 22, 2014; Linda Flanagan, "Hey, High School Senior: Dartmouth Wants YOU!" *HuffPost*, November 6, 2014; Rachel Toor, *Admissions Confidential: An Insider's Guide to the Elite College Selection Process* (New York: St. Martin's Griffin, 2002), 27.

47. Peter Schmidt, "Researchers Accuse Selective Colleges of Giving Admissions Tests Too Much Weight," *Chronicle of Higher Education*, May 9, 2008; Eric Hoover, "The Testing Hall of Shame," *Chronicle of Higher Education*, June 23, 2010.

48. Michael N. Bastedo, "Enrollment Management and the Low-Income Student: How Holistic Admissions and Market Competition Can Impede Equity," *Matching Students to Opportunity: Expanding College Choice, Access, and Quality*, eds. Andrew P. Kelly, Jessica S. Howell, and Carolyn Sattin-Bajaj (Cambridge, MA: Harvard Education Press, 2016), 121–34; Andrew S. Belasco, Kelly O. Rosinger, and James C. Hearn, "The Test-Optional Movement at America's Selective Liberal Arts Colleges: A Boon for Equity or Something Else?" *Educational Evaluation and Policy Analysis* 37, no. 2 (June 2015): 206–23.

49. Max Kutner, "How to Game the College Rankings," *Boston Magazine*, August 26, 2014.

50. Gregory R. Wegner, Lloyd Thacker, Jerome A. Lucido, and Scott Andrew Schulz, *The Case for Change in College Admissions: A Call for Individual and Collective Leadership* (Los Angeles, CA: USC Center for Enrollment Research, Policy and Practice, 2011). Available at http://www.thecollegesolution.com/wp-content/uploads/2011/09/USC-report.pdf.

51. Wegner et al., *The Case for Change*, 6.

52. Michael Fabricant and Stephen Brier, *Austerity Blues: Fighting for the Soul of Public Higher Education* (Baltimore: Johns Hopkins University Press, 2016), 8.

53. Charles T. Clotfelter, "How Rich Universities Get Richer," *Chronicle of Higher Education*, October 27, 2017.

54. Clotfelter, "How Rich Universities Get Richer."

55. Eric Stirgus, "Georgia to Mark 25 Years of Lottery, HOPE Grants," *Atlanta Journal-Constitution*, June 19, 2018.

56. Danette Gerald and Kati Haycock, *Engines of Inequality: Diminished Equity in the Nation's Premier Public Universities* (Washington, DC: The Education Trust, 2006), 3. The study found that in 2003, flagships spent $237 million

on aid to students from families that earned over $100,000 annually and $171 million on aid to students from families that earned less than $20,000.

57. The number of colleges in the three most selective categories, as measured by *Barron's Profiles of American Colleges*, grew from 326 in 1995 to 509 in 2015. Barron's College Division Staff, *Barron's Profiles of American Colleges 1995* (Hauppauge, NY: Barron's Educational Series, 1995); Barron's College Division Staff, *Barron's Profiles of American Colleges 2015* (Hauppauge, NY: Barron's Educational Series, 2015). For broader discussion of the increase in the number of competitive colleges and decline in the number of less-competitive colleges, see Anthony P. Carnevale and Jeff Strohl, "How Increasing College Access Is Increasing Inequality, and What to Do About It," in *Rewarding Strivers: Helping Low-Income Students Succeed in College*, ed. Richard D. Kahlenberg (New York: Century Foundation Books, 2010), 71–190.

58. Wegner et al., *The Case for Change.*

59. Richard V. Reeves, *Dream Hoarders: How the American Upper Middle Class Is Leaving Everyone Else in the Dust, Why That Is a Problem, and What You Can Do About It* (Washington, DC: Brookings Institution Press, 2017), 88–89.

60. Ry Rivard, "About-Face on Rankings," *Inside Higher Ed*, January 6, 2014.

61. Van Der Werf, "Researcher Offers Unusually Candid Description."

Chapter 3: Understanding the Odds

1. Robert D. Putnam, *Our Kids: The American Dream in Crisis* (New York: Simon & Schuster, 2015), 31.

2. Putnam, *Our Kids.*

3. Putnam, *Our Kids.*

4. Bhu Srinivasan, *Americana: A 400-Year History of American Capitalism* (New York: Penguin Press, 2017).

5. James D. Lutz, *Lest We Forget, a Short History of Housing in the United States* (Oakland, CA: Lawrence Berkeley National Laboratory, 2011).

6. Optimism about the potential for "the mass expansion of higher education" to lift all boats infuses such works as Yossi Shavit, Richard Arum, and Adam Gamoran, eds., *Stratification in Higher Education: A Comparative Study* (Palo Alto, CA: Stanford University Press, 2007).

7. Richard V. Reeves, *Dream Hoarders: How the American Upper Middle Class Is Leaving Everyone Else in the Dust, Why That Is a Problem, and What You Can Do About It* (Washington, DC: Brookings Institution Press, 2017), 61.

8. Reeves, *Dream Hoarders*, 58, 59.

9. Susan T. Fiske and Shelley E. Taylor, *Social Cognition: From Brains to Culture* (Thousand Oaks, CA: Sage, 2013); Daniel Kahneman and Patrick Egan, *Thinking, Fast and Slow* (New York: Farrar, Straus and Giroux, 2011).

10. See Joe R. Feagin and Melvin P. Sikes, *Living with Racism: The Black*

Middle-Class Experience (Boston: Beacon Press, 1994), and Joe R. Feagin, *Racist America: Roots, Current Realities, and Future Reparations* (New York: Routledge, 2000).

11. Nalini Ambady, Margaret Shih, Amy Kim, and Todd L. Pittinsky, "Stereotype Susceptibility in Children: Effects of Identity Activation on Quantitative Performance," *Psychological Science* 12, no. 5 (2001): 385–90.

12. Lincoln Quillian, Devah Pager, Ole Hexel, and Arnfinn H. Midtbøen, "Meta-analysis of Field Experiments Shows No Change in Racial Discrimination in Hiring Over Time," *Proceedings of the National Academy of Sciences* 114, no. 41 (2017): 10870–5. See also Devah Pager and Hana Shepherd, "The Sociology of Discrimination: Racial Discrimination in Employment, Housing, Credit, and Consumer Markets," *Annual Review of Sociology* 34 (2008): 181–209.

13. See David N. Figlio, "Names, Expectations and the Black-White Test Score Gap," NBER Working Paper No. 11195 (Cambridge, MA: National Bureau of Economic Research, 2005).

14. Timothy D. Wilson and Nancy Brekke, "Mental Contamination and Mental Correction: Unwanted Influences on Judgments and Evaluations," *Psychological Bulletin* 116, no. 1 (1994): 117–42.

15. Kriston Capps and Kate Rabinowitz, "How the Fair Housing Act Failed Black Homeowners," *City Lab*, April 11, 2018; Aaron Glantz and Emmanuel Martinez, "Modern-Day Redlining: How Banks Block People of Color from Homeownership," *Chicago Tribune*, February 17, 2018; Alexis C. Madrigal, "The Racist Housing Policy That Made Your Neighborhood," *The Atlantic*, May 22, 2014; Margery Austin Turner, Stephen L. Ross, George C. Galster, and John Yinger, *Discrimination in the Metropolitan Housing Markets: National Results from Phase 1 HDS 2000* (Washington, DC: Urban Institute Metropolitan Housing and Communities Policy Center, 2002); and National Fair Housing Alliance, *Unequal Opportunity—Perpetuating Housing Segregation in America: 2006 Fair Housing Trends Report* (Washington, DC: National Fair Housing Alliance, 2006).

16. Camille Zubrinsky Charles, "Can We Live Together? Racial Preferences and Neighborhood Outcomes," in *The Geography of Opportunity: Race and Housing Choices in Metropolitan America,* ed. Xavier de Souza Briggs (Washington, DC: Brookings Institution Press, 2005), 45–80, as summarized in Peter Schmidt, *Color and Money: How Rich White Kids Are Winning the War Over College Affirmative Action* (New York: Palgrave Macmillan, 2007).

17. John R. Logan, *Separate and Unequal: The Neighborhood Gaps for Blacks and Hispanics in Metropolitan America* (Albany, NY: Lewis Mumford Center for Comparative Urban and Regional Research, 2002).

18. See Douglas S. Massey and Mary J. Fischer, "How Segregation Concentrates Poverty," *Ethnic and Racial Studies* 23, no. 4 (2000): 670–91; and Douglas S. Massey and Mary J. Fischer, "The Geography of Inequality in the United States, 1950–2000," in *Brookings-Wharton Papers on Urban Affairs: 2003*, ed. William G. Gale and Janet Rothenberg Pack (Washington, DC: Brookings Institution Press, 2003), 1–40.

19. Kevin M. Cruse, "What Does a Traffic Jam in Atlanta Have to Do with Segregation? Quite a Lot," *New York Times*, August 14, 2019.

20. Kendra Bischoff and Sean F. Reardon, "Residential Segregation by Income, 1970–2009," *Diversity and Disparities: America Enters a New Century*, ed. John Logan (New York: Russell Sage Foundation, 2014), as cited in Putnam, *Our Kids*, 38.

21. Bill Bishop, *The Big Sort: Why the Clustering of Like-Minded America Is Tearing Us Apart* (New York: Houghton Mifflin, 2008).

22. Anthony P. Carnevale, Tanya I. Garcia, and Artem Gulish, *Career Pathways: Five Ways to Connect College and Careers* (Washington, DC: Georgetown University Center on Education and the Workforce, 2017).

23. See "Spatial Deconcentration in D.C.—Yulanda Ward," *Midnight Notes* II, no. 2 (July 1981); also Kenneth F. Warren, "Spatial Deconcentration: A Problem Greater Than School Desegregation, *Administrative Law Review* 29, no. 4 (Fall 1977).

24. Robert Greenbaum, "An Evaluation of State Enterprise Zone Policies: Measuring the Impact on Business Decisions and Housing Market Outcomes," W.E. Upjohn Institute, 1999.

25. Russell H. Jackson and others, "Youth Opportunity Grant Initiative: Impact and Synthesis Report," submitted to the United States Department of Labor, 2007, https://wdr.doleta.gov/research/FullText_Documents/YO%20 Impact%20and%20Synthesis%20Report.pdf.

26. Susan T. Fiske, *Social Beings: A Core Motives Approach to Social Psychology* (New York: Wiley, 2004).

27. Claude M. Steele, *Whistling Vivaldi: How Stereotypes Affect Us and What We Can Do* (New York: W.W. Norton, 2010).

28. Vanessa Siddle Walker, *The Lost Education of Horace Tate* (New York: New Press, 2018); and Noliwe Rooks, *Cutting School: Privatization, Segregation, and the End of Public Schools* (New York: New Press, 2017).

29. Annette Lareau, *Unequal Childhoods: Class, Race, and Family Life* (Berkeley, CA: University of California Press, 2003), as summarized in Schmidt, *Color and Money*.

30. Reeves, *Dream Hoarders*, 36.

31. Thomas S. Dee and Emily K. Penner, "The Causal Effects of Cultural Relevance: Evidence from an Ethnic Studies Curriculum," *American Educational Research Journal* 54, no. 1 (2017): 127–66.

32. Lisa Delpit, *Other People's Children: Cultural Conflict in the Classroom* (New York: New Press, 2006); and Lisa Delpit, *"Multiplication Is for White People": Raising Expectations for Other People's Children* (New York: New Press, 2012).

33. Douglas Massey, *Categorically Unequal: The American Stratification System* (New York: Russell Sage Foundation, 2007), 259.

34. Anthony P. Carnevale, Megan L. Fasules, Michael C. Quinn, and Kathryn Peltier Campbell, *Born to Win, Schooled to Lose: Why Equally Talented Students Don't Get Equal Chances to Be All They Can Be* (Washington, DC: Georgetown University Center on Education and the Workforce, 2019).

35. Kati Haycock, "Closing the Achievement Gap," *Educational Leadership* 58, no. 6 (2001): 6–11; Kati Haycock, "The Opportunity Gap: No Matter How You Look at It, Low-Income and Minority Students Get Fewer Good Teachers," *Thinking K–16* 8, no. 1 (2004): 36–42; Carnevale et al., *Born to Win, Schooled to Lose*.

36. Tom Loveless, *Ability Grouping, Tracking, and How Schools Work* (Washington, DC: The Brookings Institution, 2013).

37. Carnevale et al., *Born to Win, Schooled to Lose*.

38. See Paul E. Barton, *One-Third of a Nation: Rising Dropout Rates and Declining Opportunities* (Princeton, NJ: Educational Testing Service, 2005).

39. Anthony P. Carnevale, Andrew R. Hanson, and Artem Gulish, *Failure to Launch: Structural Shift and the New Lost Generation* (Washington, DC: Georgetown University Center on Education and the Workforce, 2013).

40. Anthony P. Carnevale and Jeff Strohl, "How Increasing College Access Is Increasing Inequality, and What to Do About It," in *Rewarding Strivers: Helping Low-Income Students Succeed in College*, ed. Richard D. Kahlenberg (New York: Century Foundation Books, 2010), 71–190.

41. Carnevale and Strohl, "How Increasing College Access."

42. For a detailed elaboration of the genesis and current evidence in these arguments, see William Julius Wilson, *When Work Disappears: The World of the New Urban Poor* (New York: Vintage Books, 2011), and Douglas S. Massey and Nancy A. Denton, *American Apartheid: Segregation and the Making of the Underclass* (Cambridge, MA: Harvard University Press, 1993).

43. Putnam, *Our Kids*, 36.

44. Douglas Belkin, Jennifer Levitz, and Melissa Korn, "Many More Students, Especially the Affluent, Get Extra Time to Take the SAT," *Wall Street Journal*, May 21, 2019.

45. Kenneth R. Weiss, "New Test-Taking Skill: Working the System," *Los Angeles Times*, January 9, 2000, as summarized in Schmidt, *Color and Money*.

46. Emily Nelson and Laurie P. Cohen, "Why Jack Grubman Was So Keen to Get His Twins into the Y," *Wall Street Journal*, November 15, 2002; and Tamar Lewin, "How I Spent Summer Vacation: Going to Get-into-College Camp," *New York Times*, April 18, 2004, as summarized in Schmidt, *Color and Money*.

47. Ellen Brantlinger, *Dividing Classes: How the Middle Class Negotiates and Rationalizes School Advantage* (New York: Routledge Falmer, 2003), as summarized in Schmidt, *Color and Money*.

48. Gunnar Myrdal, *An American Dilemma: The Negro Problem and Modern Democracy* (New York: Harper & Brothers, 1944), xliii.

49. Daniel Markovits, "A New Meritocracy," Yale Law School Commencement Address, May 2015.

50. Sharon Otterman, "Diversity Debate Convulses Elite High School," *New York Times*, August 4, 2010.

51. Justin Hudson, "The Brick Tower," speech delivered at the 2010 commencement of Hunter College High School.

Chapter 4: Standardized Bias

1. Anthony P. Carnevale, Jeff Strohl, Martin Van Der Werf, Michael C. Quinn, and Kathryn P. Campbell, *SAT-Only Admission: How Would It Change College Campuses?* (Washington, DC: Georgetown University Center on Education and the Workforce, 2019).

2. Sara Harberson, "The Cowards and Heroes of the SAT and ACT," sara harberson.com, April 30, 2018, http://www.saraharberson.com/blog/the -cowards-and-heroes-of-the-sat-and-act.

3. Eric Hoover, "Application Inflation," *Chronicle of Higher Education*, November 5, 2010.

4. Jerome Karabel, *The Chosen: The Hidden History of Admission and Exclusion at Harvard, Yale, and Princeton* (New York: Houghton Mifflin, 2005), 2.

5. Paul Tough explored how these competing considerations affect admissions decisions at Connecticut's Trinity College in "What College Admissions Offices Really Want," *New York Times*, September 10, 2019.

6. Donald Hossler and David Kalsbeek, "Enrollment Management and Managing Enrollments: Revisiting the Context for Institutional Strategy," *Strategic Enrollment Management Quarterly*, April 4, 2013.

7. Matthew Quirk, "The Best Class Money Can Buy," *The Atlantic*, November 2005.

8. Melissa Clinedinst and Anna-Maria Korentang, *2017 State of College Admission* (Arlington, VA: National Association for College Admission Counseling, 2017).

9. Hossler and Kalsbeek, "Enrollment Management and Managing Enrollments"; Eric Hoover, "The Enrollment Manager as Bogeyman," *Chronicle of Higher Education*, July 28, 2016.

10. Judy Phair, "Career Paths for Admissions Officers: A Survey Report," National Association for College Admission Counseling, July 2014; College and University Professional Association for Human Resources (CUPA-HR), *2010–11 Mid-Level Salary Survey* and *2010–11 Administrative Compensation Survey*.

11. Phair, "Career Paths."

12. Phair, "Career Paths."

13. Alia Wong, "Where College Admissions Went Wrong," *The Atlantic*, March 29, 2016.

14. Phair, "Career Paths," 33.

15. Phair, "Career Paths," 33.

16. Eric Hoover, "The Hottest Seat on Campus," *Chronicle of Higher Education*, September 15, 2014.

17. Michael N. Bastedo, "Enrollment Management and the Low-Income Student: How Holistic Admissions and Market Competition Can Impede Equity," in *Matching Students to Opportunity: Expanding College Choice, Access, and Quality*, ed. Andrew P. Kelly, Jessica S. Howell, and Carolyn Sattin-Bajaj (Cambridge, MA: Harvard Education Press, 2016), 121–34.

18. For a discussion of the relationship between the SAT and socioeconomic

status, see Jesse M. Rothstein, "College Performance Predictions and the SAT," *Journal of Econometrics* 121, no. 1–2 (2004): 297–317.

19. Donald R. Hossler, "How Enrollment Management Has Transformed—or Ruined—Higher Education," *Chronicle of Higher Education*, April 30, 2004.

20. Anthony P. Carnevale, "The Admissions System Is Worse Than Broken. It's Fixed," *Washington Post*, March 19, 2019.

21. For in-depth discussion of interference in admissions decisions, see Peter Schmidt, *Color and Money: How Rich White Kids Are Winning the War Over College Affirmative Action* (New York: Palgrave Macmillan, 2007); and Daniel Golden, *The Price of Admission: How America's Ruling Class Buys Its Way into Elite Colleges, and Who Gets Left Outside the Gates* (New York: Crown Publishers, 2006).

22. Peter Schmidt, "U. of Cal. Regents Accused of Pulling Strings for Applicants," *Chronicle of Higher Education*, March 29, 1996; Schmidt, *Color and Money*, 145.

23. Charles Huckabee, "U. of Illinois Chancellor and Several Trustees Are Reluctant to Resign," *Chronicle of Higher Education*, August 11, 2009; Elyse Ashburn, "U. of Illinois Takes Heat for Newspaper's Report About Political Influence on Admissions," *Chronicle of Higher Education*, June 1, 2009; Stacy St. Clair and Jodi S. Cohen, "University of Illinois Application Clout List Fallout Grows," *Chicago Tribune*, June 8, 2009.

24. Jack Stripling, "Admissions Report Chips at Austin Chief's Uncompromising Reputation," *Chronicle of Higher Education*, February 13, 2015; Kroll Associates, "University of Texas at Austin—Investigation of Admissions Practices and Allegations of Undue Influence: Summary of Key Findings," University of Texas System, February 6, 2015.

25. Michael N. Bastedo, "Conflicts, Commitments, and Cliques in the University: Moral Seduction as a Threat to Trustee Independence," *American Educational Research Journal* 46, no. 2 (June 2009): 354–86.

26. Jack Stripling and Eric Hoover, "In Admissions, the Powerful Weigh In," *Chronicle of Higher Education*, November 29, 2015.

27. Stripling and Hoover, "In Admissions, the Powerful Weigh In."

28. Mitch Daniels, "When Transparency Goes Too Far," *Washington Post*, August 14, 2018.

29. Peter Schmidt, "An Admissions Scandal Shows How Administrators' Ethics 'Fade,'" *Chronicle of Higher Education*, April 17, 2015; Nathan F. Harris, "The Organizational Trap of Ethical Fading: Privileging Clout in Admissions at the University of Illinois," working paper presented April 16, 2015, at the annual conference of the American Educational Research Association in Chicago, Illinois.

30. Peter Schmidt, "Supreme Court Weighs Constitutionality of Bans on Race-Conscious Admissions," *Chronicle of Higher Education*, October 14, 2013; Peter Schmidt, "Legality of Racial-Preference Bans Is Disputed in Federal Court," *Chronicle of Higher Education*, November 15, 2009; *Bill Schuette v. Coalition to Defend Affirmative Action, Integration and Immigrant Rights and*

Fight for Equality By Any Means Necessary (BAMN), et al., filed before the U.S. Supreme Court on August 30, 2013.

31. Daniel Kahneman and Amos Tversky, "On the Psychology of Prediction," *Psychological Review* 80, no. 4 (1973): 237.

32. Jennifer Crocker and Ian Schwartz, "Prejudice and Ingroup Favoritism in a Minimal Intergroup Situation: Effects of Self-Esteem," *Personality and Social Psychology Bulletin* 11, no. 4 (1985): 379–86; Charles W. Perdue, John F. Dovidio, Michael B. Gurtman, and Richard B. Tyler, "Us and Them: Social Categorization and the Process of Intergroup Bias," *Journal of Personality and Social Psychology* 59, no. 3 (1990): 475.

33. David A. Wilder, "Perceiving Persons as a Group: Categorization and Intergroup Relations," *Cognitive Processes in Stereotyping and Intergroup Behavior* 213, no. 1 (1981): 258.

34. Daniel Kahneman and Amos Tversky, "On the Psychology of Prediction," *Psychological Review* 80, no. 4 (1973): 237; Henri Tajfel, Michael G. Billig, Robert P. Bundy, and Claude Flament, "Social Categorization and Intergroup Behavior," *European Journal of Social Psychology* 1, no. 2 (1971): 149–78.

35. Anemona Hartocollis, "Harvard Rated Asian-American Applicants Lower on Personality Traits, Suit Says," *New York Times*, June 15, 2018; Jonathan Zimmerman, "One Group That Definitely Faces Prejudice in College Admissions," *Washington Post*, August 5, 2018.

36. Michael N. Bastedo, "Enrollment Management and the Low-Income Student: How Holistic Admissions and Market Competition Can Impede Equity," in *Matching Students to Opportunity: Expanding College Choice, Access, and Quality*, ed. Andrew P. Kelly, Jessica S. Howell, and Carolyn Sattin-Bajaj (Cambridge, MA: Harvard Education Press, 2016), 121–34.

37. Peter Schmidt, "In Admission Decisions, the Deciders' Own Backgrounds Play a Big Role," *Chronicle of Higher Education*, April 12, 2016.

38. See David Karen, "The Politics of Class, Race, and Gender: Access to Education in the United States, 1960–1986," *American Journal of Education* 99 (February 1991).

39. Karabel, *The Chosen*, 2, 87, 120. As summarized in Schmidt, *Color and Money*.

40. Karabel, *The Chosen*, 23, 39–76. As summarized in Schmidt, *Color and Money*.

41. Karabel, *The Chosen*, 36; David O. Levine, *The American College and the Culture of Aspiration, 1915–1940* (Ithaca, NY: Cornell University Press, 1986), 138, 139; as summarized in Peter Schmidt, "A History of Legacy Preferences and Privilege," in *Affirmative Action for the Rich: Legacy Preferences in College Admissions*, ed. Richard Kahlenberg (New York: The Century Foundation, 2010), 38–43.

42. Richard M. Freeland, *Academia's Golden Age: Universities in Massachusetts, 1945–1970* (New York: Oxford University Press, 1992), 44, as summarized in Schmidt, "A History of Legacy Preferences and Privilege."

43. Karabel, *The Chosen*, 48, 76, 114–15, 123–126, as summarized in Schmidt, "A History of Legacy Preferences and Privilege."

44. Freeland, *Academia's Golden Age*, 41–45, as summarized in Schmidt, "A History of Legacy Preferences and Privilege."

45. Hugh Hawkins, "The Making of the Liberal Arts College Identity," *Daedalus* 128, no. 1 (Winter 1999): 1–25, as summarized in Schmidt, "A History of Legacy Preferences and Privilege."

46. Benjamin Fine, *Admission to American Colleges: A Study of Current Policy and Practice* (New York: Harper and Brothers, 1946), 68–73, 121–24, as summarized in Schmidt, "A History of Legacy Preferences and Privilege."

47. Figures derived by comparing colleges' enrollment numbers with Jewish enrollment figures tracked by the national Jewish campus organization Hillel, as summarized in Schmidt, *Color and Money*, 202.

48. Kevin Eagan, Ellen Bara Stolzenberg, Hilary B. Zimmerman, Melissa C. Aragon, Hannah Whang Sayson, and Cecilia Rios-Aguilar, *The American Freshman: National Norms Fall 2016* (Los Angeles: Higher Education Research Institute at the University of California–Los Angeles, 2017).

49. Clinedinst and Korentang, *2017 State of College Admission*. Based on data from U.S. Department of Education, National Center for Education Statistics, Integrated Postsecondary Education Data System (IPEDS) Data Center (Washington, DC: National Center for Education Statistics, 2015–16). (Includes Title-IV participating, four-year public and private not-for-profit, degree-granting (primarily baccalaureate) institutions in the United States that enroll first-time freshmen and are not open admission.)

50. Schmidt, "In Admissions Decisions, the Deciders' Own Backgrounds Play a Big Role."

51. Clinedinst and Korentang, *2017 State of College Admission*.

52. Schmidt, "In Admissions Decisions, the Deciders' Own Backgrounds Play a Big Role."

53. Saul Geiser with Roger Studley, "UC and the SAT: Predictive Validity and Differential Impact of the SAT I and SAT II at the University of California," University of California Office of the President, October 29, 2001.

54. Rothstein, "College Performance Predictions and the SAT."

55. Nicholas Lemann, *The Big Test: The Secret History of American Meritocracy* (New York: Farrar, Straus & Giroux, 1999); David Owen and Marilyn Doerr, *None of the Above: The Truth Behind the SATs* (Lanham, MD; Rowman & Littlefield, 1999); Schmidt, *Color and Money*.

56. See Lemann, *The Big Test*, and Owen and Doerr, *None of the Above*, for extensive discussions of the debates over question validity. See also Maria Veronica Santelices and Mark Wilson, "Unfair Treatment? The Case of Freedle, the SAT, and the Standardization Approach to Differential Item Functioning," *Harvard Educational Review* 80, no. 1 (Spring 2010).

57. Anemona Hartocollis, "SAT 'Adversity Score' Is Abandoned in Wake of Criticism," *New York Times*, August 27, 2019.

58. Lemann, *The Big Test*, 344.

59. Owen and Doerr, *None of the Above*, 190.

60. The abbreviation originally stood for American College Testing.

61. Richard C. Atkinson and Saul Geiser, "Reflections on a Century of College Admissions Tests," *Educational Researcher* 38, no. 9 (December 2009): 665–76.

62. E.F. Lindquist, "The Nature of the Problem of Improving Scholarship and College Entrance Examinations," paper presented at Educational Testing Service invitational conference on testing problems, November 1, 1958 (Princeton, NJ: Educational Testing Service, 1958). As quoted in Atkinson and Geiser, "Reflections on a Century of College Admissions Tests."

63. Atkinson and Geiser, "Reflections on a Century of College Admissions Tests."

64. Atkinson and Geiser, "Reflections on a Century of College Admissions Tests."

65. Emily J. Shaw, Jessica P. Marini, Jonathan Beard, Doron Shmueli, Linda Young, and Helen Ng, "The Redesigned SAT Pilot Predictive Validity Study: A First Look" (College Board, 2016), 6.

66. Geiser with Studley, "UC and the SAT."

67. Anthony P. Carnevale, Martin Van Der Werf, Michael C. Quinn, Jeff Strohl, and Dmitri Repnikov, *Our Separate & Unequal Public Colleges: How Public Colleges Reinforce White Racial Privilege and Marginalize Black and Latino Students* (Washington, DC: Georgetown University Center on Education and the Workforce, 2018).

68. Carnevale et al., *Our Separate & Unequal Public Colleges.*

69. Anthony P. Carnevale and Jeff Strohl, "How Increasing College Access Is Increasing Inequality," in *Rewarding Strivers: Helping Low-Income Students Succeed in College,* ed. Richard D. Kahlenberg (New York: Century Foundation Books, 2010).

70. Josh Zumbrun, "SAT Scores and Income Inequality: How Wealthier Kids Rank Higher," *Wall Street Journal,* October 7, 2014.

71. Jesse M. Rothstein, "College Performance Predictions and the SAT," *Journal of Econometrics* 121, no. 1–2 (2004): 297–317.

72. Eric Turkheimer, Andreana Haley, Mary Waldron, Brian D'Onofrio, and Irving I. Gottesman, "Socioeconomic Status Modifies Heritability of IQ in Young Children," *Psychological Science* 14, no. 6 (November 2003): 623–28; Richard E. Nisbett, *Intelligence and How to Get It: Why Schools and Cultures Count* (New York: W.W. Norton, 2009).

73. Turkheimer et al., "Socioeconomic Status Modifies Heritability of IQ in Young Children."

74. Federal education data as summarized in Schmidt, *Color and Money,* 42. See also Richard D. Kahlenberg, *All Together Now: Creating Middle-Class Schools Through Public-School Choice* (Washington, DC: Brookings Institution Press, 2001); Anthony P. Carnevale, Megan L. Fasules, Michael C Quinn, and Kathryn Peltier Campbell, *Born to Win, Schooled to Lose: Why Equally Talented Students Don't Get Equal Chances to Be All They Can Be* (Washington, DC: Georgetown University Center on Education and the Workforce, 2019).

75. Paul Attewell and Thurston Domina, "Raising the Bar: Curricular

Intensity and Academic Performance," *Educational Evaluation and Policy Analysis* 30, no. 1 (March 2008): 51–71; Kristen Klopfenstein, "Advanced Placement: Do Minorities Have Equal Opportunity?," *Economics of Education Review* 23 (2004): 115–31.

76. Michael N. Bastedo, Joseph E. Howard, and Allyson Flaster, "Holistic Admissions After Affirmative Action: Does 'Maximizing' the High School Curriculum Matter?," *Educational Evaluation and Policy Analysis* 38, no. 2 (June 2016): 389–409.

77. Joshua Klugman, "The Advanced Placement Arms Race and the Reproduction of Educational Inequality," *Teachers College Record* 115 (May 2013).

78. Atkinson and Geiser, "Reflections on a Century of College Admissions Tests."

79. Pamela R. Bennett, Amy C. Lutz, and Lakshmi Jayaram, "Beyond the Schoolyard: The Role of Parenting Logics, Financial Resources, and Social Institutions in the Social Class Gap in Structured Activity Participation," *Sociology of Education* 85, no. 2 (2012): 131–57 (as cited in Bastedo, "Enrollment Management and the Low-Income Student"); Anthony P. Carnevale, Nicole Smith, Michelle Melton, and Eric W. Price, *Learning While Earning: The New Normal* (Washington, DC: Georgetown University Center on Education and the Workforce, 2015); Anthony P. Carnevale and Nicole Smith, *Balancing Work and Learning: Implications for Low-Income Students* (Washington, DC: Georgetown University Center on Education and the Workforce, 2018).

80. Elizabeth Stearns and Elizabeth J. Glennie, "Opportunities to Participate: Extracurricular Activities' Distribution Across and Academic Correlates in High Schools," *Social Science Research* 39, no. 2 (2010): 296–309.

81. Bastedo, "Enrollment Management and the Low-Income Student," citing Patricia M. McDonough, *Choosing Colleges: How Social Class and Schools Structure Opportunity* (Albany: SUNY Press, 1997).

82. Clinedinst and Korentang, *2017 State of College Admission*; Schmidt, *Color and Money*; Paul E. Barton, *One-Third of a Nation: Rising Dropout Rates and Declining Opportunities* (Princeton, NJ: Educational Testing Service, 2005).

83. Caroline Hodges Persell and Peter W. Cookson Jr., "Chartering and Bartering," in *The High-Status Track: Studies of Elite Schools and Stratification*, ed. Paul W. Kingston and Lionel S. Lewis (Albany: SUNY Press, 1990), 25–49.

84. Melissa Clinedinst, *2014 State of College Admission* (Washington, DC: National Association for College Admission Counseling, 2015).

85. Carnevale and Strohl, "How Increasing College Access Is Increasing Inequality."

86. Christopher Avery, Andrew Fairbanks, and Richard J. Zeckhauser, "What Worms for the Early Bird: Early Admissions at Elite Colleges," August 2001, John F. Kennedy School of Government Faculty Research Working Papers Series RWP01-049, available at https://ssrn.com/abstract=295569; see also Christopher Avery, Andrew Fairbanks, and Richard Zeckhauser, *The*

Early Admissions Game: Joining the Elite (Cambridge, MA: Harvard University Press, 2003).

87. Clinedinst and Korentang, *2017 State of College Admission*.

88. *U.S. News & World Report* ceased factoring yield rates into its rankings in 2003 in an attempt to extricate the magazine from the debate over early admissions policies. See Jeffrey R. Young, "In Response to Critics, U.S. News Changes Its Formula for Ranking Colleges," *Chronicle of Higher Education*, July 18, 2003.

89. Schmidt, *Color and Money*.

90. Daniel Golden, "'Buying' Your Way Into College," *Wall Street Journal*, March 12, 2003.

91. Jacques Steinberg, "Of Sheepskin and Greenbacks," *New York Times*, February 13, 2003.

92. Daniel Golden, "'Buying' Your Way Into College."

93. Rachel Toor, *Admissions Confidential: An Insider's Account of the Elite College Selection Process* (New York: St. Martin's Griffin, 2002), 209–21.

94. William G. Bowen and Sarah A. Levin, *Reclaiming the Game: College Sports and Educational Values* (Princeton, NJ: Princeton University Press, 2003).

95. William G. Bowen, Martin A. Kurzweil, and Eugene M. Tobin, *Equity and Excellence in American Higher Education* (Charlottesville, VA: University of Virginia Press, 2005), 106.

96. Jack Stripling, "'It's an Aristocracy': What the Admissions-Bribery Scandal Has Exposed About Class on Campus," *Chronicle of Higher Education*, April 17, 2019; Eric Hoover, "Bribery Scandal Reveals 'Weak Spots' in the Admissions System. Don't Be So Shocked," *Chronicle of Higher Education*, March 13, 2019.

97. Douglas S. Massey, Camille Z. Charles, Garvey F. Lundy, and Mary J. Fischer, *The Source of the River: The Social Origins of Freshmen at America's Selective Colleges and Universities* (Princeton, NJ: Princeton University Press, 2003).

98. Peter Schmidt, "Affirmative Action, Relatively Speaking," *Chronicle of Higher Education*, January 14, 2005. Cornell University told the newspaper it had recently admitted 29 percent of all applicants, but 58 percent of those were the children of employees.

99. Bastedo, "Enrollment Management and the Low-Income Student."

100. See Carol L. Elam and Norma E. Wagoner, "Legacy Admissions in Medical School," American Medical Association *Virtual Mentor* 14, no. 12 (December 2012): 946–49.

101. Daniel Golden, "An Analytic Survey of Legacy Preference," *Affirmative Action for the Rich*; Chad Coffman, Tara O'Neil, and Brian Starr, "An Empirical Analysis of the Impact of Legacy Preferences on Alumni Giving at Top Universities," *Affirmative Action for the Rich* (New York: Century Foundation Press, 2010).

102. Michael Hurwitz, "The Impact of Legacy Status on Undergraduate Admissions at Elite Colleges and Universities," *Economics of Education*

Review 30 (2011): 480–92; Elyse Ashburn, "At Elite Colleges, Legacy Status May Count More Than Was Previously Thought," *Chronicle of Higher Education*, January 5, 2011.

103. Cameron Howell and Sarah E. Turner, "Legacies in Black and White: The Racial Composition of the Legacy Pool," *Research in Higher Education* 45, no. 4 (June 2004): 325–51.

104. Unpublished analysis conducted as part of other research. Anthony P. Carnevale and Stephen J. Rose, "Socioeconomic Status, Race/Ethnicity, and Selective College Admissions," *America's Untapped Resource: Low-Income Students in Higher Education*, ed. Richard D. Kahlenberg (New York: Century Foundation, 2003).

105. Bastedo, "Enrollment Management and the Low-Income Student."

106. Hossler, "How Enrollment Management Has Transformed—or Ruined—Higher Education."

107. Ronald G. Ehrenberg, Liang Zhang, and Jared M. Levin, "Crafting a Class: The Trade-Off Between Merit Scholarships and Enrolling Lower-Income Students," *Review of Higher Education* 29, no. 2 (2006): 195–211.

108. Ozan Jaquette and Bradley R. Curs, "Creating the Out-of-State University: Do Public Universities Increase Nonresident Freshman Enrollment in Response to Declining State Appropriations?," *Research in Higher Education* 56 (2015): 535–65.

109. Ozan Jaquette, Bradley R. Curs, and Julie R. Posselt, "Tuition Rich, Mission Poor: Nonresident Enrollment Growth and the Socioeconomic and Racial Composition of Public Research Universities," *Journal of Higher Education* 87, no. 5 (September/October 2016): 635–73.

110. Matthew Quirk, "The Best Class Money Can Buy."

Chapter 5: Separate and Unequal

1. 2018 National Association of College and University Business Officers (NACUBO)-TIAA Study of Endowments, January 31, 2019.

2. Georgetown University Center on Education and the Workforce analysis of data from the Integrated Postsecondary Education Data System (IPEDS), U.S. Department of Education.

3. Georgetown University Center on Education and the Workforce analysis of data from the Integrated Postsecondary Education Data System (IPEDS), U.S. Department of Education.

4. *Digest of Education Statistics*, 2017 edition, web table 317.10.

5. Thomas D. Snyder, ed., *120 Years of American Education: A Statistical Portrait* (Washington, DC: U.S. Department of Education, Office of Educational Research and Improvement, National Center for Education Statistics, 1993).

6. *Digest of Education Statistics*, 2017 edition, web table 302.10.

7. *Digest of Education Statistics*, 2017 edition, web table 302.20 (three-year moving average).

8. Women make up about 55 percent of full-time undergraduate students

and first outnumbered men among full-time undergraduates in 1985. U.S. Department of Education, National Center for Education Statistics, Higher Education General Information Survey (HEGIS), "Fall Enrollment in Colleges and Universities" surveys, 1970 through 1985; Integrated Postsecondary Education Data System (IPEDS), "Fall Enrollment Survey" (IPEDS-EF:86-99); IPEDS Spring 2001 through Spring 2016, Fall Enrollment component; and Enrollment in Degree-Granting Institutions Projection Model, 2000 through 2026.

9. Authors' analysis of Education Longitudinal Study and High School and Beyond final follow-up. Analysis conducted using National Center for Education Statistics public access files with Powerstats.

10. National Center for Education Statistics, *Digest of Education Statistics* tables, table 303.10, 2017; Joshua Hatch and Brian O'Leary, "Where Does Your Freshman Class Come From?," *Chronicle of Higher Education*, August 16, 2016.

11. Georgetown University Center on Education and the Workforce analysis of data from the Integrated Postsecondary Education Data System (IPEDS), U.S. Department of Education, 2016–17.

12. Kevin J. Delaney, "New Data Show How Hard It Was to Get into an Elite US College This Year," *Quartz*, March 31, 2019.

13. "Best Colleges Rankings—Southern Connecticut University," *U.S. News & World Report*, 2019.

14. Georgetown University Center on Education and the Workforce analysis of data from the Integrated Postsecondary Education Data System (IPEDS), U.S. Department of Education, 2016–17.

15. In terms of absolute mobility, the share of twenty-five-to-sixty-four-year-olds who exceeded their parents' educational attainment was only smaller in three countries (Austria, Germany, and the Czech Republic) in the Organisation for Economic Co-operation and Development (OECD). See Chart A4.3 in OECD, *Education at a Glance 2014: OECD Indicators* (OECD Publishing, 2014). Also see OECD, "A Family Affair: Intergenerational Social Mobility across OECD Countries," in *Economic Policy Reforms 2010: Going for Growth* (Paris: OECD Publishing, 2010).

16. Anthony P. Carnevale, Megan L. Fasules, Michael C. Quinn, and Kathryn Peltier Campbell, *Born to Win, Schooled to Lose: Why Equally Talented Students Don't Get Equal Chances to Be All They Can Be* (Washington, DC: Georgetown University Center on Education and the Workforce, 2019).

17. Anthony P. Carnevale and Jeff Strohl, *Separate & Unequal: How Higher Education Reinforces the Intergenerational Reproduction of White Racial Privilege* (Washington, DC: Georgetown University Center on Education and the Workforce, 2013); Carnevale et al., *Born to Win, Schooled to Lose*.

18. Carnevale and Strohl, *Separate & Unequal*; Eric R. Eide, Michael J. Hilmer, and Mark H. Showalter, "Is It Where You Go or What You Study? The Relative Influence of College Selectivity and College Major on Earnings," *Contemporary Economic Policy* 34, no. 1 (2016): 37–46.

19. See Anthony P. Carnevale, Artem Gulish, and Jeff Strohl, *Educational*

Adequacy in the Twenty-First Century (Washington, DC: The Century Foundation and Georgetown University Center on Education and the Workforce, 2018); Dirk Krueger and Krishna B. Kumar, "Skill-Specific Rather Than General Education: A Reason for US-Europe Growth Differences?," *Journal of Economic Growth* 9, no. 2 (2004): 167–207; Eric A. Hanushek, Ludger Woessmann, and Zhang Lei, "General Education, Vocational Education, and Labor-Market Outcomes Over the Life-Cycle," CESifo working paper no. 3614 (2011); Eric Gould, "Rising Wage Inequality, Comparative Advantage, and the Growing Importance of General Skills in the United States," *Journal of Labor Economics* 20, no. 1 (2002): 105–47; and Thomas Bailey and Clive R. Belfield, "Community College Occupational Degrees: Are They Worth It?," in *Preparing Today's Students for Tomorrow's Jobs in Metropolitan America*, ed. Laura Perna (Philadelphia, PA: University of Pennsylvania Press, 2012): 121–48.

20. Carnevale and Strohl, *Separate & Unequal*.

21. Anthony P. Carnevale, Martin Van Der Werf, Michael C. Quinn, Jeff Strohl, and Dmitri Repnikov, *Our Separate & Unequal Public Colleges: How Public Colleges Reinforce White Racial Privilege and Marginalize Black and Latino Students* (Washington, DC: Georgetown University Center on Education and the Workforce, 2018).

22. For a discussion of the focus on employment-oriented education at less-prestigious institutions, see Steven Brint, Mark Riddle, Lori Turk-Bicakci, and Charles S. Levy, "From the Liberal to the Practical Arts in American Colleges and Universities: Organizational Analysis and Curricular Change," *Journal of Higher Education* 76, no. 2 (2005): 151–80; for a discussion of racial and class stratification across different educational tracks, see National Leadership Council for Liberal Education and America's Promise, *College Learning for the New Global Century* (Washington, DC: Association of American Colleges and Universities, 2007), 9.

23. Carnevale and Strohl, *Separate & Unequal*.

24. Lawrence Biemiller, "Small, Rural Colleges Grapple with Their Geography," *Chronicle of Higher Education,* June 10, 2016; Lee Gardner, "Where Does the Regional State University Go From Here?" *Chronicle of Higher Education*, May 22, 2016; Eric Kelderman, "The Plight of the Regional Public College," *Chronicle of Higher Education,* November 19, 2014; "Private Colleges with Low Scores on the U.S. Department of Education's Financial-Responsibility Test, 2014–15," *Chronicle of Higher Education,* August 13, 2017; Lee Gardner, "Public Regional Colleges Never Die. Can They Be Saved?" *Chronicle of Higher Education,* April 30, 2017; Jon Marcus, "Why Some Small Colleges Are in Big Trouble," *Boston Globe,* April 14, 2013; Jeffrey J. Selingo, "Colleges Struggling to Stay Afloat," *New York Times,* April 12, 2013.

25. William C. Boland and Marybeth Gasman, "State Funding Cuts Routinely Hurt Certain Colleges More Than Others," *The Hill,* February 20, 2017.

26. See, for example, Henry T. Kasper, "The Changing Role of Community College," *Occupational Outlook Quarterly* (Winter 2002–3): 14–21.

27. Caroline M. Hoxby and Bridget Terry Long, "Explaining Rising Income

and Wage Inequality among the College Educated," NBER Working Paper No. 6873, January 1999; Michael S. McPherson and Morton O. Schapiro, *Reinforcing Stratification in American Higher Education: Some Disturbing Trends* (Stanford, CA: National Center for Postsecondary Improvement, Stanford University, 1999); Gordon C. Winston, "Subsidies, Hierarchy and Peers: The Awkward Economics of Higher Education," *Journal of Economic Perspectives* 13, no. 1 (Winter 1999): 13–36; Gordon C. Winston, "Economic Stratification and Hierarchy in U.S. Colleges and Universities," Williams Project on the Economics of Higher Education Discussion Paper No. 58, November 2000; Gordon C. Winston and Catharine B. Hill, "Access to the Most Selective Private Colleges by High-Ability, Low-Income Students: Are They Out There?," Williams Project on the Economics of Higher Education Discussion Paper No. 69, October 2005; Caroline Hoxby, "The Changing Selectivity of American Colleges," 2009, NBER Working Paper 15446.

28. Winston, "Subsidies, Hierarchy and Peers."

29. The remaining 24 percent of public enrollments are at middle-tier institutions.

30. Carnevale et al., *Our Separate & Unequal Public Colleges*.

31. Anthony P. Carnevale and Jeff Strohl, "How Increasing College Access Is Increasing Inequality, and What to Do About It," in *Rewarding Strivers: Helping Low-Income Students Succeed in College*, ed. Richard D. Kahlenberg (New York: Century Foundation Press, 2010).

32. Gordon C. Winston, "Subsidies, Hierarchy and Peers." A subsequent study found that there still remains a disparity in institutional subsidies of educational expenditures: the bottom 10 percent of colleges spend less than 70 cents on education-related expenses for every $1 they collect in tuition and fees, while the top 10 percent of colleges spend more than $2 on education-related expenses for every $1 they collect in tuition. John J. Cheslock, "Examining Instructional Spending for Accountability and Consumer Information Purposes," The Century Foundation, February 28, 2019.

33. John W. Curtis, *The Employment Status of Instructional Staff Members in Higher Education, Fall 2011* (Washington, DC: The American Association of University Professors, 2014).

34. Peter Schmidt, "Accreditation Is Eyed as a Means to Aid Adjuncts," *Chronicle of Higher Education*, March 25, 2012; Peter Schmidt, "Summit on Adjuncts Yields Tentative Framework for Campaign to Improve Their Conditions," *Chronicle of Higher Education*, January 29, 2012.

35. For a thorough critique of this trend, see Michael Fabricant and Stephen Brier, *Austerity Blues*.

36. Carnevale et al., *Our Separate & Unequal Public Colleges*.

37. See, for example, Daniel de Vise, "State Colleges Accepting More Nonresidents to Keep Up Revenue," *Washington Post*, November 14, 2009.

38. Stephen Burd, *Undermining Pell: Volume IV* (Washington, DC: New America, 2018).

39. See, for example, Patrick M. Callan, *California Higher Education, the Master Plan, and the Erosion of College Opportunity*, National Center Report

#09-1 (San Jose, CA: The National Center for Public Policy and Higher Education, 2009).

40. Burd, *Undermining Pell: Volume IV*.

41. Steven Burd, ed., "Introduction," *Moving on Up?: What a Groundbreaking Study Tells Us About Access, Success, and Mobility in Higher Ed* (Washington, DC: New America, 2017).

42. Students' eligibility for Pell Grants is based on several factors, including family income, government benefits received, and number of siblings in college at the time. See Ernest Ezeugo and Clare McCann, "Chetty vs. Pell: What's the Best Way to Measure a College's Commitment to Low-Income Students?," in *Moving on Up?: What a Groundbreaking Study Tells Us About Access, Success, and Mobility in Higher Ed*, ed. Steven Burd, 25–27 (Washington, DC: New America, 2018).

43. Ezeugo and McCann, "Chetty vs. Pell."

44. Matt Reed, "Beyond FTE's: Formulas, Budgets and Community Colleges," *Inside Higher Ed*, May 19, 2016.

45. Steven W. Hemelt, Kevin M. Strange, Fernando Furquim, Andrew Simon, and John E. Sawyer, "Why Is Math Cheaper Than English? Understanding Cost Differences in Higher Education," National Bureau of Economic Research Working Paper No. 25314, November 2018.

46. Kevin Strange, "Ability Sorting and the Importance of College Quality to Student Achievement: Evidence from Community Colleges," Working Paper, University of Michigan, Ann Arbor, 2009.

47. Patrick M. Callan, "Stewards of Opportunity: America's Public Community Colleges," *Daedalus* 126, no. 4 (1997): 95–112.

48. Eleanor Wiske Dillon and Jeffrey Andrew Smith, "Determinants of the Match Between Student Ability and College Quality," *Journal of Labor Economics* 35, no. 1 (January 2017).

49. Caroline M. Hoxby and Christopher Avery, "The Missing 'One-Offs': The Hidden Supply of High-Achieving, Low-Income Students," *Brookings Papers on Economic Activity*, Spring 2013, 1–65.

50. Hoxby and Avery, "The Missing 'One-Offs.'"

51. David T. Ellwood and Thomas J. Kane, "Who Is Getting a College Education? Family Background and the Growing Gap in Enrollment," paper written for the Macalester Forum on Higher Education Conference, Macalester College, St. Paul, Minnesota, June 1999; Brian K. Fitzgerald and Jennifer A. Delaney, "Educational Opportunity in America," in *Condition of Access: Higher Education for Lower Income Students*, ed. Donald E. Heller (Westport, CT: American Council on Education, Praeger Series on Higher Education, 2003); Thomas Mortenson, "Pell Grant Enrollment at State Flagship Universities 1992–93 and 2001–02," *Postsecondary Education Opportunity* 140 (February 2004); Anthony P. Carnevale and Stephen J. Rose, "Socioeconomic Status, Race/Ethnicity, and Selective College Admissions," in *America's Untapped Resource: Low-Income Students in Higher Education*, ed. Richard D. Kahlenberg (New York: The Century Foundation, 2004); Winston and Hill, "Access to the Most Selective Private Colleges"; Danette Gerald and Kati Haycock, *Engines*

of Inequality: Diminishing Equity in the Nation's Premier Public Universities (Washington, DC: Education Trust, 2006); William G. Bowen, Martin A. Kurzweil, and Eugene M. Tobin, *Equity and Excellence in American Higher Education* (Charlottesville, VA: University of Virginia Press, 2006); William G. Bowen, Matthew M. Chingos, and Michael S. McPherson, *Crossing the Finish Line: Completing College at America's Public Universities* (Princeton, NJ: Princeton University Press, 2009).

52. Andrew S. Belasco and Michael J. Trivette, "Aiming Low: Estimating the Scope and Predictors of Postsecondary Undermatch," *Journal of Higher Education* 86, no. 2 (March/April 2015): 233–63; Jonathan Smith, Matea Pender, and Jessica Howell, "The Full Extent of Student-College Academic Undermatch," *Economics of Education Review* 32 (2013): 247–61.

53. Smith, Pender, and Howell, "The Full Extent of Student-College Academic Undermatch."

54. Belasco and Trivette, "Aiming Low."

55. Steven G. Brint and Jerome Karabel, *The Diverted Dream: Community Colleges and the Promise of Educational Opportunity in America, 1900–1985* (Oxford: Oxford University Press, 1989); Yossi Shavit, Richard Arum, and Adam Gamoran, *Stratification in Higher Education: A Comparative Study* (Palo Alto, CA: Stanford University Press, 2007).

56. Adam Looney and Constantine Yannelis, "A Crisis in Student Loans? How Changes in the Characteristics of Borrowers and the Institutions They Attended Contributed to Rising Loan Defaults," *Brookings Papers on Economic Activity*, Fall 2015.

57. Gregory R. Wegner, Lloyd Thacker, Jerome A. Lucido, and Scott Andrew Schulz, *The Case for Change in College Admissions: A Call for Individual and Collective Leadership* (Los Angeles, CA: University of Southern California Center for Enrollment Research, Policy and Practice, 2011), 7.

58. For discussion of the costs associated with college applications, see Jennifer Glynn, *Opening Doors: How Selective Colleges and Universities Are Expanding Access for High-Achieving, Low-Income Students* (Jack Kent Cooke Foundation, 2017).

59. Wegner et al., *The Case for Change in College Admissions.*

60. Glynn, *Opening Doors.*

61. Raj Chetty, John N. Friedman, Emmanual Saez, Nicholas Turner, and Danny Yagan, "Mobility Report Cards: The Role of Colleges in Intergenerational Mobility," NBER Working Paper No. 23618, July 2017, http://www.equality-of-opportunity.org/papers/coll_mrc_paper.pdf.

62. Chetty et al., "Mobility Report Cards."

63. Stephen Burd, "Even at Private Colleges, Low-Income Students Tend to Go to the Poorest Schools," in *Moving on Up?: What a Groundbreaking Study Tells Us About Access, Success, and Mobility in Higher Ed*, ed. Stephen Burd (Washington, DC: New America, 2017).

64. Ezeugo and McCann, "Chetty vs. Pell."

65. Peter Sacks, "How Colleges Perpetuate Inequality," *Chronicle of Higher Education*, January 12, 2007.

66. Sacks, "How Colleges Perpetuate Inequality."
67. Carnevale et al., *Our Separate & Unequal Public Colleges.*
68. Carnevale and Strohl, *Separate & Unequal*; Carnevale et al., *Our Separate & Unequal Public Colleges*; Anthony P. Carnevale, Stephen J. Rose, and Jeff Strohl, "Achieving Racial and Economic Diversity with Race-Blind Admissions Policy," in *The Future of Affirmative Action: New Paths to Higher Education Diversity After Fisher v. University of Texas*, ed. Richard D. Kahlenberg (New York: Century Foundation Press, 2014); Anthony P. Carnevale and Stephen J. Rose, "Socioeconomic Status, Race/Ethnicity, and Selective College Admissions," in *America's Untapped Resource: Low-Income Students in Higher Education*, ed. Richard D. Kahlenberg (New York: Century Foundation Press, 2004); Anthony P. Carnevale, "The Admissions System Is Worse Than Broken. It's Fixed," *Washington Post*, March 19, 2019.
69. Michael N. Bastedo and Ozan Jaquette, "Running in Place: Low-Income Students and the Dynamics of Higher Education Stratification," *Educational Evaluation and Policy Analysis* 33, no. 3 (September 2011): 318–39.
70. Bastedo and Jaquette, "Running in Place."
71. Michael Rothschild and Lawrence J. White, "The University in the Marketplace: Some Insights and Some Puzzles," in *Studies of Supply and Demand in Higher Education*, ed. Charles T. Clotfelter and Michael Rothschild (Chicago: University of Chicago Press, 1993); Michael Rothschild and Lawrence J. White, "The Analytics of the Pricing of Higher Education and Other Services in Which the Customers Are Inputs," *Journal of Political Economy* 103, no. 3 (1995): 573–86; Caroline M. Hoxby, "The Changing Selectivity of American Colleges," National Bureau of Economic Research Working Paper No. 15446, 2009; Michael N. Bastedo, "Convergent Institutional Logics in Public Higher Education: State Policymakers and Governing Board Activism," *Review of Higher Education* 32, no. 2 (2009): 209–34; Michael N. Bastedo, "Cascading in Higher Education: Examining Longitudinal Evidence on Institutional Stratification," Seminar Presentation at the University of Illinois, February 13, 2009.
72. For more discussion of these claims, see Rothschild and White, "The University in the Marketplace"; Rothschild and White, "The Analytics of the Pricing of Higher Education"; Hoxby, "The Changing Selectivity of American Colleges"; Bastedo, "Convergent Institutional Logics"; Bastedo, "Cascading in Higher Education"; Charles T. Clotfelter, *Buying the Best: Cost Escalation in Elite Higher Education*, NBER Monograph (Princeton, NJ: Princeton University Press, 1996); and Dan A. Black and Jeffrey A. Smith, *How Robust Is the Evidence on the Effects of College Quality? Evidence from Matching*, CIBC Human Capital and Productivity Project Working Papers no. 20033 (London, Ontario: University of Western Ontario, CIBC Human Capital and Productivity Project, 2006).
73. Hoxby, "The Changing Selectivity of American Colleges."
74. Stacy Berg Dale and Alan B. Krueger, "Estimating the Payoff to Attending a More Selective College," NBER Working Paper No. 7332, August 1999; Winston, "Economic Stratification and Hierarchy in U.S. Colleges and Universities"; Adam S. Booij, Edwin Leuven, and Hessel Oosterbeek, "Ability

NOTES 257

Peer Effects in University: Evidence from a Randomized Experiment," *Review of Economic Studies* 84, no. 2 (April 2017), 547–78; Joshua D. Angrist, "The Perils of Peer Effects," *Labour Economics* 30 (2014): 98–108.

75. Dale and Krueger, "Estimating the Payoff to Attending a More Selective College."

76. Caroline Hoxby, "The Changing Selectivity of American Colleges," *Journal of Economic Perspectives* 23, no. 4 (2009): 13.

77. Georgetown University Center on Education and the Workforce analysis of the Education Longitudinal Study of 2002 (public-use data), 2012.

78. Georgetown University Center on Education and the Workforce, *The Forgotten 500,000 College-Ready Students* (video), https://www.youtube.com/watch?v=K-vGcqowMyg.

79. Carnevale and Strohl, *Separate & Unequal.*

80. Georgetown University Center on Education and the Workforce analysis of data from the Education Longitudinal Study of 2002.

81. Georgetown University Center on Education and the Workforce analysis of data from the Education Longitudinal Study of 2002.

82. Thomas R. Bailey, Davis Jenkins, and D. Timothy Leinbach, *Is Student Success Labeled Institutional Failure? Student Goals and Graduation Rates in the Accountability Debate at Community Colleges,* CCRC Working Paper 1 (New York: Community College Research Center, Teachers College, Columbia University, 2006); Ellen M. Bradburn, David G. Hurst, and Samuel Peng, *Community College Transfer Rates to 4-Year Institutions Using Alternative Definitions of Transfer,* NCES Report 2001-197 (Washington, DC: National Center for Education Statistics, Institute of Education Sciences, U.S. Department of Education, 2001); Jane V. Wellman, *State Policy and Community College–Baccalaureate Transfer,* National Center Report #02-6 (San Jose, CA: National Center for Public Policy and Higher Education, 2002); John Bound, Michael Lovenheim, and Sarah Turner, "Why Have College Completion Rates Declined?," NBER Working Paper No. 15566, December 2009.

83. Scott A. Ginder, Janice E. Kelly-Reid, and Farrah B. Mann, *Graduation Rates for Selected Cohorts, 2008–13; Outcome Measures for Cohort Year 2008; Student Financial Aid, Academic Year 2015–16; and Admissions in Postsecondary Institutions, Fall 2016* (Washington, DC: National Center for Education Statistics Institute of Education Sciences, 2017). Georgetown University Center on Education and the Workforce analysis of data from the 2003–04 Beginning Postsecondary Students Longitudinal Study, Second Follow-Up, 2008–09.

84. Sam Peltzman, "The Effect of Government Subsidies-in-Kind on Private Expenditures: The Case of Higher Education," *Journal of Political Economy* 81, no. 5 (1973): 1049–91; Paul N. Courant, Michael McPherson, and Alexandra M. Resch, "The Public Role in Higher Education," *National Tax Journal* 59, no. 2 (2006): 291–318.

85. Students at the most selective colleges are more likely to attend graduate school and have higher annual earnings ten years after graduation than those at less-selective two- and four-year colleges; see Carnevale and Strohl, *Separate & Unequal.*

86. Anthony P. Carnevale, Stephen J. Rose, and Ban Cheah, *The College Payoff: Education, Occupations, and Lifetime Earnings* (Washington, DC: Georgetown University Center on Education and the Workforce, 2011).

87. Claudia Goldin and Lawrence F. Katz, "Long-Run Changes in the U.S. Wage Structure: Narrowing, Widening, Polarizing," *Brookings Papers on Economic Activity* no. 2 (2007): 135–67; see also David Autor, "Skills, Education, and the Rise of Earnings Inequality Among the 'Other 99 Percent,'" *Science* 344, no. 6186 (May 2014): 843–51.

88. Carnevale et al., *Born to Win, Schooled to Lose.*

Chapter 6: The Fight for Fairness

1. Laura Isensee, "How a Dad Helped Start the Fight for Better Public School Funding in Texas," Houston Public Media, September 7, 2015, https://www.houstonpublicmedia.org/articles/news/2015/09/07/59720/how-a-dad-helped-start-the-fight-for-better-public-school-funding-in-texas-2; Elaine Ayala, "Rodriguez, Who Fought for Equality, Dies at 87," *MySA* (*San Antonio Express-News*), April 23, 2013, https://www.mysanantonio.com/news/local_news/article/Rodriguez-who-fought-for-equality-dies-at-87-4456618.php.

2. *San Antonio Indep. Sch. Dist. v. Rodriguez*, 411 U.S. 1 (1973), https://supreme.justia.com/cases/federal/us/411/1/#tab-opinion-1950219.

3. Daniel Bell, "On Meritocracy and Equality," *The Public Interest*, Fall 1972, 29–68.

4. Bell, "On Meritocracy and Equality."

5. U.S. Commission on Civil Rights, *Toward Equal Educational Opportunity: Affirmative Action Programs in Law and Medical Schools* (Washington, DC: U.S. Government Printing Office, 1978), as cited in Peter Schmidt, *Color and Money: How Rich White Kids Are Winning the War Over College Affirmative Action* (New York: Palgrave Macmillan, 2007).

6. William G. Bowen, Martin A. Kurzweil, and Eugene M. Tobin, *Equity and Excellence in American Higher Education* (Charlottesville, VA: University of Virginia Press, 2005), 20–23; Schmidt, *Color and Money.*

7. Jerome Karabel, *The Chosen: The Hidden History of Admission and Exclusion at Harvard, Yale, and Princeton* (New York: Houghton Mifflin, 2005), 397–409; Schmidt, *Color and Money.*

8. Charles T. Clotfelter, *After Brown: The Rise and Retreat of School Desegregation* (Princeton, NJ: Princeton University Press, 2004), 7; Schmidt, *Color and Money.*

9. Clotfelter, *After Brown*, 22; U.S. Commission on Civil Rights, *Toward Equal Educational Opportunity*; Schmidt, *Color and Money.*

10. Sheryll Cashin, *The Failures of Integration: How Race and Class Are Undermining the American Dream* (New York: Public Affairs, 2004), 83–124; Stephen Richard Higley, *Privilege, Power & Place: The Geography of the American Upper Class* (Lanham, MD: Rowman & Littlefield, 1995), 31–47; Schmidt, *Color and Money.*

11. Cashin, *Failures of Integration.*

12. Higley, *Privilege, Power & Place*, 1–30.

13. Sarah Mervosh, "Minneapolis, Tackling Housing Crisis and Inequity, Votes to End Single-Family Zoning," *New York Times*, December 13, 2018.

14. Higley, *Privilege, Power & Place.*

15. Clotfelter, *After Brown*, 16–17.

16. James Bryant Conant, *Slums and Suburbs: A Commentary on Schools in Metropolitan Areas* (New York: McGraw-Hill, 1961).

17. Karabel, *The Chosen*, 407–9.

18. John D. Skrentny, *The Ironies of Affirmative Action: Politics, Culture, and Justice in America* (Chicago: University of Chicago Press, 1996), 67–110; Schmidt, *Color and Money.*

19. Karabel, *The Chosen*, 380–409.

20. Karabel, *The Chosen*, 380–409.

21. Skrentny, *The Ironies of Affirmative Action*, 67–110; Schmidt, *Color and Money.*

22. Peter Schmidt, "Historically Black Colleges Seek Congress's Help in Desegregation Disputes," *Chronicle of Higher Education*, March 30, 2007; Adam Harris, "They Wanted Desegregation. They Settled for Money, and It's About to Run Out," *Chronicle of Higher Education*, March 26, 2018.

23. Clotfelter, *After Brown*, 37, 100–25; Schmidt, *Color and Money.*

24. John D. Skrentny, *The Minority Rights Revolution* (Cambridge, MA: Belknap Press of Harvard University Press, 2002), 278; Skrentny, *The Ironies of Affirmative Action*, 182; Kevin P. Philips, *The Emerging Republican Majority* (New Rochelle, NY: Arlington House, 1969); Thomas Byrne Edsall with Mary D. Edsall, *Chain Reaction: The Impact of Race, Rights, and Taxes on American Politics* (New York: W.W. Norton, 1992).

25. Terry H. Anderson, *The Pursuit of Fairness: A History of Affirmative Action* (New York: Oxford University Press, 2004); Schmidt, *Color and Money.*

26. Nathan Glazer, *Affirmative Action: Ethnic Inequality and Public Policy* (New York: Basic Books, 1975), 220–21; Schmidt, *Color and Money.*

27. Carol A. Horton, *Race and the Making of American Liberalism* (New York: Oxford University Press, 2005), 219.

28. Horton, *Race and the Making of American Liberalism.*

29. Schmidt, *Color and Money*, 115–16.

30. *Sweezy v. New Hampshire*, 354 U.S. 243 (1957).

31. Schmidt, *Color and Money*, 81.

32. Nancy Weiss Malkiel, *"Keep the Damned Women Out": The Struggle for Coeducation* (Princeton, NJ: Princeton University Press, 2016).

33. Anthony P. Carnevale, Nicole Smith, and Artem Gulish, *Women Can't Win: Despite Making Educational Gains and Pursuing High-Wage Majors, Women Still Earn Less Than Men* (Washington, DC: Georgetown University Center on Education and the Workforce, 2018); Nick Anderson, "The Gender Factor in College Admissions: Do Men or Women Have an Edge?," *Washington Post*, March 26, 2014; Terrance F. Ross, "What Gender Inequality Looks Like in Collegiate Sports," *The Atlantic*, March 18, 2015.

34. Peter Schmidt, "'Bakke' Set a New Path to Diversity for Colleges," *Chronicle of Higher Education*, June 20, 2008.

35. Dana Y. Takagi, *The Retreat from Race: Asian-American Admissions and Racial Politics* (New Brunswick, NJ: Rutgers University Press, 1992), 9, 27–28; Karabel, *The Chosen*, 501.

36. Schmidt, *Color and Money*.

37. Schmidt, *Color and Money*, and Schmidt, "For Asians, Affirmative Action Cuts Both Ways," *Chronicle of Higher Education*, June 6, 2003.

38. Peter Schmidt, "Lawsuits Against Harvard and UNC-Chapel Hill Urge an End to Race-Conscious Admissions," *Chronicle of Higher Education*, November 18, 2014.

39. Daniel Hertz, "You've Probably Never Heard of One of the Worst Supreme Court Decisions," *Washington Post*, July 24, 2014.

40. Karabel, *The Chosen*, 380–409.

41. Karabel, *The Chosen*, 397–409, 483–84; Schmidt, *Color and Money*.

42. *Grutter v. Bollinger*, 288 F.3d 732 (6th Cir. 2002).

43. Black and Latino students who score above 1000 on the SAT graduate at a rate of 73 percent at the 500 most selective colleges, compared to 40 percent at open-access colleges. Anthony P. Carnevale and Jeff Strohl, *Separate & Unequal: How Higher Education Reinforces the Intergenerational Reproduction of White Racial Privilege* (Georgetown University Center on Education and the Workforce, 2013.

44. Robert L. Jacobson, "Admissions Help Urged," *Chronicle of Higher Education*, November 8, 1967.

45. See, for example, John Aubrey Douglass, "Anatomy of a Conflict: The Making and Unmaking of Affirmative Action at the University of California," in *Color Lines: Affirmative Action, Immigration, and Civil Rights Options for America*, ed. John D. Skrentny (Chicago: University of Chicago Press, 2001), 118–44; and Schmidt, *Color and Money*.

46. Julie Renee Posselt, Ozan Jacquette, Rob Bielby, and Michael N. Bastedo, "Access Without Equity: Longitudinal Analyses of Institutional Stratification by Race and Ethnicity, 1972–2004," *American Educational Research Journal* 49, no. 6 (December 2012): 1074–11.

47. *Board of Education of Oklahoma City v. Dowell*, 498 U.S. 237 (1991).

48. *Freeman v. Pitts*, 498 U.S. 1081 (1992); Peter Schmidt, "Desegregation Study Spurs Debate Over Equity Remedies," *Education Week*, January 12, 1993.

49. *Missouri v. Jenkins*, 515 U.S. 70 (1995).

50. *Parents Involved in Community Schools v. Seattle School District No. 1*, 551 U.S. 701 (2007); Peter Schmidt, "Supreme Court Leaves Affirmative-Action Precedents Intact in Striking Down School-Integration Plans," *Chronicle of Higher Education*, June 28, 2017.

51. Schmidt, "Historically Black Colleges Seek Congress's Help in Desegregation Disputes."

52. *Alexander v. Sandoval*, 532 U.S. 275 (2001).

53. *DeFunis v. Odegaard*, 416 U.S. 312 (1974).

54. *Regents of the University of California v. Bakke*, 438 U.S. 265 (1978).

55. Carnegie Council on Policy Studies in Higher Education, *The Relevance of Race in Admissions* (Berkeley, CA: Carnegie Council on Policy Studies in Higher Education, 1977); Schmidt, *Color and Money*.

56. Schmidt, *Color and Money*, 116.

57. Schmidt, "'Bakke' Set a New Path to Diversity for Colleges."

58. Schmidt, "'Bakke' Set a New Path to Diversity for Colleges."

59. Schmidt, "'Bakke' Set a New Path to Diversity for Colleges."

60. Schmidt, "'Bakke' Set a New Path to Diversity for Colleges."

61. *Wygant v. Jackson Board of Education*, 476 U.S. 267 (1986); *City of Richmond v. J.A. Croson Co.*, 488 U.S. 469 (1989).

62. Schmidt, *Color and Money*, 175–76; *Adarand Constructors, Inc. v. Peña*, 515 U.S. 200 (1995).

63. Schmidt, *Color and Money*, 118–119; *Podberesky v. Kirwan*, 38 F.3d 147 (4th Cir. 1994).

64. Peter Schmidt, "From 'Minority' to 'Diversity,'" *Chronicle of Higher Education*, February 3, 2006.

65. Peter Schmidt, "As Colleges Open Race-Exclusive Programs to All, Some Minority Students May Be Left Out in the Cold," *Chronicle of Higher Education*, January 26, 2006; Daniel Golden, "Colleges Cut Back Minority Programs After Court Rulings," *Wall Street Journal*, December 30, 2003; Brian Kladko, "Princeton Cuts Minority-Only Summer Program," *The Record*, February 11, 2003.

66. Schmidt, *Color and Money*, 87–96.

67. *Hopwood v. Texas*, 78 F.3d 932.

68. Peter Schmidt, "Cal. Vote to Ban Racial Preferences Sparks Lawsuits, Protests," *Chronicle of Higher Education*, November 15, 1996; Peter Schmidt, "An End to Affirmative Action? Californians Prepare to Vote," *Chronicle of Higher Education*, October 25, 1996; Kit Lively, "University of California Ends Race-Based Hirings, Admissions," *Chronicle of Higher Education*, July 28, 1995.

69. Schmidt, *Color and Money*, 145.

70. Schmidt, *Color and Money*.

71. Markus Kemmelmeier and David G. Winter, "Putting Threat into Perspective: Experimental Studies on Perceptual Distortion in International Conflict," *Personality and Social Psychology Bulletin* 26, no. 7 (2000): 795–809; Kazuho Ozawa, Matthew Crosby, and Faye Crosby, "Individualism and Resistance to Affirmative Action: A Comparison of Japanese and American Samples 1," *Journal of Applied Social Psychology* 26, no. 13 (1996): 1138–52.

72. John T. Jost and Erik P. Thompson, "Group-Based Dominance and Opposition to Equality as Independent Predictors of Self-Esteem, Ethnocentrism, and Social Policy Attitudes Among African Americans and European Americans," *Journal of Experimental Social Psychology* 36, no. 3 (2000): 209–32; see also Felicia Pratto, James Sidanius, Lisa M. Stallworth, and Bertram F. Malle, "Social Dominance Orientation: A Personality Variable Predicting Social and Political Attitudes," *Journal of Personality and Social Psychology* 67, no. 4 (1994): 741–63; James Sidanius, Felicia Pratto, and Lawrence Bobo,

"Racism, Conservatism, Affirmative Action, and Intellectual Sophistication: A Matter of Principled Conservatism or Group Dominance?," *Journal of Personality and Social Psychology* 70, no. 3 (1996): 476; James Sidanius and Felicia Pratto, *Social Dominance: An Intergroup Theory of Social Hierarchy and Oppression* (Cambridge, UK: Cambridge University Press, 1999); Christopher M. Federico and Jim Sidanius, "Racism, Ideology, and Affirmative Action Revisited: The Antecedents and Consequences of 'Principled Objections' to Affirmative Action," *Journal of Personality and Social Psychology* 82, no. 4 (2002): 488; Yesilernis Peña and Jim Sidanius, "US Patriotism and Ideologies of Group Dominance: A Tale of Asymmetry," *Journal of Social Psychology* 142, no. 6 (2002): 782–90.

73. Schmidt, *Color and Money*, 126.

74. *Johnson v. Board of Regents of the University System of Georgia*, 106 F. Supp. 2d 1362 (S.D. Ga. 2000); Schmidt, *Color and Money*, 150, 176–78.

75. *Smith v. University of Washington, Law School*, 233 F.3d 1188 (9th Cir. 2000); *Grutter v. Bollinger*, 288 F.3d 732 (6th Cir. 2002).

76. Schmidt, *Color and Money*, 111–30, 173–80.

77. See also Eric Grodsky and Demetra Kalogrides, "The Declining Significance of Race in College Admissions Decisions," *American Journal of Education* 115, no. 1 (2008): 1–33.

78. National Association for College Admissions Counseling, *Diversity and College Admissions in 2003: A Survey Report*, September 2003.

79. Schmidt, *Color and Money*, 203–10.

80. Peter Schmidt, "'Fisher' Ruling May Open a 'Wave of Litigation Against Colleges,'" *Chronicle of Higher Education*, June 26, 2013.

81. *Fisher v. University of Texas at Austin*, 579 U.S. ___ (2016).

82. Peter Schmidt, "Supreme Court Upholds Bans on Racial Preferences in College Admissions," *Chronicle of Higher Education*, April 22, 2014.

83. Eight states have banned race-based affirmative action: California, Washington, Michigan, Nebraska, Arizona, Oklahoma, Florida, and New Hampshire; see Halley Potter, "What Can We Learn from States That Ban Affirmative Action?" Century Foundation website, June 26, 2014. The demographic analysis is based on the population of people ages eighteen to twenty-four in these states; Georgetown University Center on Education and the Workforce analysis of data from U.S. Census Bureau, American Community Survey, 2014–16 (pooled).

84. Richard Kahlenberg, "Economic Affirmative Action in College Admissions: A Progressive Alternative to Racial Preferences and Class Rank Admissions Plans," Issue Brief Series, Century Foundation, New York, 2003.

85. Peter Schmidt, "New Research Complicates Discussions of Campus Diversity—in a Good Way," *Chronicle of Higher Education*, January 31, 2010; Camille Z. Charles, Mary J. Fischer, Margarita A. Mooney, and Douglas S. Massey, "Affirmative-Action Programs for Minority Students: Right in Theory, Wrong in Practice," *Chronicle of Higher Education*, March 27, 2009; Peter Schmidt, "Study Offers Mixed Assessment of Race-Conscious Admissions Policies," *Chronicle of Higher Education*, March 4, 2005.

86. See, for example, Peter Schmidt, "New Study Fuels Debate Over 'Mismatch' Theory in Race-Conscious Admissions," *Chronicle of Higher Education*, December 17, 2015; Peter Schmidt, "What Color Is an A?" *Chronicle of Higher Education*, June 1, 2007; Kevin Kiley, "Civil-Rights Panel Weighs In on Where Minorities Fare Best in STEM Fields," *Chronicle of Higher Education*, December 6, 2010; David Glenn, "Minority Students Fare Better at Selective Colleges, Sociologists Find," *Chronicle of Higher Education*, August 16, 2004.

87. Katherine S. Mangan, "Does Affirmative Action Hurt Black Law Students?," *Chronicle of Higher Education*, November 12, 2004; Paulette Walker Campbell, "Minority Applications to Medical School Drop in States Without Affirmative Action," *Chronicle of Higher Education*, November 14, 1997; Katherine S. Mangan, "The Unusual Rules for Affirmative Action in Medical Schools," *Chronicle of Higher Education*, November 24, 2000.

88. Lorelle E. Espinosa, Matthew N. Gaertner, and Gary Orfield, *Race, Class, and College Access: Achieving Diversity in a Shifting Legal Landscape* (Washington, DC: American Council on Education, 2015).

89. Lani Guinier, "Saving Affirmative Action," *Village Voice*, July 8, 2003.

90. Lani Guinier, *The Tyranny of the Meritocracy: Democratizing Higher Education in America* (Boston: Beacon Press, 2015), 41.

Chapter 7: Built to Collapse

1. Reporting based on interviews by one of this book's co-authors, Peter Schmidt, who attended this conference.

2. Figures based on Independent Educational Consultants Association literature distributed at the conference site.

3. Peace Bransberger and Demarée K. Michelau, *Knocking at the College Door: Projections of High School Graduates* (Boulder, CO: Western Interstate Commission for Higher Education, 2016).

4. For the report referenced here, see Making Caring Common Project, "Turning the Tide: Inspiring Concern for Others and the Common Good Through College Admissions," Harvard Graduate School of Education, January 2016, http://mcc.gse.harvard.edu/files/gse-mcc/files/20160120_mcc_ttt_report_interactive.pdf?m=1453303517.

5. Georgetown University Center on Education and the Workforce analysis of data from the Education Longitudinal Study of 2002. In this instance, top-scoring refers to SAT scores of at least 1250 and "most affluent" refers to the top quartile of socioeconomic status.

6. Emma Pettit, "A Fifth of Private Colleges Report First-Year Discount Rate of 60 Percent, Moody's Says," *Chronicle of Higher Education*, November 14, 2018.

7. Adam Harris, "Moody's Downgrades Higher Ed's Outlook From 'Stable' to 'Negative,'" *Chronicle of Higher Education*, December 5, 2017.

8. Rick Seltzer, "Ratings Agencies Post Mixed Outlooks for Higher Education," *Inside Higher Ed*, December 11, 2019.

9. Anthony P. Carnevale, "Graduate Education and the Knowledge

Economy," in *Graduate Education in 2020: What Does the Future Hold?* (Washington, DC: Council of Graduate Schools, 2009).

10. Richard V. Reeves, *Dream Hoarders: How the American Upper Middle Class Is Leaving Everyone Else in the Dust, Why That Is a Problem, and What You Can Do About It* (Washington, DC: Brookings Institution Press, 2017), 57, 58.

11. Daniel Bell, "On Meritocracy and Equality," *The Public Interest*, Fall 1972, 29–68.

12. Jason England, "Admissions Confidential," *Chronicle of Higher Education*, December 3, 2017; italics in original.

13. Jason England, "Admissions Confidential," *Chronicle of Higher Education*, December 3, 2017; italics in original.

14. Caroline Hoxby, "The Changing Selectivity of American Colleges," *Journal of Economic Perspectives* 23, no. 4 (2009): 95–118.

15. Rebecca Zwick, "Is the SAT a 'Wealth Test'? The Link Between Educational Achievement and Socioeconomic Status" in *Rethinking the SAT*, ed. Rebecca Zwick (New York: Routledge, 2013).

16. Michael Rothschild and Lawrence J. White, "The University in the Marketplace: Some Insights and Some Puzzles," in *Studies of Supply and Demand in Higher Education*, eds. Charles T. Clotfelter and Michael Rothschild (Chicago: University of Chicago Press, 1993); Michael Rothschild and Lawrence J. White, "The Analytics of the Pricing of Higher Education and Other Services in Which the Customers Are Inputs," *Journal of Political Economy* 103, no. 3 (1995): 573–86; Hoxby, "The Changing Selectivity of American Colleges"; Michael N. Bastedo, "Convergent Institutional Logics in Public Higher Education: State Policymakers and Governing Board Activism," *Review of Higher Education* 32, no. 2 (2009), 209–34; Michael N. Bastedo, "Cascading in Higher Education: Examining Longitudinal Evidence on Institutional Stratification," Seminar Presentation at the University of Illinois, February 13, 2009.

17. Jesse M. Rothstein, "College Performance Predictions and the SAT," *Journal of Econometrics* 121, nos. 1–2 (2004): 297–317.

18. Calculated based on statistics in Anthony P. Carnevale, Martin Van Der Werf, Michael C. Quinn, Jeff Strohl, and Dmitri Repnikov, *Our Separate & Unequal Public Colleges: How Public Colleges Reinforce White Racial Privilege and Marginalize Black and Latino Students* (Washington, DC: Georgetown University Center on Education and the Workforce, 2018).

19. Anthony P. Carnevale and Jeff Strohl, *Separate & Unequal: How Higher Education Reinforces the Intergenerational Reproduction of White Racial Privilege* (Washington, DC: Georgetown University Center on Education and the Workforce, 2013). For more on the relationship between funding and student outcomes, see Douglas A. Webber and Ronald G. Ehrenberg, "Do Expenditures Other Than Instructional Expenditures Affect Graduation and Persistence Rates in American Higher Education?," *Economics of Education Review* 29, no. 6 (2010): 947–58; John Bound, Michael F. Lovenheim, and Sarah Turner, "Why Have College Completion Rates Declined? An Analysis of Changing Student Preparation and Collegiate Resources," *American*

Economic Journal: Applied Economics 2, no. 3 (2010): 129–57; Richard Kahlenberg, *Policy Strategies for Pursuing Adequate Funding of Community Colleges* (New York: The Century Foundation, 2018); Richard D. Kahlenberg, "Community of Equals?," *Democracy Journal*, Spring 2014; David J. Deming and Christopher R. Walters, "The Impact of Price Caps and Spending Cuts on U.S. Postsecondary Attainment," National Bureau of Economic Research, Working Paper No. 23736, August 2017.

20. Carnevale and Strohl, *Separate & Unequal.*

21. Corbin Campbell, Marisol Jimenez, and Christine Arlene N. Arrozal, "Prestige or Education: College Teaching and Rigor of Courses in Prestigious and Non-prestigious Institutions in the US," *Higher Education* (2018): 1–22.

22. Ruffalo Noel Levitz, *2018 Cost of Recruiting an Undergraduate Student Report* (Cedar Rapids, IA: Ruffalo Noel Levitz, 2018).

23. Donald Hossler and David Kalsbeek, "Enrollment Management and Managing Enrollments: Revisiting the Context for Institutional Strategy," *Strategic Enrollment Management Quarterly*, April 4, 2013.

24. Don Hossler, Jacob P. K. Gross, and Brandi M. Beck, *Putting the College Admission "Arms Race" in Context: An Analysis of Recent Trends in College Admission and Their Effects on Institutional Policies and Practices* (Arlington, VA: National Association for College Admissions Counseling, 2010).

25. Study by Luke Behaunek of Simpson College and Ann M. Gansemer-Topf of Iowa State University, as quoted in Peter Schmidt, "Is Tuition Discounting Leading Some Colleges Off a Cliff?," *Chronicle of Higher Education*, April 28, 2017.

26. Kellie Woodhouse, "Discount Much?," *Inside Higher Ed*, November 25, 2015.

27. The University of Akron in 2018 eliminated eighty degree tracks, or 19 percent of its total offerings. This came a few months after the University of Wisconsin–Stevens Point eliminated many of its majors in the humanities. Colleen Flaherty, "U of Akron Cuts 80 Degree Tracks," *Inside Higher Ed*, August 16, 2018.

28. Christina Tkacik, "Maryland's Goucher College Eliminating Several Majors, Including Math," *Baltimore Sun*, August 15, 2018.

29. Mickey Shuey, "Amid Financial Strains, Earlham Puts $100 Million into Campus Updates," *Richmond (Ind.) Palladium-Item*, August 9, 2018.

30. Anthony P. Carnevale and Jeff Strohl, "How Increasing College Access Is Increasing Inequality, and What to Do About It," in *Rewarding Strivers: Helping Low-Income Students Succeed in College*, ed. Richard D. Kahlenberg (New York: Century Foundation Press, 2010).

31. Anthony P. Carnevale, "Every Year, Half a Million Top Scoring Students Never Get a College Credential," LinkedIn (blog post), April 12, 2018.

32. Georgetown University Center on Education and the Workforce analysis of Current Population Survey March Supplement, 1971–2017.

33. Anthony P. Carnevale, Stephen J. Rose, and Ban Cheah, *The College Payoff: Education, Occupations, Lifetime Earnings* (Washington, DC: Georgetown University Center on Education and the Workforce, 2011).

34. Georgetown University Center on Education and the Workforce analysis of Current Population Survey March Supplement, 1971–2017.

35. In 1967, the middle class included almost half of families headed by high school dropouts and 70 percent of those headed by people who ceased their educations after high school. By 2004, middle-class status could be claimed by only a third of families headed by dropouts and half of those headed by people with no more than a high school diploma. During that period, the share of families in the highest-paid 30 percent headed by people with bachelor's degrees rose from 22 percent to 39 percent, by someone with a graduate degree, from 32 percent to 56 percent. See Anthony P. Carnevale, "Access to Opportunity: The Need for Universal Education and Training After High School," *Education Week*, June 12, 2007.

36. Anthony P. Carnevale, Tamara Jayasundera, and Artem Gulish, *America's Divided Recovery: College Haves and Have-Nots* (Washington, DC: Georgetown University Center on Education and the Workforce, 2016).

37. Thomas R. Dye, *Who's Running America? The Bush Restoration*, 7th ed. (Upper Saddle River, NJ: Prentice Hall, 2002), 148.

38. Anthony P. Carnevale, Jeff Strohl, Artem Gulish, Martin Van Der Werf, and Kathryn Peltier Campbell, *The Unequal Race for Good Jobs: How Whites Made Outsized Gains in Education and Good Jobs Compared to Blacks and Latinos* (Washington, DC: Georgetown University Center on Education and the Workforce, 2019). While there is no official or universally accepted definition of an earnings level that renders a U.S. resident self-sustaining, this report defines a good job for workers ages twenty-five to forty-four as one that pays at least $35,000 annually, or $17 per hour for full-time work. For workers ages forty-five to sixty-four, this report identifies a good job as one paying at least $45,000 annually, or $22 per hour for full-time work. We use this two-tiered system based on the presumption that higher earnings levels are required for self-sufficiency among older workers. All earnings are reported in 2016 dollars. The jobs that meet either of the two age-based good-job standards pay a median of $65,000 annually.

39. Willard Waller, *The Sociology of Teaching* (New York: John Wiley and Sons, 1965).

40. Gregory R. Wegner, Lloyd Thacker, Jerome A. Lucido, Scott Andrew Schulz, *The Case for Change in College Admissions: A Call for Individual and Collective Leadership* (Los Angeles, CA: USC Center for Enrollment Research, Policy and Practice, 2011), 5.

41. Carnevale et al., *Our Separate & Unequal Public Colleges.*

42. Pamela R. Bennett and Amy Lutz, "How African American Is the Net Black Advantage? Differences in College Attendance Among Immigrant Blacks, Native Blacks, and Whites," *Sociology of Education* 82, no. 1 (2009): 70–100.

43. Thomas J. Espenshade, Chang Y. Chung, and Joan L. Walling, "Admission Preferences for Minority Students, Athletes, and Legacies at Elite Universities," *Social Science Quarterly* 85, no. 5 (2004): 1422–46; Thomas J. Espenshade and Alexandria Walton Radford, *No Longer Separate, Not Yet*

Equal: Race and Class in Elite College Admission and Campus Life (Princeton, NJ: Princeton University Press, 2009).

44. See, for example, Peter Schmidt, "How the Missouri Protests Might Change the Game for Other Colleges," *Chronicle of Higher Education*, November 13, 2015; Peter Schmidt, "Demand Surges for Diversity Consultants," *Chronicle of Higher Education*, May 15, 2016; Peter Schmidt, "University of California's Proposed Statement on Intolerance Is Widely Found Intolerable," *Chronicle of Higher Education*, September 16, 2015; Peter Schmidt, "New Insights on What Psychologically Rattles Graduate Students," *Chronicle of Higher Education*, November 12, 2016; Peter Schmidt, "A University Examines Underlying Problems After Racist Incidents," *Chronicle of Higher Education*, March 14, 2008; Peter Schmidt, "Study Offers Mixed Assessment of Race-Conscious Admissions Policies," *Chronicle of Higher Education*, March 4, 2005.

45. Raj Chetty, John N. Friedman, Emmanual Saez, Nicholas Turner, and Danny Yagan, "Mobility Report Cards: The Role of Colleges in Intergenerational Mobility" (The Equality of Opportunity Project, January 2017).

46. Ernest Ezeugo and Clare McCann, "Chetty vs. Pell: What's the Best Way to Measure a College's Commitment to Low-Income Students?," in *Moving on Up: What a Groundbreaking Study Tells Us About Access, Success, and Mobility in Higher Ed*, ed. Stephen Burd (Washington DC: New America, 2017).

47. Chetty et al., "Mobility Report Cards."

48. Peter Sacks, "How Colleges Perpetuate Inequality," *Chronicle of Higher Education*, January 12, 2007.

49. David R. Johnson and Jared L. Peifer, "How Public Confidence in Higher Education Varies by Social Context," *Journal of Higher Education*, April 2017.

50. Sara Hebel, "From Public Good to Private Good," *Chronicle of Higher Education*, March 2, 2014.

51. Peter Schmidt, "Faculty Foe: Scott Walker," *Chronicle of Higher Education*, December 13, 2015.

52. Eric Gould, *The University in a Corporate Culture* (New Haven, CT: Yale University Press, 1999), 102.

53. Gordon Lafer, "The Corporate Assault on Higher Education," *Chronicle of Higher Education*, April 30, 2017.

54. Mark G. Yudof, "Is the Public Research University Dead?," *Chronicle of Higher Education*, January 11, 2002.

55. Federal Reserve Bank of New York, Quarterly Report on Household Debt and Credit, 2019: Q2 (August 2019).

56. U.S. Department of Education, "Official Cohort Default Rates for Schools," 2018, https://www2.ed.gov/offices/OSFAP/defaultmanagement/cdr.html.

57. Kim Clark, "A Record Number of People Aren't Paying Back Their Student Loans," *Money*, March 14, 2017.

58. Adam Looney and Constantine Yannelis, "A Crisis in Student Loans? How Changes in the Characteristics of Borrowers and in the Institutions They Attended Contributed to Rising Loan Defaults," *Brookings Papers on Economic Activity*, Fall 2015.

59. Organisation for Economic Co-operation and Development, *Education at a Glance 2019* (Paris: OECD Publishing, 2019).

60. David Card and Thomas Lemieux, "Can Falling Supply Explain the Rising Return to College for Younger Men?," *Quarterly Journal of Economics* 116, no. 2 (May 2001): 70–46; Claudia Goldin and Lawrence F. Katz, *The Race Between Education and Technology* (Cambridge, MA: Harvard University Press, 2010).

61. Alexander Monge-Naranjo, "Workers Abroad Are Catching Up to U.S. Skill Levels," *The Regional Economist* (Third Quarter, 2017): 6–7, https://www.stlouisfed.org/~/media/publications/regional-economist/2017/third_quarter_2017/monje.pdf.

62. *Grutter v. Bollinger*, 288 F.3d 732 (6th Cir. 2002).

63. Christopher Hayes, *Twilight of the Elites: America After Meritocracy* (New York: Crown Publishers, 2012), 2–13.

64. Michael Young, *The Rise of the Meritocracy, 1870–2033* (London: Penguin Books, 1962).

65. Gregory R. Wegner, Lloyd Thacker, Jerome A. Lucido, Scott Andrew Schulz, *The Case for Change in College Admissions: A Call for Individual and Collective Leadership* (Los Angeles, CA: USC Center for Enrollment Research, Policy and Practice, 2011), 5.

66. Wegner et al., *The Case for Change in College Admissions*, 9.

67. Raymond Fisman, Pamela Jakiela, Shacher Kariv, and Daniel Markovits, "The Distributional Preferences of an Elite," *Science* 349, no. 6254 (September 18, 2015). This study compared the behavior of Yale Law School students, undergraduates at the University of California at Berkeley, and members of the public at large in a simulation involving decisions on how to distribute wealth. The Yale Law students were far more likely than others to disregard considerations of fairness and focus on their selfish gain. The Berkeley students fell between Yale students and the public.

68. Rosa Rodríguez-Bailón, Miguel Moya, and Vincent Yzerbyt, "Who Do Superiors Attend to Negative Stereotypic Information About Their Subordinates? Effects of Power Legitimacy on Social Perception," *European Journal of Social Psychology*, 30 (2000), 651–71.

69. Valerie Alexandra, Miguel M. Torres, Olga Kovbasyuk, Theophilus B.A. Addo, and Maria Cristina Ferreira, "The Relationship Between Social Cynicism Belief, Social Dominance Orientation, and the Perception of Unethical Behavior: A Cross-Cultural Examination in Russia, Portugal, and the United States," *Journal of Business Ethics* 146 (2017): 545–62.

70. In the United States, the distinction between cosmopolitans and locals dates back to the work of sociologist Robert K. Merton. When Merton first described this distinction in the mid-twentieth century, he wrote of locals who lived their lives in the context of the town and cosmopolitans who identified more strongly with the nation. Since Merton's day, the cosmopolitan social identity has grown in complexity and gone global. Today, the local and nationalist perspectives are aligned with the localism of previous generations. See Robert K. Merton, *Social Theory and Social Structure* (New York: The Free

11. Stacy Berg Dale and Alan B. Krueger, "Estimating the Payoff to Attending a More Selective College: An Application of Selection on Observables and Unobservables," *Quarterly Journal of Economics* 117, no. 4 (2002): 1491–1527.

12. Gregory R. Wegner, Lloyd Thacker, Jerome A. Lucido, and Scott Andrew Schulz, *The Case for Change in College Admissions: A Call for Individual and Collective Leadership* (Los Angeles: University of Southern California Center for Enrollment Research, Policy and Practice, 2011), 14.

13. Anthony P. Carnevale and Jeff Strohl, *Separate & Unequal: How Higher Education Reinforces the Intergenerational Reproduction of White Racial Privilege* (Washington, DC: Georgetown University Center on Education and the Workforce, 2013).

14. Anthony P. Carnevale, Martin Van Der Werf, Michael C. Quinn, and Dmitri Repnikov, *Our Separate & Unequal Public Colleges: How Public Colleges Reinforce White Racial Privilege and Marginalize Black and Latino Students* (Washington, DC: Georgetown University Center on Education and the Workforce, 2018).

15. Claudia Goldin and Lawrence F. Katz, "Long-Run Changes in the US Wage Structure: Narrowing, Widening, Polarizing," *Brookings Papers on Economic Activity*, 2 (2007), 135–67.

16. Anthony P. Carnevale, "The Sweet Spot on Free College: Why 14 Is the New 12," *Washington Post*, March 4, 2019.

17. Carnevale and Strohl, *Separate & Unequal*.

18. Carnevale and Strohl, *Separate & Unequal*.

19. Leon Botstein, "College President: SAT Is Part Hoax, Part Fraud," *Time*, March 7, 2014.

20. Carnevale, Van Der Werf, et al., *Our Separate & Unequal Public Colleges*.

21. Anthony P. Carnevale and Stephen J. Rose, "Socioeconomic Status, Race/Ethnicity, and Selective College Admissions," The Century Foundation, 2003.

22. For a lengthier discussion of this point, see Sara Harberson, "The Cowards and Heroes of the SAT and ACT," saraharberson.com, April 30, 2018, http://www.saraharberson.com/blog/the-cowards-and-heroes-of-the-sat-and-act.

23. Richard C. Atkinson and Saul Geiser, "Reflections on a Century of College Admissions Tests," *Educational Researcher* 38, no. 9 (December 2009): 665–76.

24. Catherine B. Hill and Gordon C. Winston, "Low-Income Students and Highly Selective Private Colleges: Geography, Searching, and Recruiting," *Economics of Education Review* 29 (2010): 495–503.

25. New York Times Editorial Board, "End Legacy College Admissions," *New York Times*, September 7, 2019.

26. New York Times Editorial Board, "End Legacy College Admissions."

27. Chuck Grassley, "Some Tax-Exempt Hospitals Are Lax at Providing Charitable Care and Accountability," *STAT*, September 18, 2017.

Press, 1948, 1957); for updates, see Christopher Lasch, *The Revolt of the Eli* *and the Betrayal of Democracy* (New York: W.W. Norton, 1995), and Mi Featherstone, *Undoing Culture: Globalization, Postmodernism and Ident* (London: Sage Publications, 1995).

71. Karen Stenner, *The Authoritarian Dynamic* (New York: Cambrid University Press, 2005); Lenka Dražanová, *Education and Tolerance: A Co* *parative Quantitative Analysis of the Educational Effect on Tolerance* (N< York: Peter Lang, 2017).

72. Dražanová, *Education and Tolerance.*

73. Dražanová, *Education and Tolerance.*

74. Edward L. Glaeser, Giacomo A. M. Ponzetto, and Andrei Schleif< "Why Does Democracy Need Education?," *Journal of Economic Growth* 1 no. 2 (May 2007): 77–99, 79.

75. Patrick J. Deneen, *Why Liberalism Failed* (New Haven, CT: Yale Unive sity Press, 2018), 126–7.

76. Carlos Santos, "Bad Boys: Tales of the University's Tumultuous Ear Years," *Virginia*, Winter 2013, http://uvamagazine.org/articles/bad_boy More recently, Alan Taylor writes of how Jefferson's racist ideas and person commitment to slavery undermined his ability to create the university he ha envisioned; see *Thomas Jefferson's Education* (New York: W.W. Norton, 2019

Chapter 8: College for All

1. Anthony P. Carnevale and Stephen J. Rose, *The Economy Goes to Colleg* *The Hidden Promise of Higher Education in the Post-industrial Service Econ* *omy* (Washington, DC: Georgetown University Center on Education and th Workforce, 2015).

2. David F. Labaree, "Public Goods, Private Goods: The American Strug gle over Educational Goals," *American Educational Research Journal* 34, no. (Spring 1997): 39–91.

3. Labaree, "Public Goods, Private Goods."

4. *San Antonio v. Rodriguez*, 411 U.S. 1 (1973).

5. Emily Parker, *50-State Review: Constitutional Obligations for Publi* *Education* (Denver, CO: Education Commission of the States, 2016).

6. Louisa Diffey and Sarah Steffes, *50-State Review: Age Requirements fo* *Free and Compulsory Education* (Denver, CO: Education Commission of the States, 2017).

7. Labaree, "Public Goods, Private Goods."

8. Anthony P. Carnevale, Jeff Strohl, Martin Van Der Werf, Michael C. Quinn, and Kathryn Peltier Campbell, *SAT-Only Admission: How Would It* *Change College Campuses?* (Washington, DC: Georgetown University Center on Education and the Workforce, 2019).

9. Carnevale et al., *SAT-Only Admission.*

10. Georgetown University Center on Education and the Workforce analy- sis of data from National Center for Education Statistics, Education Longitu- dinal Study of 2002, 2012.

28. For example, the proportion of legacy students or recruited athletes who were admitted to Harvard ranged from 41 percent to 48 percent annually from 2000 to 2017, even while the overall admission rate to Harvard was about 4.5 percent in 2019. Peter Arcidiacono, Josh Kinsler, and Tyler Ransom, "Divergent: The Time Path of Legacy and Athlete Admissions at Harvard," NBER Working Paper 26315, Washington, DC: National Bureau of Economic Research, September 2019.

29. Chad Coffman, Tara O'Neil, and Brian Starr, "An Empirical Analysis of the Impact of Legacy Preferences on Alumni Giving at Top Universities," in *Affirmative Action for the Rich: Legacy Preferences in College Admissions,* ed. Richard D. Kahlenberg (New York: Century Foundation Press, 2010), 101–22.

30. Richard D. Kahlenberg, "10 Myths About Legacy Preferences in College Admissions," *Chronicle of Higher Education,* September 22, 2010.

31. Jack Stripling and Eric Hoover, "In Admissions, the Powerful Weigh In," *Chronicle of Higher Education,* November 29, 2015.

32. Eric Hoover, "'Welcome to the Wild West': The Competition for College Applicants Just Intensified," *Chronicle of Higher Education,* September 29, 2019.

33. Louis Menand, "Is Meritocracy Making Everyone Miserable?," *The New Yorker,* September 23, 2019.

34. Carnevale and Strohl, *Separate & Unequal.*

35. Anthony P. Carnevale and Martin Van Der Werf, *The 20% Solution: Selective Colleges Can Afford to Admit More Pell Grant Recipients* (Washington, DC: Georgetown University Center on Education and the Workforce, 2017).

36. U.S. Department of Education, National Center for Education Statistics. In the 2016–17 academic year, 34.9 percent of undergraduates received a Pell Grant.

37. Carnevale and Van Der Werf, *The 20% Solution.*

38. Carnevale and Van Der Werf, *The 20% Solution.*

39. Peter Sacks, "How Colleges Perpetuate Inequality," *Chronicle of Higher Education,* January 12, 2007.

40. Donald Hossler and David Kalsbeek, "Enrollment Management and Managing Enrollments: Revisiting the Context for Institutional Strategy," *Strategic Enrollment Management Quarterly,* April 4, 2013.

41. Ernest Ezeugo and Clare McCann, "Chetty vs. Pell: What's the Best Way to Measure a College's Commitment to Low-Income Students?" in *Moving on Up: What a Groundbreaking Study Tells Us About Access, Success, and Mobility in Higher Ed,* ed. Stephen Burd (Washington, DC: New America, 2017).

42. Georgetown University Center on Education and the Workforce analysis of data from National Center for Education Statistics, Education Longitudinal Study of 2002, 2012.

43. Richard B. Kahlenberg, *Rewarding Strivers: Helping Low-Income Students Succeed in College* (New York: The Century Foundation, 2010).

44. Peter Schmidt, "In Admission Decisions, the Deciders' Own Backgrounds Play a Big Role," *Chronicle of Higher Education*, April 12, 2016.

45. Warren W. Willingham, *Success in College: The Role of Personal Qualities and Academic Ability* (New York: The College Board, 1985); Warren W. Willingham and Hunter M. Breland, *Personal Qualities and College Admissions* (New York: The College Board, 1982).

46. Richard D. Kahlenberg, *Achieving Better Diversity: Reforming Affirmative Action in Higher Education* (New York: The Century Foundation, 2015).

47. Lani Guinier, *The Tyranny of the Meritocracy: Democratizing Higher Education in America* (Boston: Beacon Press, 2015), 23.

48. Eight states have banned race-based affirmative action: California, Washington, Michigan, Nebraska, Arizona, Oklahoma, Florida, and New Hampshire; see Halley Potter, "What Can We Learn from States That Ban Affirmative Action?," *The Century Foundation*, June 26, 2014. The demographic analysis is based on the population ages 18 to 24 in these states, according to Georgetown University Center on Education and the Workforce analysis of data from the U.S. Census Bureau, American Community Survey, 2014–16 (pooled).

49. Selective public colleges are getting much more difficult to get into in recent years. Fourteen selective public colleges had acceptance rates of 40 percent or less in 2016–17, compared to six selective public colleges with that acceptance rate ten years earlier. Farran Powell, "It's Tougher to Get into These Public Schools," *U.S. News & World Report*, September 27, 2017.

50. Lisa J. Dettling, Joanne W. Hsu, Lindsay Jacobs, Kevin B. Moore, and Jeffrey P. Thompson, "Recent Trends in Wealth-Holding by Race and Ethnicity: Evidence from Survey of Consumer Finances," *Board of Governors of the Federal Reserve System*, September 27, 2017. https://www.federalreserve.gov/econres/notes/feds-notes/recent-trends-in-wealth-holding-by-race-and-ethnicity-evidence-from-the-survey-of-consumer-finances-20170927.htm.

51. Ezekiel J. Dixon-Román, Howard T. Everson, and John J. McArdle, "Race, Poverty and SAT Scores: Modeling the Influences of Family Income on Black and White High School Students' SAT Performance," *Teachers College Record* 115, no. 4 (2013): 1–33.

52. Georgetown University Center on Education and the Workforce analysis of data from National Center for Education Statistics, Education Longitudinal Study of 2002, 2012.

53. Carnevale and Strohl, *Separate & Unequal*.

54. Scott Jaschik, "Survey: Americans Back Diversity, Not Consideration of Race," *Inside Higher Ed*, September 17, 2018. See also Paul M. Sniderman and Edward G. Carmines, *Reaching Beyond Race* (Cambridge, MA: Harvard University Press, 1999).

55. Thomas J. Espenshade and Alexandria Walton Radford, *No Longer Separate, Not Yet Equal: Race and Class in Elite College Admission and Campus Life* (Princeton, NJ: Princeton University Press, 2009).

56. Anthony P. Carnevale, Stephen J. Rose, and Jeff Strohl, "Achieving Racial and Economic Diversity with Race-Blind Admissions Policy," in *The Future of Affirmative Action: New Paths to Higher Education Diversity After Fisher v. University of Texas*, ed. Richard D. Kahlenberg (The Century Foundation, 2014).

57. Anthony P. Carnevale, "Testimony of Anthony P. Carnevale in Front of U.S. Senate Committee on Health Education and Pensions; Hearing on Reauthorizing the Higher Education Act: Accountability and Risk to Taxpayers," January 30, 2018.

58. For a thorough discussion of how the *U.S. News* rankings promote such behavior, see Kevin Carey, "College Rankings Reformed: The Case for a New Order in Higher Education," *Education Sector Reports*, September 2006.

59. For in-depth looks at what an outcomes-based, value-added accountability system might look like, see Siddharth Kulkarni and Jonathan Rothwell, *Beyond College Rankings: A Value-Added Approach to Assessing Two- and Four-Year Schools*, Brookings Institution, April 29, 2015; and Jonathan Rothwell, *Using Earnings Data to Rank Colleges: A Value-Added Approach Updated with College Scorecard Data*, Brookings Institution, October 29, 2015.

60. Carnevale, "Testimony of Anthony P. Carnevale."

61. Anthony P. Carnevale, Stephen J. Rose, and Ban Cheah, *The College Payoff* (Washington, DC: Georgetown University Center on Education and the Workforce, 2011).

62. National Leadership Council for Liberal Education and America's Promise, *College Learning for the New Global Century* (Washington, DC: Association of American Colleges and Universities, 2007).

63. Anthony P. Carnevale, Artem Gulish, and Jeff Strohl, *Educational Adequacy in the Twenty-First Century* (Washington, DC: Georgetown University Center on Education and the Workforce and The Century Foundation, 2018).

64. Anthony P. Carnevale, Nicole Smith, Lenka Dražanová, Artem Gulish, and Kathryn Peltier Campbell, *The Role of Education in Taming Authoritarian Attitudes* (Washington, DC: Georgetown University Center on Education and the Workforce, forthcoming).

65. Anthony P. Carnevale, *We Need a New Deal Between Higher Education and Democratic Capitalism* (Washington, DC: Georgetown University Center on Education and the Workforce, 2017).

66. Ronald J. Daniels, "Don't Underestimate the Value of Humanities," *Hartford Courant*, September 24, 2016.

67. Stephanie Marken and Zac Auter, "Half of U.S. Adults Would Change at Least One Education Decision" (Washington, DC: Gallup, 2017).

68. Carnevale, Rose, and Cheah, *The College Payoff*.

69. Based on extrapolation of difference in average annual salaries from analysis in Anthony P. Carnevale and Ban Cheah, *Five Rules of the College and*

Career Game (Washington, DC: Georgetown University Center on Education and the Workforce, 2018).

70. Carnevale, Rose, and Cheah, *The College Payoff.*

71. Anthony P. Carnevale, Tanya I. Garcia, and Artem Gulish, *Career Pathways: Five Ways to Connect College and Careers* (Washington, DC: Georgetown University Center on Education and the Workforce, 2017).

72. Carnevale, Garcia, and Gulish, *Career Pathways.*

73. Credential Engine, "Counting U.S. Postsecondary and Secondary Credentials," September 2019.

74. Anthony P. Carnevale, Andrew R. Hanson, and Artem Gulish, *Failure to Launch: Structural Shift and the New Lost Generation* (Washington, DC: Georgetown University Center on Education and the Workforce, 2013).

75. We learned this summary vision in much greater detail in conversation with Dan Greenstein, who led the Gates Foundation efforts in higher education reform for many years and is currently the chancellor of the Pennsylvania State System of Higher Education.

76. Farran Powell, "17 States Offer Tuition-Free College Programs," *U.S. News & World Report*, September 19, 2018, https://www.usnews.com/education/best-colleges/paying-for-college/articles/2018-02-01/these-states-offer-tuition-free-college-programs.

77. Meredith Billings, "Understanding the Design of College Promise Programs and Where to Go from Here," *Brown Center Chalkboard* (Washington, DC: The Brookings Institution, September 18, 2018).

78. Anthony P. Carnevale, "Every Year, Half a Million Top-Scoring Students Never Get a College Credential," LinkedIn blog post, April 12, 2018, https://www.linkedin.com/pulse/every-year-half-million-top-scoring-students-never-get-carnevale.

79. Anthony P. Carnevale, "The Promise of O*Net," in *Minding the Gap: Why Integrating High School with College Makes Sense and How to Do It*, ed. Nancy Hoffman, Joel Vargas, Andrea Venezia, and Marc S. Miller (Cambridge, MA: Harvard University Press, 2007).

80. Thomas Humphrey Marshall and Tom Bottomore, *Citizenship and Social Class* (London: Pluto Press, 1992), 49.

81. Christopher Hayes, *Twilight of the Elites: America After Meritocracy* (New York: Crown Publishers, 2012), 18–19.

82. Ralph Waldo Emerson, "Power," in *The Complete Writings* (New York: Wise & Co., 1929), 541.

83. Georgetown University Center on Education and the Workforce analysis of data from National Center for Education Statistics, Education Longitudinal Study of 2002, 2012.

84. Annette Lareau, Elliot B. Weininger, and Amanda Barrett Cox, "How Entitled Parents Hurt Schools," *New York Times*, June 24, 2018.

85. Robert D. Putnam, *Our Kids: The American Dream in Crisis* (New York: Simon & Schuster, 2015), 234–35.

86. Peter Schmidt, *Color and Money: How Rich White Kids Are Winning the War Over College Affirmative Action* (New York: Palgrave Macmillan, 2007).

87. Colin Diver, "Is There Life After Rankings?" *The Atlantic*, November 2005.

INDEX

admission acceptance rates
and probabilities (by applicant
characteristic) (*cont.*)
  donor ties ("development admits"),
    14, 70, 96, 97, 110, 112, 127, 169,
    173, 186, 202, 203, 214
  "early action" or "early decision,"
    109–110, 248n86, 249n88
  employment of parent by college,
    14, 90, 95, 111–112, 127,
    249n98
  geographic area, 18, 70, 88, 97, 99,
    258n10, 270n24
  grades in high school, 88, 102,
    104–105, 272n45
  high school attended, 14, 56,
    207–208
  legacy status, 10, 14, 90, 100, 112,
    127, 202–204, 214, 249n101,
    245n41, 249n102, 271n28,
    271n30
  personal qualities, 272n45
  political ties, 14, 90, 95–97, 110,
    127, 173, 202, 204, 244n20,
    244n21, 244n22, 244n23,
    244n24, 244n25, 244n26,
    244n28, 244n29, 244n30
  race, 18, 84, 111–112, 116,
    138–139, 141–146, 149–166,
    182–183, 187, 207–211,
    221–222, 245n35, 250n104,
    260n35, 260n38, 261n55,
    261n68, 262n77, 262n78,
    262n82, 262n85, 263n86,
    273n56. *See also* affirmative
    action
  recruited athlete, 5–6, 63–64, 88,
    90, 95, 110–112, 127, 152, 203,
    214, 237n23, 259n33, 266n43,
    271n28
  religion, 99–101
  sex, 18, 29, 99, 116, 141, 148,
    150–151, 230n46, 250n8,
    259n32, 259n33
  socioeconomic status, 13–14,
    16, 62, 84, 88–89, 92–93, 113,
    129–130, 149, 183, 204–205,
    207–211, 222, 229n35, 243n17,
    250n104, 262n84, 271n35

standardized test scores, 13–14,
  18, 87, 88–89, 102–105, 170,
  200–202, 238n47, 243n1,
  247n61
admissions considerations. *See*
  admissions acceptance rates
  and probabilities
admissions bias or favoritism, 6, 10,
  14, 21, 82, 95–101, 137–166,
  249n98, 249n101. *See also*
  admission acceptance rates and
  probabilities
admissions consultants, 83, 110
admissions counselors, 5
admissions cycles, 91
admissions deans and directors, 89,
  93–94, 96–97, 169, 172–173,
  176–177
admissions "hooks," 90, 95–97,
  152, 222. *See also* admissions
  acceptance rates and
  probabilities
admissions officers and offices, 4,
  6, 17, 45, 89, 92–99, 101–102,
  108, 110, 167–169, 176–177,
  243n5, 243n8, 243n10, 245n37,
  246n46, 246n49, 249n93,
  265n24, 272n44
admissions policies, 5, 17, 23, 35,
  54–57, 62, 64, 67, 87–114,
  255n57, 256n68, 262n85,
  263n4, 264n12, 265n24. *See
  also* admission acceptance rates
admissions processes, 5, 6, 17, 35,
  54–55, 64, 82, 83, 87–114,
  255n57, 263n4. *See also*
  admission acceptance rates
admissions scandals, 5–7, 95–97,
  110, 227n7, 227n8, 249n96
admissions standards, 54
admissions summer camps, 83
admissions system, 6, 17, 95, 97,
  100, 204, 227n8, 244n20
admissions tests (institutional), 13,
  56–57, 100
"admit-deny" (use of low
  financial aid awards to deter
  matriculation), 114
adult basic education, 125

income, 4, 7, 10, 18, 27, 34, 47,
  52, 65, 70–71, 75–76, 80, 88,
  106, 108, 118–119, 122–126,
  129–130, 132–133, 135, 172,
  175, 179–181, 183–184, 189,
  192, 198, 201, 209, 211–216,
  218, 225, 228n16, 236n7,
  238n56, 241n20, 251n18,
  252n27, 257n85, 258n86,
  258n87, 259n33, 265n33,
  266n38, 272n51, 273n59. *See
  also* low-income
indentured servitude, 36
independent college counselors, 5,
  168
Independent Educational
  Consultants Association, 168,
  263n2. *See also* admissions
  consultants
Indiana, 142, 177
Indiana University, 84
individual liberty, 21, 32, 172
individualism, 11–12, 20, 22, 24,
  27–35, 38, 41, 53, 79, 139–140,
  161, 190, 192, 194, 231n6,
  261n71
Industrial Era, 34, 37, 40, 42–43
industrial order, 42
industrial organization, 216,
Industrial Revolution, 38–39
industrial society, 46
industrialism and industrialization,
  20, 34, 38, 39–40, 233n46
industrialists, 40, 60
industry, 17, 39, 53, 179, 211
inequality. *See also* low-income,
  high-income, middle class,
  upper middle class, African
  Americans, Asian American,
  black people, Latino, white
  people, women, admission
  acceptance rates, graduation
  college access, in, 3–4, 16, 21,
    71–72, 77, 79–80, 120–123,
    138, 172, 183- 184, 190,
    197–198, 237n41, 238n56,
    239n57, 248n77, 254n51
  college preparation, in, 3–4, 16,
    21, 71–72, 77, 79–80, 120–123,

138, 184, 190, 237n41, 238n56,
  247n70, 248n77, 254n51
economic, 3–4, 10, 16, 21, 27,
  30–31, 35, 38–39, 40, 46–47,
  66, 70, 72, 77, 89, 103, 106, 117,
  120–123, 139, 172, 182, 184,
  188, 197–200, 239n57, 247n70,
  251n19, 252n27, 254n51,
  258n87
gender, 40, 89, 106, 259n33
housing, in, 3–4, 16, 21, 77,
  240n18
political representation and
  power, in, 3–4, 16, 27, 31, 77
racial, 3–4, 21, 38, 40, 47, 79–80,
  89, 106, 117, 120–123, 139, 143,
  172, 199, 254n51
schools, in, 3–4, 16, 18, 21, 47,
  71–72, 77, 79–80, 138, 190, 199,
  247n70, 248n77
Information Age, 20
information systems, 216, 218
infrastructure
  college, 121
  residential, 75
  school, 137
innate intelligence, 12, 21, 58,
  103–106, 174, 200–201
inputs vs. outcomes as measures of
  college performance, 51, 62–63,
  184, 211–213, 256n71
institutionalists, 219–220, 222
instructional technology, 222
insurrectionists, 219–220
intelligence, 12, 21, 38, 55, 58, 70,
  79, 84–86, 98, 103–105, 141,
  237n28, 247n72
interest groups, 1
intergenerational reproduction
  of advantage or privilege, 7,
  14–15, 53, 132, 136, 199, 221,
  229n30
intergenerational social mobility,
  71–72, 118, 171, 228n9
Internal Revenue Service (IRS), 124,
  203
international students, 124
internships, 10, 82, 217
interracial marriage, 150

controversies, 64, 103–106, 221,
    246n56, 246n57, 270n19
history, 45, 55–58, 103, 105, 130,
    145, 235n64
influence on schools, 104–105,
    201–202
preparation, 50, 105, 168,
    201–202, 247n70
rankings of colleges, influence on,
    51, 62, 67–68, 94, 200
research on, 13–14, 80–81,
    102–103, 105–106, 131–132,
    134, 155, 174, 201, 208–209,
    229n32, 229n33, 243n18,
    246n53, 247n65, 247n71,
    260n43, 263n5, 264n15,
    264n17, 270n51
score influences, 80–81, 104,
    106, 130, 209, 243n18, 247n70,
    264n15, 270n51
use by colleges, 54, 64, 67, 87–89,
    102, 106, 109, 131, 174, 178,
    195–196, 200–202, 205,
    208–209, 243n1, 243n2, 269n8
Scalia, Antonin (U.S. Supreme Court
    Justice), 154
Scholastic Aptitude Test. *See* SAT
Scholastic Assessment Test. *See* SAT
school districts and systems, 37,
    139–140, 144, 153, 155–156
science, 17, 32, 45, 57, 115, 125, 165,
    214
Seattle, Wash., 156, 260n50
secessionism, 11
Second Industrial Revolution, 38–39
Second Treatise of Civil Government,
    30, 231n7
secularization, 30, 189
self-segregation, 75
"separate but equal" doctrine,
    141–144
Servicemen's Readjustment Act of
    1944 (G.I. Bill), 57
Shain, William M., 90
"The Significance of the Frontier
    in American History," 38, 41,
    233n40
slavery, 4, 11–12, 28, 37–38, 78, 103,
    141, 182, 230n1, 269n76

Slums and Suburbs, 144,
    230n42
Smith, Adam, 30, 32
Smith-Hughes National Vocational
    Education Act of 1917, 43
"snowflakes," 8
social cognition, 73–74, 239n9
social efficiency, 193
Social Darwinism, 38, 233n38
social mechanisms, 72–81
    cognitive mechanisms, 72–74, 98,
        245n32
    cultural mechanisms, 73,
        77–79
    educational mechanisms, 73,
        79–81
    market mechanisms, 72, 76–77
    policy mechanisms, 73, 77
    spatial mechanisms, 72, 74–77,
        241n23
social media, 1, 168
social mobility, 3–4, 7–8, 13–19,
    20, 22–23, 27, 35–36, 43, 47,
    53, 56, 59, 69–86, 119, 133,
    145, 171–174, 181–184, 187,
    190–191, 193–195, 197, 204,
    208, 228n9, 251n15, 252n42,
    255n61, 255n63, 277n41
social networks, 61
social stratification, 39, 45–47,
    187
social unrest, 2, 3
socialism, 39, 44
socioeconomic. *See also* class,
    income, high-income, low-
    income, wealth
    diversity, 19, 81, 85–86, 103, 111,
        129, 178, 183, 195–196,
        206–211, 221, 250n104,
        250n109
    status, 7, 13, 16, 19, 21, 81, 82,
        85–86, 94, 103, 106, 117, 119,
        133, 135, 174, 178, 195–196,
        206–211, 221, 228n16, 228n17,
        243n18, 247n72, 250n104,
        250n109, 263n5, 2564n15
The Sociology of Teaching, 181
Socrates, 30–31
"soft" competencies, 180

sorting mechanisms ("sorting
machine"), 4, 12, 20–21, 45,
49–68, 79–82, 93, 118, 166,
174–175, 185–186, 188, 214,
254n46
South (region of United States), 2,
36, 78, 81, 141–149, 190, 230n1
South Bronx (New York), 86
South Carolina, 49
Southern Connecticut State
University, 115, 117–118,
251n13
Soviet Union, 17, 47, 57
speech codes, 149, 183
Spencer, Richard B., 2
spatial deconcentration, 77, 241n23
sports, collegiate. *See* athletes,
athletics departments
sports stadiums, professional, 75
St. Bonaventure College, 60
standardized admission tests, 7, 18,
21, 45, 46, 57, 65, 83, 92, 99,
101–107, 123, 127, 130–131,
152, 170, 178, 181, 200–202.
See also ACT, SAT
Stanford University, 5, 60, 63, 116,
129, 132, 158, 173
state constitutions, 139, 160, 194
state legislatures and lawmakers, 8,
124, 138, 160, 185
State Longitudinal Dating Systems,
218
state lotteries, 66, 238n55
state public college systems, 54, 123,
147, 156
state school systems, 37
State University of New York, 149
stereotyping, 73–74, 153, 188,
240n11, 241n27, 268n68
stock market, 71
stock ownership, 76
stratification of higher education,
21–22, 49–68, 115–136,
175–176, 182–185, 192, 239n6,
241n33, 248n83, 252m22,
251n27, 256n69, 256n71,
256n74, 260n46
strategic planning, 90
"strict scrutiny" legal tests, 159, 163

"strivers," 3, 7, 14, 23, 196, 207–208,
239n57
student services, 91, 115
student loans, 62, 128, 186, 255n56,
267n57
Students for Fair Admissions,
152–153
suburbs, 83, 129, 142, 144, 153–154,
230n42
summer remediation programs, 64
superstition, 32
Supreme Court of the United States,
97, 138–144, 146, 149–164, 187,
194, 209–211, 244n30, 260n39,
260n50, 262n82
*Swann v. Charlotte-Mecklenburg
Board of Education*, 146
Sweatt, Heman Marion, 143–144
Sweatt v. Painter, 143–144
Sweezy v. New Hampshire, 149,
259n30
syndicalism, 39
Syracuse University, 67
Syverud, Kent, 68

Taplin, Ian, 7
tax jurisdictions, 75
tax policies, 77
teaching, 37, 65, 67, 133, 141,
174–175, 181, 184–185, 194,
201–202, 213, 222, 265n21,
266n39
technical colleges, 54, 59, 116,
125–126, 127
technology, 17, 33, 39, 42, 48, 65, 93,
116, 119, 177, 180, 189, 222,
228n14
tennis, collegiate, 111
Texas, 110, 138–139, 142, 143,
160–164, 258n1
Texas Board of Education, 137
Texas Ten Percent Plan, 160, 164,
testing and tests, 4–5, 7, 13–14, 16,
18, 20–21, 45–46, 55, 57–59,
64–65, 81, 83, 85, 88–89, 92,
99–107, 110, 112, 122–123,
127–128, 130–131, 135,
152, 164–166, 170, 174, 178,
181, 184, 194, 198, 200–202,

ABOUT THE AUTHORS

Anthony Carnevale, the chairman under President Bill Clinton of the National Commission for Employment Policy, is the director of the Georgetown University Center on Education and the Workforce. **Peter Schmidt**, the author of *Color and Money*, is an award-winning reporter and editor who covered education policy and student access at *Education Week* and the *Chronicle of Higher Education*. **Jeff Strohl** is the director of research at the Georgetown University Center on Education and the Workforce. All three authors live in Washington, DC.

PUBLISHING IN THE
PUBLIC INTEREST

Thank you for reading this book published by The New Press. The New Press is a nonprofit, public interest publisher. New Press books and authors play a crucial role in sparking conversations about the key political and social issues of our day.

We hope you enjoyed this book and that you will stay in touch with The New Press. Here are a few ways to stay up to date with our books, events, and the issues we cover:

- Sign up at www.thenewpress.com/subscribe to receive updates on New Press authors and issues and to be notified about local events
- Like us on Facebook: www.facebook.com/newpressbooks
- Follow us on Twitter: www.twitter.com/thenewpress

Please consider buying New Press books for yourself; for friends and family; or to donate to schools, libraries, community centers, prison libraries, and other organizations involved with the issues our authors write about.

The New Press is a 501(c)(3) nonprofit organization. You can also support our work with a tax-deductible gift by visiting www .thenewpress.com/donate.